HAPPY FATHER'S
DAY
POP!

XO,
JULIANNA
ROGER
MARTINA

REBEL GIANTS

REBEL GIANTS

The Revolutionary Lives of
ABRAHAM LINCOLN & CHARLES DARWIN

DAVID R.
CONTOSTA

Prometheus Books

59 John Glenn Drive
Amherst, New York 14228–2119

Published 2008 by Prometheus Books

Inquiries should be addressed to
Prometheus Books
59 John Glenn Drive
Amherst, New York 14228–2119
VOICE: 716–691–0133, ext. 210
FAX: 716–691–0137
WWW.PROMETHEUSBOOKS.COM

12 11 10 09 08   5 4 3 2 1

Library of Congress Cataloging-in-Publication Data

Contosta, David R.
    Rebel giants : the revolutionary lives of Abraham Lincoln and Charles Darwin / David
R. Contosta.
        p. cm.
    Includes bibliographical references and index.
    ISBN 978–1–59102–610–5 (hardcover)
    1. Lincoln, Abraham, 1809–1865. 2. Lincoln, Abraham, 1809–1865—Philosophy.
3. Lincoln, Abraham, 1809–1865—Influence. 4. Presidents—United States—Biography.
5. United States—Intellectual life—19th century. 6. Darwin, Charles, 1809–1882.
7. Darwin, Charles, 1809–1882—Philosophy. 8. Darwin, Charles, 1809–1882—Influence.
9. Naturalists—England—Biography. 10. England—Intellectual life—19th century.
I. Title.

E457.2.C76 2008
973.7092—dc22

2008005598

Printed in the United States of America on acid-free paper

To the teachers, friends, family, colleagues, and mentors
who have helped me on the journey through life.

CONTENTS

ACKNOWLEDGMENTS

am grateful to the many individuals who believed in this project and encouraged me to continue with it. David Fahey, one of my former professors at Miami University, read the manuscript, gave helpful suggestions, and cheered me on. My friend and sometime coauthor, Robert Muccigrosso, likewise read and critiqued the manuscript with his keen historical insight and writer's skill. Lakshmi Atchison, Peggy Vogelson, William Walker, and Jennifer Wofford—all colleagues at Chestnut Hill College—were also among my readers. Colleagues and friends who attended the series of three lectures on Lincoln and Darwin that I gave at the college in February 2007 assisted in focusing my approach to these towering figures and offered several new insights. Christy Fletcher and Emma Parry, of the Fletcher & Parry literary agency, were extremely adept in helping to shape the book proposal.

As always, I enlisted my entire family in this project. My wife, Mary, and daughters, Nicole, Alexandra, and Jessica, commented freely on the manuscript and discussed my ideas as they evolved. Our teenage sons,

David and John, shared their home with the ghosts of Lincoln and Darwin without complaint and showed great enthusiasm for Dad's latest writing passion. They and their mother joined me at the end of my research time at Cambridge University and experienced the magic of a place that meant so much to Charles Darwin.

The staff of the Logue Library at Chestnut Hill College went out of their way to find and secure any requested materials, no matter how obscure. I am beholden to Thomas F. Schwartz, Illinois state historian at the Lincoln Library in Springfield, Illinois, who guided me during a research trip there in the summer of 2005 and who has continued to give valuable suggestions. Adam Perkins, curator of scientific manuscripts at the Cambridge University Library, helped to arrange my research visit during the summer of 2006, advised me about the Darwin Papers once I arrived, and has continued to be available to answer questions. During both my Lincoln and Darwin journeys, dozens of individuals at museums, libraries, and historic sites could not have been more cordial and interested in what I was doing. Liz Gordon, house manager of Westcott House in Cambridge, and her assistant, Sharon Jones, made me feel very much at home from the beginning of my stay with them, as did the many wonderful people that I met there and who frequently invited me to join in their activities. A special thanks to Sergio, who kept me well fed with his superb pasta dishes and Tuscan wines, and to Adrian, for his "full English breakfasts" every morning in the hall.

I am indebted to Sister Carol Jean Vale, president of Chestnut Hill College, who has shared my excitement about Lincoln and Darwin from the first day I told her about the idea for a book and who granted me a leave of absence from teaching in the fall of 2006 so that I could finish the writing. Sister Carol, along with William Walker, vice president for academic affairs, and the college's faculty development committee, who also supported requests for a course reduction in my teaching assignment each term.

Robert "Bob" Stephens, president of the nonprofit Darwin Day

Celebration, enthusiastically welcomed a book on Lincoln and Darwin and made successful recommendations about a publisher. Steven L. Mitchell, editor-in-chief at Prometheus Books, understood from the start of our collaboration just what I was trying to accomplish and did everything possible to make this book an attractive reality. I shall always be indebted to him and his excellent staff.

INTRODUCTION

Coincidence may be described as the chance encounter of two unrelated causal chains which—miraculously, it seems—merge into a significant event.

—Arthur Koestler, *Janus: A Summing Up*

Almost two centuries ago, two men, one an American and one an Englishman, turned their world—and ours—upside down. They were Abraham Lincoln and Charles Darwin.

Astonishingly, both men were born on the same day, February 12, 1809. While this might seem the kind of coincidence that fills astrologers with glee, further reflection points to many parallels and intersections in their lives. These offer insights into the wellsprings of greatness and the crucial intersection between individuals and events in monumental paradigm shifts.

This book addresses the question of how and why paradigm shifts occur and how some "rebels" are especially equipped to lead or nurture such changes. In so doing, the book also shows that there is little difference between paradigm shifts in the sciences and in politics. The struggles of Lincoln and Darwin to understand and promote the basic humanity of all people, despite their own prejudices, offer hope for global understanding and universal human dignity. The ways in which their ideas and accomplishments have been twisted, exploited, and misunderstood are excellent examples of how the continuing dialogue between past and present is impacted by changing worldviews and special interests.

In fact, the timing of the men's births was important—not because of any celestial forces at play—but because their being born ten or a dozen years earlier or later would have made a big difference: Lincoln could not have grasped the political opportunities and extraordinary events—the ferment over slavery and the breakdown of party alignments—that came his way at just the right time and during just the right circumstances. In Darwin's case, the advances in scientific knowledge pointed to a plausible theory of evolution in the second half of the nineteenth century that someone was sure to formulate.

Given their identical ages, the dates of crucial events in their lives were often very close. The year 1858 seemed a devastating year for both men: In Illinois, Lincoln lost his bid for the United States Senate despite his broiling ambition and his impressive performance in a series of debates against Stephen A. Douglas. In England, Darwin was stunned to receive a packet in the mail from Alfred Russel Wallace announcing a theory of evolution that appeared to undo his own years of hard work and block any possibility of scientific preeminence.

Yet these setbacks were only turning points. Within two years both men would touch off revolutions that continue to shake the world: Darwin published his path-breaking *Origin of Species* in November 1859, and a year later, in November 1860, Lincoln was elected president of the United States. Darwin's book launched a continuing debate about the place of human beings in the universe that had implications for racial and individual equality, while Lincoln's election led to a bloody Civil War that ultimately was about human dignity and human rights.

Although there have been many books about these men as individual subjects, no one has written about the two of them under one cover. Impressive though Lincoln and Darwin were and remain, there is nothing magical about their fame. Studying both men and their often intersecting needs, methods, and timing explains and demystifies them in ways that examining each one in isolation cannot do.

Both left home in search of who they were and who they might become. They found different ways of postponing careers, and at the end of the same half dozen years, each discovered his life's work. As young men, they both said no to the conventional truths of the day. In rejecting these commonplace views, they were able to lead others to face the contradictions between traditional practices and beliefs and the needs and realities of a new age—what a later generation would call thinking and acting "outside the box."

At first glance, Lincoln and Darwin would seem to have little in common—one born to a struggling and obscure family on the American frontier, the other to a wealthy and prominent English family; one with less than a year's formal education, the other with a degree from Cambridge University; one a lawyer and politician, the other a scientist and country gentleman; one seeking the approval of the crowd, the other a partial recluse.

But the similarities are striking, and studying these (along with the differences) helps us to understand each man better. Both lost their mothers in childhood and both lost beloved children at young ages, both had strained relations with their fathers, both struggled with religious doubt, both hated slavery, both read and admired William Shakespeare, both were latter-day sons of the Enlightenment who elevated reason over religious revelation, both were ambitious as well as patient men, both had sure and steady mental powers rather than quick minds, and despite vast differences in their formal educations, both were in many ways self-taught. Both were skillful "politicians" who could persuade others to support them and help lay the groundwork for future triumphs. They also shared a common political inheritance, rooted in the Whig traditions of both countries. Perhaps most importantly, they each possessed an excellent sense of pacing that allowed them to wait until the time was ripe for their ideas and leadership.

These common factors—especially difficulties in childhood, burning ambitions, a willingness to postpone decisions about careers and to reject the familiar notions of their age, a superb sense of timing, and dogged determination—set Lincoln and Darwin apart from others of their time. Although these men worked in different fields, their qualities allowed them to stand out from the several thousand other individuals born in the English-speaking world on February 12, 1809.

Lincoln and Darwin were also fortunate in when and where they lived. Darwin came from a country where gentlemen scientists had the wealth and leisure to explore and experiment. Lincoln flourished in a place where individuals—if they were white and male—could rise as far as their native abilities, hard work, and incidents of luck would take them. Religious dissent and political and social reform movements stirred minds on both sides of the Atlantic.

Along with the good fortunes of time and place, both men suffered from serious depression throughout their adult lives. Both seem to have inherited tendencies toward melancholia, but ambition, overwork, and the stresses of their controversial causes contributed to emotional breakdowns. Yet these sufferings may have offered deeper insights, even as these insights provoked additional ill health. In the end, both maintained a will to live by throwing themselves into a line of work that might ensure lasting fame.

Lincoln and Darwin never met, though there is no doubt that Darwin, who faithfully followed world events through the English newspapers and who corresponded with Harvard botanist Asa Gray about Lincoln and the Civil War (often disapprovingly), knew about the American president's struggles to save the Union and abolish slavery. It is unclear if Lincoln knew about Darwin's *Origin of Species* in 1859, but he was fascinated by the idea of evolution and had devoured an earlier book on the subject called *Vestiges of Creation* by Robert Chambers. There is every reason to believe that the publication of *Origin*, given all the publicity it received in the United States, came to Lincoln's attention at some point.

Two centuries after the births of these remarkable men, and nearly a century and a half after their greatest achievements, the period in which they lived—before automobiles, airplanes, space travel, the electronic media, antibiotics, and even a germ theory of disease—seems very remote from our own. But Abraham Lincoln and Charles Darwin were asking and answering questions that we continue to ask: What is the meaning of human freedom and how can we best achieve it? How did the incredibly complex and interrelated life forms on our planet come to exist and how can we best save this precious biological inheritance? Is evolution a random process without any ultimate purpose or has it been directed by some kind of intelligent design? How do paradigm shifts occur and why do some extraordinary individuals gather the strength and courage to lead them?

The writings of these two men became instant classics. Darwin's *Origin of Species* and Lincoln's Gettysburg Address and Second Inaugural Address continue to inspire and provoke. During the lifetimes of these two men—and after—cartoonists never tired of depicting the two distinctive-looking men, whose faces remain among the best known of all historical figures. In the United States, Lincoln has long appeared on the five-dollar bill and the penny, and in England, Darwin graces the widely circulated ten-pound note. Places and institutions all over the world bear their names.

Both men have been subjects of great controversy over the years. Darwin's work was criticized within the scientific community, though mainly in the two generations after his death, before the breakthroughs in genetics that occurred during the first half of the twentieth century. Not unexpectedly, Lincoln was excoriated in the South. More surprisingly, some historians on both sides of the Mason-Dixon Line played down his commitment to human equality and accused him of undue sympathies with the Southern way of life. This was partly the result of a growing spirit of reconciliation between the North and South around 1900. Many progressive reformers, on the other hand, were inspired by Lincoln's idealism and use of vigorous executive authority to bring about change.

During the past century, debates over Lincoln and Darwin have run into new and unexpected channels, and have sometimes come full circle, as earlier praises and condemnations reappeared and then faded away. Religious opposition to Darwin remained and even intensified in some parts of the faith community, particularly in the United States, where the Scopes "Monkey Trial" of 1925 riveted the attention of a nation. Eight decades later, the struggles over teaching evolution in the public schools erupted when parents sued the Dover, Pennsylvania, school board in federal court for requiring the presentation of intelligent design claims in biology classes. In England, where religious fundamentalism has been less prominent and where the national school curriculum has long mandated the teaching of evolution, there has been much less controversy.

During World War II and the cold war against communism, Darwin's reputation suffered as Lincoln's rose. Critics of both Nazi Germany and Communist Russia unfairly linked Darwin with the materialism and violence of these regimes. Lincoln, on the other hand, was used to personify everything that was good about the American way of life.

During the war years, historian Richard Hofstadter took social Darwinists to task for bolstering cutthroat capitalism and thwarting progressive reforms. Soon after the war, Hofstadter also turned his critical guns on Lincoln, whose praise of capitalistic competition, he charged, furthered the cause of the robber barons.

By the 1960s, Lincoln's image was suffering, ironically, among many African American historians who renewed the charge that Lincoln was a racist and Southern sympathizer. Later, those who wanted to strengthen the power of the national executive, including President

George W. Bush, pointed to Lincoln's wartime suspension of habeas corpus to justify the withdrawal of certain constitutional protections in "the war against terror."

Debates over what Lincoln and Darwin said, did, and represented remained intense on the approach of their two-hundredth birthday anniversaries in 2009. Hardly a day passes without some mention of Abraham Lincoln and Charles Darwin in the mass media. To know ourselves in today's world, we must come to terms with these two rebel giants of the nineteenth century.

Chapter 1

INTERSECTING WORLDS

The Anglo-American connection transcended the facts of economic geography. Along the North Atlantic trade route there moved, not only goods, but people, the carriers of technical, philanthropic, religious and political ideas. The Atlantic economy supported a structure of social relations which bound together important elements in Britain and the United States.

—Frank Thistlethwaite, *The Anglo-American Connection in the Early Nineteenth Century*

From the moment they came into the world, Abraham Lincoln and Charles Darwin belonged to an Anglo-American community. Although they were born into very different families and economic circumstances, they were formed by many of the same influences and shaped their intertwined worlds more than any other two individuals of their time.

In 1809, the year Lincoln and Darwin were born, George III remained on the British throne, as much admired by his subjects at home as reviled by the American rebels a generation earlier. Three weeks after the births of Lincoln and Darwin, Thomas Jefferson stepped down from eight years as president of the United States, after persuading Congress to place an embargo on all trade with Europe and the British Isles in hopes of avoiding war with either England or France, both of which had violated American neutral rights on the high seas. That same year, Arthur Wellesley, soon to become the Duke of Wellington, delivered stunning blows against the French in both Portugal and Spain that proved crucial to the final defeat of Napoleon.

Just two years before that, in 1807, Great Britain had outlawed the international slave trade, and a year later, the United States followed suit, though slavery itself remained legal in the United States and in Britain's West Indian colonies. Four years earlier, in 1803, the United States had purchased the vast Louisiana Territory from France. This was possible, in part, because the ongoing conflict between Britain and France had flared up again in Europe, and Napoleon was happy to be rid of Louisiana. Between 1804 and 1806, Meriwether Lewis and William Clark explored the vast new territory and pushed beyond to the Pacific Northwest, land later claimed by both the United States and Great Britain, which nearly caused another war. Conflict about slavery in the Louisiana Territory would, a half century later, become a key to Lincoln's successful bid for the presidency.

In 1812, just three years after Lincoln and Darwin were born, their two countries did go to war over British impressments of American sailors, violations of American maritime rights, and disputed boundaries between the United States and British Canada. American troops invaded Canada, and British forces attacked Washington, DC, where they burned the White House. Neither side won a clear-cut victory, but the end of this Anglo-American conflict in 1814—and the final defeat of Napoleon a year later—left both countries with a new sense of pride and national unity. Peace also allowed the United States and Great Britain to settle a number of disputes over boundaries and trade. In 1823, when Lincoln and Darwin both turned fourteen, Britain even proposed a joint declaration with the United States against any European interference with the newly independent countries of Latin America. Not wanting to be bound so closely to British policy, the United States issued its own unilateral declaration known famously as the Monroe Doctrine, but it was the British Navy that enforced the policy for many years.

Peace also brought new prosperity to both countries, helped along by an industrial revolution that had begun in the British Isles and then was copied, sometimes literally, by American entrepreneurs. The textile industry in the United States and Great Britain created a voracious demand for cotton, which, in turn, stimulated the growth of slavery in the United States, as planters moved south and west to create vast cotton plantations. Governments in both countries that were favorable to individual entrepreneurship stoked the fires of financial and manufacturing enterprise; and although the class system was far more firmly entrenched in Great Britain, economic and social mobility became more possible than ever before in both countries. There would be winners and losers in this high-stakes atmosphere, creating a sense of struggle, uncertainty, and individual anxiety. The image of the self-made man that Lincoln came to personify, as well as the competition that was so crucial to Darwin's theory of natural selection, was at the center of this paradigm shift.

Despite ongoing animosities, Great Britain would remain America's most important trading partner; and Britain, which began its industrial revolution a generation or two earlier than the United States, supplied much of the investment capital to build the railroads and canals of its former colonies. But money, raw materials, and finished goods were not the only items exchanged between the two countries. Books, periodicals, people, and ideas also passed back and forth. Religious toleration in Britain and religious freedom in the United States had unleashed a proliferation of denominations that cross-fertilized each other across the Atlantic, which was as much a broad highway as it was a watery barrier.

American abolitionists were encouraged by Britain's abolition of slavery in its West Indian colonies in 1833, after which their British counterparts provided funds and shared strategies to attack slavery in the United States. William Lloyd Garrison, America's most outspoken abolitionist, went to England to consult with sympathizers. Harriet Martineau, the avowed antislavery writer, feminist, and intimate friend of Charles Darwin's brother, Erasmus, traveled to America to observe and speak about slavery and other telling aspects of American society.

Those in Britain who campaigned for electoral reform pointed to the success of universal white male suffrage in the United States by the 1820s, a factor that helped Andrew Jackson win the presidency at the end of the decade. Although Jacksonian democracy differed in many ways from the Whig reform program in Britain, both assailed social privilege and unfair economic advantages—the urban banking establishment in America and the established church and other bastions of aristocratic power in England.

The English common law remained the basis for the American legal system and courtroom procedure. Protestant Christians on both sides of the ocean read from the revered 1611 King James Version of the Bible. Many of the most socially prominent and politically powerful citizens of the United States belonged to the Episcopal Church, the American branch of the Anglican Communion, and used a liturgical language based in sixteenth-century Tudor English. It was a language well known to Abraham Lincoln and Charles Darwin—through the Bible and a common love of Shakespeare.[1] But the two men would share much more than an Anglo-American culture while they were growing up, including the deaths of their mothers, difficult relations with their fathers, an ability to attract others, religious skepticism, habits of self-education, and the bases for reaching beyond the commonplace truths of their day.

The lands around Shrewsbury, England, where Charles Darwin was born, had been cultivated for hundreds of years and by 1809 they had a long-settled appearance, still largely untouched by the smokestacks of early British industry. Just outside the town, on a hundred-foot embankment above a bend in the Severn River, Charles Darwin's father had built a large, five-bay redbrick house called "The Mount." Designed in the late Georgian style, it was two and a half stories high and contained over a dozen rooms. The ancient town of Shrewsbury, with its eleventh-century castle and numerous black-and-white stucco and half-timbered buildings surviving from the late Middle Ages, lay along the river in the valley below the house.

There, Charles Robert Darwin, the fifth child of Robert and Susannah Darwin, was born into a world of wealth, comfort, and powerful family connections. The boy was named for his father, Robert, and his dead Uncle Charles, both medical doctors. He joined a network of three sisters, Marianne, Caroline, and Susan, and one brother, Erasmus. The girls were six to eleven years older than Charles, and Erasmus was a little more than four years his senior. Catherine, the last of the six Darwin children, was born just fifteen months after Charles.

Their father, Dr. Robert Darwin, was one of the most successful rural physicians of his day, with a knack for winning the trust of his wealthy patients, a number of them titled nobility. Robert chose well when he married Susannah Wedgwood, the beautiful daughter of Josiah Wedgwood, the immensely wealthy founder of the Wedgwood pottery works. A year before her marriage in 1796, Susannah had inherited twenty-five thousand pounds, equal to several million dollars two centuries later. Susannah remained loyal to her Unitarian upbringing and took the children to the Unitarian Chapel in Shrewsbury on Sundays. Robert, although a freethinker in religion, became a member of the established Church of England, where Charles and the other children were baptized. In this sense, Robert and the children were outward conformists, making it convenient many years later for Dr. Darwin to propose ordination in the Church of England for Charles.

Several generations before Charles was born, the Darwins had been yeomen farmers who held minor posts under James I and Charles I. On Darwin's mother's side, the Wedgwoods had been potters since the early 1600s, a profession at which they made only a modest living at first. Both the Darwin and the Wedgwood ancestors became religious dissenters who did not belong to the established Church of England. These Protestant dissenters were particularly strong in Scotland and the English Midlands, where they and their families formed tight-knit associations. Barred from attending Oxford or Cambridge universities, which were Church of England institutions, the dissenters opened their own academies and sent their children to study in the Scottish universities or on the Continent. Many British historians have seen this as a great boon to the country, since the dissenting academies and universities followed a more practical curriculum based in modern languages, politics, modern history, and mathematics and science (then known as natural philosophy) in contrast to the old classical studies at Oxford and Cambridge.

Charles's grandfather, Erasmus Darwin, had been a close friend to Josiah Wedgwood and, like his son, Robert, was a highly successful medical doctor with legendary diagnostic skills. Erasmus was also a poet and self-taught naturalist, whose book *Zoonomia*, a two-volume work published in 1794 and 1796, speculated on the possibilities of biological evolution. He was especially fascinated by fossils and the evidence that they offered for the extinction of some plants and animals and by the appearance of new species over a period of time—a period far longer than the six thousand years then accepted by most Christians. Erasmus was also a tinker and inventor, who designed a special windmill for grinding pigments at his friend Josiah Wedgwood's pottery factory.

Erasmus Darwin and Josiah Wedgwood were both members of Birmingham's Lunar Society, a group founded in the 1760s by prominent men interested in machinery and mechanical inventions. They met once a month, on the Monday (translated literally as "moon day") closest to the full moon, so they could see their way home in this age before artificial lighting. Among their fellow members were James Watt and Matthew Boulton, who teamed up to manufacture high-compression steam engines that powered the new industrial revolution in Britain. Like Darwin and Wedgwood, most members of the Lunar Society were religious dissenters, more specifically Unitarians. Their great hero was Joseph Priestley, a fellow Lunar man, chemist, and leading Unitarian philosopher of the day who became the minister of Birmingham's Unitarian meetinghouse in 1780. (Priestley became a political refugee in the early 1790s when he left for the United States and established the country's first Unitarian church in Philadelphia.[2])

Like many other dissenters, both Erasmus Darwin and Josiah Wedgwood despised slavery and were founding members of the British Anti-Slavery Society. Wedgwood commissioned a blue and white china medallion showing the image of a slave in chains and below it the words "Am I not a Man and a Brother," a motto that the Anti-Slavery Society adopted around 1787. Wedgwood shipped some of these medallions to Benjamin Franklin for distribution.[3]

Sending medallions to the fledgling United States made much sense, because Englishmen and Americans were more deeply involved in slavery than anyone else in the world at that time. According to historians Charlotte and Dennis Palmer, "Slaving has been called the most lucrative trade the world has ever known. Its gigantic dividends underwrote the development of the ports of Bristol and Liverpool in England, and of their New England counterparts, Boston and Newport. Later they helped to create entire industrial complexes: railways, docks, coal-mining, iron smelting. They also financed a vast range of supporting enterprises."[4] Charles Darwin inherited this family hatred of slavery, a sentiment shared by the Lincoln family on the American frontier, but neither he nor other members of his family appeared to realize that their own financial success, if only indirectly, had benefited from the wealth derived from slavery.

The contrast between Darwin's large and well-furnished family home, in a long-settled and cultivated part of England, was as great as could be imagined from the one-room, dirt-floor log cabin on the heavily forested frontier, at a place called Sinking Spring in Hardin County, Kentucky, where Abraham Lincoln came into the world. When Abraham was two, the family moved to a nearby farm on Knob Creek. Lincoln's sister, Sarah, had been born in 1807, and a younger brother had died in infancy.

Asked about his early life by a newspaper reporter during the presidential election of 1860, Lincoln responded, "It can all be condensed into a single sentence, and that sentence you will find in Gray's Elegy. The short and simple annals of the poor. That is my life; and that's all you or any one else can make of it."[5] In fact, Lincoln's childhood standard of living was very similar to that of other common people on the American frontier, and he may well have exaggerated the family's hardships to dramatize his own rise in the world and to connect with the everyday voter. Still, he was reluctant to talk about his past, as if he were ashamed of it and wanted to put it behind him. According to his longtime law partner and biographer, William Herndon, "There was something about his origin he never cared to dwell upon."[6]

A little later, Lincoln composed a brief autobiographical sketch, written in the third person, for use in his first presidential campaign. In a published collection of his writings, the sketch runs a little less than nine pages—brief, indeed, compared to Darwin's *Autobiography*, which in a recent edition fills 145 printed pages. Comparatively few of Lincoln's letters survived his prepresidential period, as opposed to the more than fifteen thousand items in the Darwin correspondence that cover every part of his life. Biographers tried to give a fuller picture of the future president's early life by interviewing people who had known him. This was especially true of William Herndon, who relied on his own conversations and experiences with Lincoln, in addition to extensive interviews with others who had known him, to give a fuller picture of the man in his 1888 biography. Yet because of limited sources, certain aspects of Lincoln's early life will always remain obscure.

Lincoln himself related that Indians killed his grandfather, also named Abraham, "about the year 1784," soon after he arrived in Kentucky. Lincoln does not explain how unfortunate his grandfather's early death was for their branch of the family. Grandfather Abraham had acquired 5,544 acres of some of the richest land in Kentucky, but because the law of primogeniture remained in effect in Virginia and its Kentucky extension, all this land went to the eldest son, Mordecai, leaving the other two sons, Josiah and Thomas (Abraham's father), with nothing. Tom Lincoln had to work hard all his life just to scratch out a living, while Mordecai became a man of substance who bred horses and became a respected resident of Washington County, Kentucky.[7]

Abraham Lincoln described his father as "a wandering laboring-boy, [who] grew up literally without education. He never did more in the way of writing than to bunglingly write his own name."[8] From all reports, Tom Lincoln was not a brutal man, but he did sometimes strike Abraham in anger and grew impatient with a son who was more interested in reading books than in doing farm work.[9] When Abraham received word in early 1851 that his father was dying and wanted to see his son one last time, he did not go to visit him. When his father did die a few weeks later, Lincoln did not attend the funeral. In every way, Tom Lincoln makes a study in contrasts to Charles Darwin's wealthy and highly successful doctor father. There is every reason to think that Abraham Lincoln would have far preferred to have Dr. Darwin as a father than Tom Lincoln.

Abraham knew almost nothing about his earlier American ancestors who could, in fact, be compared favorably to Darwin's forebears. His earliest American ancestor, Samuel Lincoln, came from County Norfolk in England, where he had been a weaver. He settled in Hingham, Massachusetts, in 1637, becoming a successful trader and businessman. Samuel's grandson Mordecai was a wealthy ironmaster and large landowner in Pennsylvania and became part of the local elite. His son John migrated down the Shenandoah Valley of Virginia and became a prosperous farmer, and it was his son Abraham (grandfather of the future president) who amassed thousands of acres in Kentucky. Although the Lincolns could not match the Darwins or Wedgwoods in wealth and social standing, they had been far from poor or unsuccessful by the mid-eighteenth century.[10]

Still, the Darwins and Wedgwoods were, by the time Charles was born, among the wealthiest and most powerful members of Britain's rising upper-middle class, with more money than many aristocrats and with every prospect of becoming even richer in the years ahead. Given such wealth from both sides of the family, young Charles Darwin enjoyed most every advantage that money and a wide network of social and familial connections could command, including several generations of well-read and very successful men, about whom Charles gradually became aware. "The Mount," his childhood home, had a large, well-stocked library and a greenhouse filled with exotic plants. In the garden were fruit trees and rare shrubs. Charles loved to fish on the riverbank behind the house, sitting there for hours at a time.

Once he gathered peaches and plums from his father's trees, hid them under some shrubbery, and then ran to tell that he "had discovered a hoard of stolen fruit." He plied other "deliberate falsehoods," like telling another boy that he could create different-colored flowers by watering them with various colored fluids.[11] The reason for these fibs, he later thought, was to cause excitement and call attention to himself as one of the younger members of the family. Very early he craved notice and recognition, needs that would follow him throughout life and play an important part in his quest for success.

Charles was also a constant collector, storing up caches of seashells, bird eggs, coins, minerals, dead insects, and anything else he could think of squirreling away, carefully labeling everything he found. This passion for collecting, he explained in his *Autobiography*, "was very strong in me, and was clearly innate."[12] Dr. Darwin indulged his son's collecting hobbies, as well as the mischief, making light of the falsehoods or playing along with them. Later Darwin felt embarrassed about these little lies, but not nearly as bad as he felt about once beating a puppy, "simply from enjoying the sense of power."[13] He felt particularly ashamed as a lifelong dog lover.

When he was eight and a half, Charles's carefree childhood was interrupted when his mother, Susannah Darwin, died in July 1817. She had suffered horribly from what may have been peritonitis. The two older sisters, Marianne and Caroline, nursed their mother, while the other children, including Charles, were banned from the sickroom. Caroline did her best to comfort him.

Charles remembered very little about his mother beyond the image of her lifeless body laid out on the bed and dressed in a black velvet gown. She had often been sick and, when not at home in bed, she was out making social calls. Like most children in well-to-do families, Charles and the others had their meals in the nursery and spent only an hour or two with their parents at the end of the day. His sister Caroline, and not his mother, had taught him his alphabet and how to read and write. Charles remembered her as clever and kind, but "too zealous in trying to improve me," and asked himself whenever he entered a room where she was, "What will she blame me for now?"[14] Yet Darwin believed that his own "humane feelings" had come from Caroline's kind examples. They more than filled the maternal void for Charles, with the result that he went on with his young life much as before. In truth, the sisters may have made better mothers than Charles's birth mother, who seemed to have been somewhat remote and emotionally unavailable to him.

Dr. Darwin's reaction to his wife's death was another matter. He had known Susannah since they were children, and she was the love of his life. Remarriage was out of the question. He was often out of sorts and suffered long bouts of depression.

Charles had mixed memories of his father, most of them from the years after his mother's death. He described him as "a remarkable man" in many ways. A large man physically, he stood "about 6 feet 2 inches . . . with broad shoulders, and very corpulent, so that he was the largest man whom I ever saw."[15] He marveled at his father's keen powers of observation, which had helped make him such a successful doctor. Charles also admired his father's habit of formulating theories to explain nearly everything in his own experience and in the world at large, an ability that Charles would also exhibit in adult life. Dr. Darwin had a strikingly good memory and was a great storyteller, which, combined with a genuine sympathy for his patients, gave him a wonderful bedside manner. Despite these traits, Charles wrote that many people feared his father because of his "art of making every one obey him to the letter . . . [and] he was easily made very angry." Charles softened this memory, adding, "His kindness was unbounded, [and] he was widely and deeply loved."[16]

As a loyal son, Charles may have held back even harsher judgments about his father. According to biographers Adrian Desmond and James Moore, Dr. Darwin became more fastidious and opinionated after his wife's death: "He interrogated and pontificated by turns; to be summoned was like being hauled before the Most High."[17] The Wedgwood cousins remembered that everyone had to go along with Dr. Darwin's "orderly and correct" standards and complained of the "stiff and awful" evenings at The Mount when he was at home.[18]

Even so, Dr. Darwin shared his love of gardening with Charles and took time to explain the names of various plants. He also took Charles in his carriage when he visited sick patients and opened his library to his son.[19] In the end, Charles's experiences with his father were mixed and probably conflicted. Dr. Darwin was critical, benevolent, and remote by turns, behaviors that may have left Charles guessing how his father might react to a particular situation and in doubt about whether his father would approve of his actions and decisions. Charles would carve out a life of his own and live on his own terms, but self-doubt would remain a constant companion and possibly an important ingredient in his later depressions.

Both Lincoln's and Darwin's fathers could become exasperated and angry, but Robert Darwin limited himself to verbal assaults. In frontier America where physical violence was widely tolerated, Tom Lincoln sometimes lashed out with his hands and fists. Yet his neighbors reported that he was an honest, hardworking man who paid his bills, supported his family adequately by the standards of his time and place, was always ready to give neighbors a helping hand, and was a good story-teller, a trait that his son mastered very early on. Later, when Lincoln had left home and wanted to emphasize the difference between his success and humble origins, his own assessments of Tom Lincoln may have been more negative than they should have been. In his psychological portrait of the future president, Charles Strozier writes, "It seemed to pain Lincoln to realize how dull his father was, which tells more about Lincoln's driving ambition than it does about Thomas's character. As a boy, Lincoln had aspirations beyond his grasp."[20]

In 1816, when Abraham was seven years old, his father decided they would leave Kentucky and move to southwestern Illinois. His reasons were opposition to slavery and the uncertainty of land titles in Kentucky. The Baptist Church to which Abraham's parents belonged opposed slavery on moral grounds. In addition, Tom Lincoln disliked competing with slave labor in a county where there were 1,007 slaves and 1,627 white males over sixteen years of age.[21] The problem of land titles stemmed from the lack of a government land survey in Kentucky, with the result that settlers had set their own boundary claims, describing them by rocks, trees, or other objects in the landscape. Tom Lincoln had trouble obtaining a clear title to any of the land he claimed in Kentucky and did not have the money to hire a lawyer and settle the matter in court. In contrast, Indiana was in the Northwest Territory, where the United States government had surveyed the land and could give accurate and clear titles, and where the Northwest Ordinance of 1787 prohibited slavery. Abraham would point to this ordinance many times in his crusades against the spread of slavery.

The Lincoln family's new home was a quarter section of land (180 acres) near Little Pigeon Creek in what became Spencer County, Indiana. They arrived in December and at first lived in a rough shelter enclosed on three sides. The fourth side faced a fire that provided some warmth while keeping away wild animals. Many years later, when Abraham revisited the site, he composed a poem that recalled "the panther's scream" that "filled night with fear and bears [that] preyed on the swine."[22] Tom Lincoln soon went to work building a one-room log house with a loft, probably with the help of some other men already settled in the area. They survived that first winter by hunting deer and bear, and in the spring began the backbreaking work of clearing the land so they could plant corn. Abraham was big for his age, and his father put him to work swinging an ax. Along with farming, Tom Lincoln supplemented the family income by making furniture and selling it, including some finely crafted and handsomely decorated corner cupboards.

Lincoln's mother, Nancy Hanks Lincoln, was illiterate and had to sign her name with an X. She clearly could not write and probably was unable to read, though there were cases of people at that time who could read but not write. Several of the individuals whom Herndon interviewed reported that Nancy Hanks Lincoln was "intellectual," no doubt meaning that she was a natively intelligent woman who may well have accumulated a store of knowledge through listening to and conversing with others. The contrast between her and Susannah Wedgwood Darwin could not have been greater, but her early death gave her son an experience that was, in some ways, similar to Charles Darwin's.

Not quite two years after the Lincoln family arrived in Indiana, on October 5, 1818, Nancy Hanks Lincoln died of the mysterious "milk sick," when Abraham was nine and a half, just a year older than Darwin was when he lost his mother. The cause of her illness, scientists discovered decades later, was the poisonous snakeroot plant (*Eupatorium rugosum*), which cows had been eating in the forest, passing the poison into their milk and to anyone who drank it. Their neighbors, Thomas and Elizabeth Hanks Sparrow, Abraham's aunt and uncle, had died of the same malady only a few weeks before. Those afflicted by this terrible and always fatal illness lay on their backs with their legs up and spread apart. Their skin turned cold and clammy, their breath becoming shorter and shorter and their pulse increasingly irregular until they fell into a coma and finally died.

Once during the 1850s, while riding in a horse-drawn buggy with Herndon, Lincoln said he thought his mother had been born out of wedlock, a belief that later genealogical researchers and Lincoln historians have generally supported. Lincoln also told Herndon that he thought his mother's father was a wealthy and successful Virginia planter. Disliking his own father and finding nothing impressive about his mother's Hanks relations, Lincoln liked to think that he inherited his successful traits from this anonymous Virginia gentleman.[23]

While Darwin had three older sisters and a battery of servants as well as a large extended family to care for him after his mother's death, Lincoln had only his eleven-year-old sister Sarah, an often angry father, and his cousin Dennis Hanks, who had been living with the Sparrows and who now moved into the Lincoln's small cabin. Like Darwin, Lincoln remembered very little about his mother in later life. He left no account of her death, of how he felt about it, or how it may have affected him. Losing a parent before reaching adulthood was not unusual in the early nineteenth century given the many infectious diseases, the rigors of everyday life, and the paucity of good medical knowledge and care, and Lincoln may have taken his mother's passing in stride. But Lincoln scholar Michael Burlingame, as well as others, believe that Nancy Hanks Lincoln's terrible suffering and death, combined with the losses of Abraham's aunt and uncle—and later his sister Sarah's death in childbirth—were among the causes of Lincoln's lifelong battle with depression.[24] Nevertheless, Lincoln seemed to take these deaths especially hard in a place and time where death was a constant companion, suggesting that he already had a predisposition to depression that was somewhat triggered by these events.

Tom Lincoln soon found that he could not make it on the frontier without a wife, and less than a year after Nancy's death, he went back to Kentucky to find a new mate. He chose Sarah Bush Johnson, a recent widow and mother of three young children whom both he and Nancy had known before setting out for Indiana. He agreed to pay her debts and to take her and her three children off to Indiana.

A stepmother could have made Abraham's life even more miserable, but Sarah brought new life and hope to the struggling frontier family. She came with several pieces of good furniture—tables, chairs, chests, and flatware—the best that Abraham had ever seen. The two stepsisters, Elizabeth and Matilda, and a stepbrother, John, were welcome and cheerful additions to the household, but it was Sarah's genuine love for Abraham that probably saved him from complete despair. He soon called her Mama and treated her with the utmost kindness and respect. She later said of him, "He was the best boy I ever saw. . . . Abe never gave me a cross word or look and never refused in fact, or Even [*sic*] in appearance, to do any thing I requested him. . . . I never gave him a cross word in all my life. . . . His mind & mine—what little I had seemed to run together—move in the same channel."[25] Like Darwin's close relationship with his sisters, Lincoln's stepmother might have had a more positive effect on him than his actual mother would have had. This can never be known, but both he and Darwin were fortunate to have mother surrogates to love and nurture them.

Although Sarah Lincoln was illiterate, she valued education. Soon after arriving in Indiana, she and Tom Lincoln enrolled all five children in a log cabin school about a mile away taught by Andrew Crawford, which Abraham attended for around three months. The school was ungraded, a so-called blab school, where the students recited their lessons while the teachers listened and pointed out mistakes. Crawford also tried to instruct the children in some everyday manners. The following year, Crawford gave up his school, and now the nearest one, run by a James Swaney, was about four miles from the Lincoln cabin. Because of his heavy chores at home, Abraham could only make the long round-trip to school every once and a while. A year later, Azel W. Dorsey opened another school in the former Crawford cabin, and Abraham attended for about six months. He was now fifteen, and his total formal education added up to no more than one year. Lincoln later looked back on these crude schools with scorn: "No qualification was ever required of a teacher, beyond '*readin, writin, and ciphern.* . . . If a straggler supposed to understand latin [*sic*], happened to sojourn in the neighborhood, he was looked upon as a wizard [*sic*]."[26]

By every standard of the time, Darwin had an education far superior to Abraham Lincoln's. In 1817, when he was eight, Charles started going to a day school taught by the Reverend George Case, the minister of the Unitarian Church in Shrewsbury that his mother attended. The next year he enrolled at the Shrewsbury School, presided over by the Reverend Samuel Butler, where Darwin's thirteen-year-old brother Erasmus, called Eras (and sometimes Ras), was already a student. Although a boarding school, it was less than a mile from The Mount, allowing Charles to make almost daily visits home. As a boarder, he had to be back at school by the time the doors were locked and he often had to run as hard as he could to return on time. Fortunately, he was a good runner, but whenever it looked like he might not make it, he "prayed earnestly to God to help me, . . . and marveled how generally I was aided."[27] It is no wonder that Charles went home frequently, even if he had to return to school at night, given the cramped quarters in the dormitory, where as many as thirty boys slept above the library, with a window at just one end of the room and the foul smells of body odor mingled with the stench of chamber pots.

The Shrewsbury School prepared the sons of wealthy families for Oxford or Cambridge, or, if they did not go to university, for the life of a country gentleman. Like other schools of the sort, it stressed the classical languages of Latin and Greek. Although Charles had no trouble memorizing lessons for daily recitations, he soon forgot what he had learned, except for the odes of Horace, which he liked very much. He later wrote to one of his professors, whose scientific lectures he had enjoyed, "I find I have utterly forgotten my whole intense stock of classical knowledge."[28] "The school as a means of education," he wrote in his *Autobiography*, "was simply a blank." Both his teachers and his father, Darwin thought, considered him "a very ordinary boy, rather below the standard in intellect." Commenting one day on Charles's love of hunting and collecting, Dr. Darwin had exploded in exasperation, "You care for nothing but shooting, dogs, and rat-catching, and you will be a disgrace to yourself and all your family." This low estimation of his younger son may well have spurred Charles to succeed, if only to prove his father wrong and win his approval.

Outside the classroom, Charles reveled in Shakespeare's historical plays (also Lincoln's favorites), along with some of the more modern poets, especially Byron and Scott. A book called *Wonders of the World*, he later thought, "first gave me a wish to travel in remote countries." As he later admitted, he had "much zeal for whatever interested [him]," and most of these interests had nothing to do with school, as was true of his chemistry experiments with Eras, carried out in a toolshed in their father's garden. Charles read several books on chemistry and often worked over them late into the night. "This was the best part of my education," he insisted, "for it showed me practically the meaning of experimental science." When word of the experiments got around at school, his schoolmates started calling him "Gas Darwin." The headmaster, who thought chemistry a waste of time, was not impressed and criticized Charles in front of his classmates as a "poco curante," or a trifler. Charles thought this unfair, both because he had learned so much while experimenting with Eras and because he did not know at the time what the rebuke was supposed to mean. More importantly, Darwin had begun a lifelong habit of self-education. When the schools did not offer what he wanted or needed, he set out to teach himself—a habit that may have helped to save him from being just another unambitious son of a wealthy and privileged family and from accepting the received verities of his time without question. To use a phrase familiar to later generations, this degree of self-education may have helped him to think and act "outside the box."

Like Eras, Charles disliked sports, preferring to ramble around the countryside for exercise and to add to his various collections. In 1819, when he was ten, his sisters took him on a three-week visit to the Welsh seacoast where he collected insects and went bird-watching.

Despite the vast differences in their formal education, Lincoln, like Darwin, managed to learn a great deal on his own. He enthusiastically took advantage of the few books his stepmother brought with her from Kentucky, including the Bible, John Bunyan's *Pilgrim's Progress*, *Aesop's Fables*, and William Scott's *Lessons on Elocution*, which was probably his first exposure to Shakespeare. Lincoln also walked great distances to borrow books and found copies of Benjamin Franklin's *Autobiography* as well as Mason Weems's *Life of George Washington*. Borrowing the Washington biography turned out to be costlier than he ever imagined. He placed the book on a shelf one night near a crack between logs in the Lincoln cabin during a storm. The rain leaked through and badly damaged the book. The lender, a man named Josiah Crawford, reckoned the loss at seventy-five cents and made Abraham work three days to pay for it by pulling fodder from his fields.

Contributing to Lincoln's informal education were the religious and political beliefs of his family—contributions only because he viewed them as mostly negative models to be rejected. Tom and Sarah Lincoln belonged to the nearby Pigeon Primitive Baptist Church, originally a log structure that Tom helped to build and that Abraham took turns in cleaning. Although Abraham sometimes attended services there, he did not join the church. Since the Baptists did not believe in infant baptism and left the decision to the individual rather than to the parents, it was up to Abraham to put himself forward for the ceremony. He never did. Lincoln may well have been frightened and then offended by the hellfire-and-brimstone sermons and the denomination's belief that God had predestined most individuals to eternal damnation, regardless of their personal faith or daily rectitude. After church Lincoln sometimes amused other youngsters by getting up on a stump and mocking what the preacher had said in his weekly sermon. In spite of this ridicule, Lincoln likely imbibed a strong dose of predestinarian determinism from the Baptists, which he later expressed in more secular terms as "the doctrine of necessity" and then, during the Civil War, as a belief in divine Providence.

In addition to rejecting his parents' church, Lincoln came to oppose his father's devotion to the Democratic Party and to its leader, Andrew Jackson, known fondly to his supporters as "Old Hickory." Most everyone in southern Indiana admired Jackson's frontier background—his duels, brawls, and military exploits, his opposition to federal spending on transportation improvements, and his defiance of the eastern banking establishment. As an adult, Lincoln would become a devoted supporter of the opposition Whig Party, which excoriated the crude persona of Andrew Jackson, championed banks and internal improvements as essential to the country's economic progress, and represented the culture and interests of the better-off classes that Lincoln aspired to join. For

Abraham, his father's political preferences and lack of education and worldly success became powerful "positive, negative" influences.

Meanwhile, Charles Darwin was also displeasing his father. He made so little progress in school that Dr. Darwin withdrew him early and sent him, at age sixteen in 1825, to Edinburgh University to join Eras in studying medicine. To prepare him during the summer before going to Edinburgh, Dr. Darwin gave him some patients to attend among the poor in Shrewsbury. He made a careful written record of their symptoms, which he later read to his father, who advised certain medicines, which Charles then prepared and delivered.

Instruction in the medical school at Edinburgh was entirely by lecture and "these were intolerably dull," with the exception of a series on chemistry, understandable, given Charles's earlier enthusiasm for the subject. He found the lectures on geology and zoology very boring. Even the course in anatomy did not include dissection, an omission that Charles would regret later in life. He visited the hospital wards, where many of the cases alarmed and unnerved him. He also watched two operations from the surgical amphitheater in this age before anesthetics and ran from the blood and screams before the operations were over. These scenes haunted him "for many a long year."[29]

For the rest of his life, Charles believed that most of what he learned of value or interest continued to take place outside the classroom. Luckily, he met several men at Edinburgh who shared his fascination with nature and scientific inquiry. One of them was Robert Edmund Grant, who later became a professor of comparative anatomy and zoology at the University of London. Grant frequently took him on collecting expeditions among the many tidal pools around Edinburgh, and Charles himself befriended some local fishermen who let him go out with them to collect marine specimens.

Charles accompanied Grant to several meetings of the Wernerian Society to hear papers on natural history, later published as part of the organization's transactions. At one meeting he heard American artist and naturalist John James Audubon (one of many transatlantic lecturers) deliver three talks on the habits of North American birds. Grant also shared his enthusiasm for Jean Baptiste Lamarck's theories of evolution. Darwin could not remember that this had any great effect on him at the time, but he later thought that "the hearing rather early in life such views maintained and praised may have favoured my upholding them under a different form in my Origin of Species." Around the same time, Charles joined the Plinian Society, a student organization at Edinburgh devoted to the natural sciences. He shared his first scientific discovery in a speech before this group: that the eggs of the flustra (a small marine coral, more commonly known as *hornwrack*) were in fact larvae with "the power of independent movement by means of cilia."

During this period, Charles learned to stuff birds from a "Negro" taxidermist in Edinburgh. He liked sitting and talking with this "very pleasant and intelligent man." This experience, and his family's long opposition to slavery on religious and humanitarian grounds, no doubt contributed to his hatred of slavery and racial cruelty.

Charles thoroughly enjoyed his summer holidays during the Edinburgh years. In 1826 he went on an extended tour of northern Wales with two friends, walking thirty miles a day with knapsacks. He spent the end of each summer shooting game at his uncle Josiah Wedgwood's estate known as Maer Hall. He was so keen on hunting that he "used to place my shooting boots open by my bed-side when I went to bed, so as not to lose half-a-minute in putting them on in the morning."[30] He kept a precise account of every bird killed, a habit of record keeping that would be of tremendous help to him later as a scientist.

Charles remembered these visits to Maer for the happy family atmosphere that filled the place:

Life there was perfectly free; the country was very pleasant for walking or riding; and in the evening there was much very agreeable conversation . . . together with music. In the summer the whole family used often to sit on the steps of the old portico, with the flower-garden in front, and with the steep wooded bank, opposite the house, reflected in the lake, with here and there a fish rising or a water-bird paddling about. Nothing has left a more vivid picture on my mind than these evenings at Maer.[31]

Charles was especially fond of his "Uncle Jos," who, ironically, could be as intimidating as his own father—more because of his silence and reserve than because of any reputation for scolding or criticizing. Yet he sometimes talked very openly with Charles, who occasionally asked for his uncle's generally good advice. If Dr. Darwin could be off-putting, Charles could always depend on his uncle's support and approval, a factor that may have helped to offset some of Charles's doubts about himself and inspire self-confidence, a role that several other male mentors would play.

Finally realizing that Charles had little aptitude for medicine, an exasperated Dr. Darwin decided that he should become a clergyman in the Church of England, a tradition for less ambitious sons of the wealthy. He could easily buy him a country parish where he could live comfortably off the tithes. Charles was not against the idea initially, especially if he settled down in a rural parish where he could hunt and continue as an amateur naturalist, not an uncommon pastime for rural parsons. Despite the fact that his mother had been a Unitarian and his father a freethinker and nominal member of the Church of England, Charles had to subscribe to the doctrines of the Anglican Church as set forth in its Thirty-Nine Articles—a requirement for ordination as well as admission to one of the English universities, from which he needed a degree to become a clergyman.

Charles had been baptized in the local Anglican parish and at the time he was considering the priesthood, he accepted on faith the "literal truth of every word in the Bible." After reading several books on theology, he also decided that the Anglican creed should be accepted without question. Still, given his family's dissenting background, affirming that he accepted these core doctrines of the church strikes the historian as something of a stretch, a point that Darwin would come to realize himself.

Later he confessed, "I had scruples about declaring my belief in all the dogmas of the Church of England," and should have stated simply that "I had no wish to dispute any dogma," which then would have been enough to gain admission to the university.[32] Whatever his precise religious beliefs at the time, Charles and his father decided that he would enter Christ's College, Cambridge, in early 1828, after several months of being tutored in Greek and Latin, much of which he had forgotten during the two years at Edinburgh.

In his *Autobiography*, Darwin claimed that his years at Cambridge were "wasted, as far as the academic studies were concerned, as completely as at Edinburgh and at school."[33] He went to few lectures, most of which were optional anyway, but he managed to do respectably in his exams because of his good showing in geometry, which he liked for its logic, and his excellent account of William Paley's *Evidences of Creation* and *Moral Philosophy*, which he also admired for its apparent order and reason. (In fact, Darwin reportedly lived in the same set of rooms at Christ's College that Paley had earlier occupied.) Darwin's good showings when examined on Paley and Euclid were largely responsible for his receiving a "respectable tenth" among graduates not competing for honors.

Darwin continued his collecting expeditions at Cambridge, mainly searching for beetles. He often hunted in the company of his second cousin, William Darwin Fox, also a student at Christ's College and an avid collector who, unlike Charles, would become a parish priest while continuing to be an amateur naturalist. At this point, Charles was maintaining a mere "passion for collecting" and did not dissect or compare the external characteristics of his findings with published descriptions. He filled his college room with specimens, including a large stuffed swan and moth pupae.

Charles's most important contact was Professor John Stevens Henslow, whom his brother Eras had described as a living encyclopedia of scientific knowledge. Charles was invited, along with other selected students and faculty, to attend Henslow's Friday Evenings at home, where they discussed a variety of scientific topics. The professor developed a special liking for Charles and took long walks with him nearly every day during his last year and a half at Cambridge; Darwin came to be known as "the man who walks with Henslow." Many evenings after their walks, Darwin stayed for dinner with the family. Another professor whose fascinating but voluntary lectures and field trips he attended was geologist Adam Sedgwick. Both Sedgwick and Henslow were committed Anglicans who believed that the apparent design in nature proved the existence of a beneficent God.[34] Henslow was so deeply orthodox that one day he told Charles, "he should be grieved if a single word of the Thirty-Nine Articles were altered."[35] It is no wonder that Darwin later hesitated to publish a scientific theory that would question everything his old professor most cherished.

Although he would disparage the formal curriculum at Cambridge as much as that of Edinburgh, Cambridge was clearly a good fit for Charles, and he had a lot of fun there. He wrote to his sister Caroline in 1831, "Cambridge, I find, is one of the few places, where if you anticipate a great deal of pleasure you do not find yourself disappointed."[36] He later wrote that he fell in with a "sporting set, including some dissipated, low-minded young men." They often dined together, and "sometimes drank too much, with jolly singing, and playing cards afterwards."[37] His indulgence in alcohol was frequent enough to prompt his friend George Simpson, who was planning to visit him in early 1831, to write, "I hope you will not get so very drunk but that you can find time to tell me a little of your future prospects."[38] With a generous annual allowance of three hundred pounds from his father, he could afford to indulge himself; and it is clear that Darwin was a very outgoing young man with many friends.

His enjoyments could also rise above drinking, card playing, and shooting. He developed a taste for music at Cambridge and used to time his walks to pass by the fifteenth-century King's College Chapel to hear the choir, which "gave me intense pleasure, so that my backbone would sometimes shiver."[39] The chapel, begun by Henry VI and completed by Henry VII, is one the glories of late perpendicular English Gothic, with its soaring fan-vaulted ceiling and luminous stained glass windows. (Nearly two centuries after Darwin attended Cambridge, the choirs still sing at Kings, and the chapel is an international tourist attraction.)

By the time Darwin started at Cambridge, Lincoln appeared to be trapped in the life of a hardscrabble farmer. If that were not enough, in 1828, just before his nineteenth birthday, Lincoln was plunged into despair. That year his sister Sarah, who had married a neighbor named Aaron Grigsby, died in childbirth. Sarah had been a source of consolation after their mother's death, and he loved her dearly. A neighbor later remembered that Lincoln was in the smokehouse when he heard the news of her death. "He came to the door and sat down, burying his face in his hands. The tears trickled through his large fingers, and sobs shook his frame."[40]

As in other periods of his life, Lincoln probably tried to escape his sorrows by throwing himself into work and by telling humorous stories. Whenever possible, he went around the countryside attending house raisings, husking bees, and log-rolling contests, where he called attention to himself with amusing stories and jokes. He was especially fond of walking to Gentryville where the main attraction was the general store. Lincoln quickly attracted a small crowd by telling one of his funny and often far-fetched stories. One man who remembered these perfor-mances said of him, "Lincoln would frequently make political speeches to the boys. . . . His jokes and stories were so odd, original, and witty all the people in town would gather around him."[41] In his own way, young Lincoln was as popular as the college boy Charles Darwin, able to draw others around him for a good time.

Meanwhile, Lincoln was always looking for a way to make some money. He got a job helping James Taylor run a ferryboat across the Ohio River near the mouth of Anderson's Creek and was paid thirty-seven cents a day, less than full wages, since he was not yet considered a man. He also plowed fields, built or fixed fences, split firewood, killed hogs, and most anything else that called for hard physical labor. In March 1828, he set out for New Orleans on a flatboat loaded with cured meat and grains belonging to storekeeper James Gentry, joined by Gentry's son, Allen, for which Lincoln received eight dollars a month and board. It was a leisurely trip, with frequent stops. The most exciting part of the trip occurred one night while the boat was tied up a few miles below Baton Rouge, Louisiana. There a group of "marauding Negroes" bent on plunder attacked the boat, but Lincoln and his partner beat them off with clubs, then cut loose and drifted down the river for the rest of the night. How this may have affected his attitudes toward blacks is unknown. He also left no record of his impressions of New Orleans—the largest city Lin-coln had ever seen, filled with slaves and people speaking French.

Despite these adventures away from home, Lincoln was still not free to do as he pleased, since he owed his father labor until he was legally an adult. Although he turned twenty-one in February 1830, he set out a month later to help his family to move once again, this time from Spencer County, Indiana, to Macon County, Illinois. The party included Abraham's father and stepmother, her two daughters, Elizabeth and Matilda, and their husbands, and cousin Dennis Hanks. It was a rough journey in a covered wagon, pulled by two yoke of oxen over still-frozen roads that thawed a little each day and then froze up at night. As the family reached Illinois, the rivers were swollen with melting snow and early spring rains, which often flooded the roads, making them impassable. Abraham walked beside the wagon, goading the oxen and keeping the family cheerful by telling jokes and spinning yarns. One day their pet dog, who walked along behind the wagon, failed to cross an ice-covered stream and was missed only after the family had reached the other side. Everyone except Abraham thought it best just to keep going, but he could not stand it. As he related years later: "Pulling off shoes and socks[,] I waded across the stream and triumphantly returned with the shivering animal under my arm. His frantic leaps of joy and other evidences of a dog's gratitude amply repaid me for all the exposure I had undergone."[42]

That spring and summer of 1830, Abraham helped to clear and fence seventeen acres with split rails. He had done everything he could to help the family, but now he was legally an adult and was determined not to follow in this father's footsteps by becoming a farmer. The next spring he left home for good with no clear plans.

In their now somewhat dated but still insightful book *Cradles of Eminence*, authors Victor and Mildred Goertzel concluded that "the comfortable and contented do not ordinarily become creative."[43] Basing their conclusions on four hundred highly successful men and women of the twentieth century, they discovered that "children in . . . turbulent and explosive homes do not always enjoy life."[44] They suffer intensely at times, and they are deeply capable of suffering, since they are sensitive and aware individuals. They freely admit that most children who experience difficult childhoods fail to become famous and may even know less success than those with a generally happy family life. But those who have the strength and imagination to develop successful coping strategies are somewhat more willing to question contemporary practices and beliefs—thinking outside the box—even if they suffer for it.

In most ways, Darwin's childhood was far more pleasant than Lincoln's, but he, too, lost his mother at a young age and had to cope with a moody and demanding father. Lincoln was determined not to be a

1959); Ida M. Tarbell, *In the Footsteps of the Lincolns* (New York: Harper and Brothers, 1924).

11. Nora Barlow, ed., *The Autobiography of Charles Darwin, 1809–1882* (New York: W. W. Norton, 1993), p. 23. Darwin composed the bulk of his autobiography in 1876, but a complete version of it was not published until 1958 because family members had objected to including some of the more controversial parts of the work, especially Darwin's statements of religious unbelief.

12. Ibid.

13. Ibid., p. 27.

14. Ibid., p. 22.

15. Ibid., pp. 28–29.

16. Ibid., pp. 39–40.

17. Adrian Desmond and James Moore, *Darwin: The Life of a Tormented Evolutionist* (New York: Warner Books, 1991), p. 14.

18. Ibid., p. 15.

19. For a more positive view of the relationship between Charles and his father, see Janet Browne, *Charles Darwin: Voyaging* (Princeton, NJ: Princeton University Press, 1995), pp. 14–17.

20. Charles B. Strozier, *Lincoln's Quest for Union* (Philadelphia: Paul Dry Books, 2001), p. 17.

21. These figures are from Donald, *Lincoln*, p. 24.

22. Lincoln, "The Bear Hunt," c. 1846, *Collected Works of Abraham Lincoln*, 1:386.

23. Herndon, *Herndon's Life of Lincoln*, p. 2. See also Donald, *Lincoln*, p. 20.

24. Michael Burlingame, *The Inner World of Abraham Lincoln* (Urbana: University of Illinois Press, 1994), pp. 93–96.

25. Sarah Bush Lincoln, interview by William Herndon, September 8, 1865, in *Herndon's Informants: Letters, Interviews, and Statements about Abraham Lincoln*, edited by Douglas L. Wilson and Rodney O. Davis (Urbana: University of Illinois Press, 1998), pp. 107–108.

26. *Collected Works of Abraham Lincoln*, 3:511.

27. Barlow, *Autobiography of Charles Darwin*, p. 25.

28. Darwin to Henslow, July 2, 1848, *The Correspondence of Charles Darwin* (Cambridge: Cambridge University Press, 1985–[2005]), 1:121.

farmer like his father, and Darwin had similar feelings toward becoming a medical doctor like his father or—as time would tell—the country clergyman that Dr. Darwin then proposed for him. Fortunately, both men would find ways to put off deciding who they were and what they wanted to do with their lives, resisting the pull to fall into more predictable paths.

NOTES

1. Although they are somewhat dated, there are two excellent studies of this Anglo-American world in the nineteenth century: Robert Kelley, *The Transatlantic Persuasion* (New York: Alfred A. Knopf, 1969) and Frank Thistlethwaite, *America and the Atlantic Community* (New York: Harper and Row, 1959).

2. For more on this group, see Jenny Uglow, *The Lunar Men* (New York: Farrar, Straus and Giroux, 2002).

3. Charlotte and Denis Palmer, *Slavery: The Anglo-American Involvement* (New York: Barnes and Noble Books, 1973), p.60.

4. Ibid., p. 9.

5. Abraham Lincoln, quoted in David Herbert Donald, *Lincoln* (New York: Quadrangle Books, 1995), p. 19. These lines are also quoted in William H. Herndon, *Herndon's Life of Lincoln* (New York: Da Capo Press, 1983), pp 1–2. Herndon's *Lincoln* was originally published in 1888.

6. Herndon, *Herndon's Life of Lincoln*, p, 1.

7. Donald, *Lincoln*, p. 21.

8. "Autobiography Written for John L. Scripps," in *The Collected Work of Abraham Lincoln*, edited by Roy P. Basler et al. (New Brunswick, NJ: Rutgers University Press, 1953), 4:61.

9. Donald, *Lincoln*, pp. 32–33.

10. On Lincoln's ancestry, see Louis A. Warren, *Lincoln's Parentage and Childhood* (New York: Century Company, 1926) and *Lincoln's Youth: Indiana Years, Seven to Twenty-One, 1816–1830* (New York: Appleton-Century-Crofts

29. Barlow, *Autobiography of Charles Darwin*, pp. 47, 48.

30. Ibid., p. 54.

31. Ibid., pp. 55–56.

32. Ibid., p. 57.

33. Ibid., p. 58.

34. On Darwin at Cambridge, see Peter J. Bowler, "Charles Darwin," in *Cambridge Scientific Minds*, edited by Peter Harman and Simon Mitton (Cambridge: Cambridge University Press, 2002), pp. 94–106.

35. Barlow, *Autobiography of Charles Darwin*, p. 65.

36. Darwin to C. S. Darwin, April 28, 1831, *Correspondence of Charles Darwin*. These letters are also available from the Darwin Correspondence Online Database, http://www.darwinproject.ac.uk/.

37. Barlow, *Autobiography of Charles Darwin*, p. 60.

38. George Simpson to Darwin, January 26, 1831, *Correspondence of Charles Darwin*, 1:113.

39. Barlow, *Autobiography of Charles Darwin*, p. 61.

40. John W. Lamar, *Footprints of Abraham Lincoln*, by J. T. Hobson (Dayton, OH: Otterbein Press, 1909), p. 24.

41. Herndon, *Herndon's Life of Lincoln*, p. 50.

42. Ibid., p. 58.

43. Victor Goertzel and Mildred Goertzel, *Cradles of Eminence* (Boston: Little, Brown, 1962), p. 131.

44. Ibid., p. 132. On page viii, the authors spelled out their research plan for choosing the four hundred famous individuals: "Include each person who has at least two books about him in the biography section of the Montclair, New Jersey, Public Library if he was born in the United States and all persons who have at least one book about them if they were born outside the United States. Include only those who lived into the twentieth century and are described in a standard reference work."

Chapter 2

WHO AND WHERE

The chosen young man extends the problem of identity to the borders of existence in the known universe; other human beings bend all their efforts to adopt and fulfill the departmentalized identities which they find prepared in their communities.

—Erik H. Erikson, *Young Man Luther*

"Who am I and where am I going?" These are questions that sensitive souls with freedom to choose have asked since the beginning of the modern age seven centuries ago. "Life is a work of art," declared Renaissance humanists, meaning that individuals were responsible for developing their human qualities to the fullest. In a more democratic age, beliefs in "equality of opportunity" or "careers open to talent" became modifications and extensions of that mentality. Freedom to choose a line of work, to compete, and to make the most of individual talents were woven into the national creeds of Lincoln's America and Darwin's England.

This freedom to shape one's own life and to rise as far as possible in the world could be a heady prospect. Young men (and eventually young women) were no longer doomed to follow the same patterns as their elders. Nor were they prisoners of a cyclical view of change, which held that each generation and each life passed in endless circles that were, in the end, essentially the same. In contrast, modern change—and modern time—was linear, indicating that the present and future were bound to be different from the past, and the experiences of each generation would be different from those that had gone before. A belief that the future would be better than the past supposedly meant progress—for the individual, for society, and for civilization as a whole.[1]

This modern worldview came at a price: traditional cues and expectations were replaced with the admonition to make one's own way in the world, for the child to be more successful than the parent. The possibility of failure was ever present and, in an age of growing individualism, failure could and often would be blamed on the seeker of success. In premodern societies, mere survival, which required following a set of long-held customs and expectations, was more than enough. Now there was the burden of choosing a path to follow and the many hurdles required to succeed on that path.

Lincoln and Darwin were willing participants in this world of ambition, despite their different social backgrounds and material resources. Now in their early twenties, just how they would succeed and where this success would take them was unclear. It is therefore not surprising that both men declared what developmental psychologist Erik Erikson has called an early adult moratorium on having to decide who they were and what they wanted to be. Putting off this crucial identity decision gave them time to explore abilities and inclinations and saved them from falling into well-worn paths and standard beliefs.

Neither Lincoln nor Darwin wanted to follow trajectories that seemed obvious or that had been indicated by parents. Lincoln rebelled against the drudgery of farmwork, however good a farm laborer he had proven himself to be, and Darwin rejected becoming either a doctor or a clergyman. Neither seemed to have a conscious plan for a time out, or moratorium, but both were fortunate to come up with possibilities at just the right times: Darwin, when he was asked to join an expedition aboard the HMS *Beagle*, and Lincoln, when he was offered a job that led him to settle in the frontier village of New Salem, Illinois. Darwin's five years aboard the *Beagle* and Lincoln's six years in New Salem occupied almost exactly the same time span, beginning in 1831, when they were both twenty-two years old. Both were at the right age for maximum exertion of physical and mental abilities, for seeking and absorbing new information and ideas.

They read, observed, sampled the possibilities, and made personal connections that would point them toward vocations and later allow them to lead revolutions that their times demanded: ending slavery and changing the social contract in the United States and formulating plausible answers to age-old questions about the origins and diversity of life. In merging their own vocational interests with the emerging needs of their age, they were able to resolve their early adult identity crises and to lay the ground for greatness.

Lincoln's moratorium began when he left home for good in the spring of 1831. His opportunity came in the form of a second trip down the Mississippi River, when Denton Offutt, a local entrepreneur who owned properties and enterprises up and down Illinois' Sangamon River, commissioned Lincoln, his stepbrother John Johnson, and his cousin John Hanks (another member of the large Hanks family) to take a load of provisions downriver to sell in New Orleans. The three men built the boat, loaded it with corn, hogs, and salted pork packed in barrels, and set off in mid-April down the Sangamon. They almost had to abort the venture when their vessel got stuck over the breast of a milldam at New

Salem, Illinois. Lincoln managed to dislodge it by moving some of the cargo from the back of the boat to the front and then by boring a hole in the front end that projected out over the dam. When the water that had leaked into the boat poured out the front, the vessel tipped down and slid over the dam, to the amazement of a crowd of onlookers perched on the hill above.

After exiting the Sangamon, the three young men swung into the Illinois River and then into the broad Mississippi. Herndon later quoted John Hanks's memory of Lincoln's horror over a slave auction in New Orleans: "A vigorous and comely mulatto girl was being sold. She underwent a thorough examination at the hands of the bidders; they pinched her flesh and made her trot up and down the room like a horse. . . . The whole thing was so revolting that Lincoln moved away from the scene with a deep feeling of 'unconquerable hate.'"[2] Although Hanks had only gone as far as St. Louis, and was not in New Orleans with Lincoln when the boat landed there in June, Lincoln may well have related something like this story to Hanks when he returned to Illinois.[3] In any case, Herndon adds that he had "also heard Mr. Lincoln refer to [this story] himself."[4] Lincoln's revulsion over seeing slavery in its most demeaning aspect appears similar to what Darwin would feel less than a year later when he confronted the cruelties of slavery in Brazil.

The trip down the river was clearly a success for Lincoln. He earned $60 and impressed his employer so much that Offutt invited him to come to New Salem to manage businesses he had acquired in the village. Gliding with the current down the broad Mississippi River also gave Lincoln plenty of time to think and dream, though he apparently kept no record of the trip.

As Lincoln was leaving home, Charles Darwin was equally uncertain about where life might take him. He finished his studies at Cambridge

University and passed his examinations for the Bachelor of Arts degree in January 1831. Because he had entered the university late in 1828, he had to stay at Cambridge until June (less than two months before Lincoln moved to New Salem) to fulfill his residency requirements. It was now time to start preparing for ordination and life as a country vicar. Professor John Stevens Henslow, an ordained Anglican clergyman and botany professor who had already taken Charles under his wing, agreed to help him; but Henslow, who had not immediately entered the church after receiving his degree, persuaded Darwin to take up the study of geology as a way of becoming either a clergyman naturalist or a clergyman professor.

All during the winter and spring of 1831, Darwin read widely. His list included *Natural Theology* (1802), the third of Paley's trilogy, which again marshaled mountains of evidence to demonstrate his "Argument from Design." Paley insisted that just as a watch must have a maker, so must the intricate design of nature prove the existence of God. Darwin later wrote that Paley's arguments "gave me as much delight as did Euclid. The careful study of these works ... was the only part of the Academical Course which, as I then felt and as I still believe, was of the least use to me in the education of my mind."[5] Darwin may not have realized it at the time, but Paley was making strenuous efforts to reconcile basic Christian beliefs with the new information that was flooding in from the biological sciences, including fossil evidence that resulted in questions about the fixity of species and the age of the earth. Paley particularly objected to proposals about biological evolution. He would continue to intrigue Darwin, who would also marvel at the wonderful adaptation of living things, but in ways that would completely undermine Paley.

At Cambridge, Darwin also read Sir John Herschell's just-published *Preliminary Discourse on the Study of Natural Philosophy* (1830), which painted a rosy picture of the prospects for scientific progress. Equally enthralling was Alexander von Humboldt's seven-volume *Personal Narrative* (1799–1804) of his explorations of South America. Together these works stirred in Darwin "a burning zeal to add even the most humble contribution to the noble structure of Natural Science."[6] This enthusiasm nearly jumps off the page in a letter he wrote from Cambridge to his sister Caroline: "All the while I am writing now my head is running about the Tropics: in the morning I go and gaze at Palm trees in the hot-house and come home and read Humboldt: my enthusiasm is so great that I cannot hardly sit still on my chair.... I have written myself into a Tropical glow."[7]

Humboldt's descriptions of Tenerife made such a powerful impression on Charles that he proposed a one-month expedition to this largest of Spain's Canary Islands that would include Henslow and three others, to be financed by his father. Dr. Darwin agreed, but the scheme fell apart when Henslow, with a new baby at home, changed his mind and one of the other interested parties unexpectedly died.

Back home at Shrewsbury, in the early summer of 1831, Darwin began investigating the local geology. One day, while examining a gravel pit, a laborer showed Darwin a "large worn tropical Volute shell" he had found there. This astonished Darwin and made him wonder how and why such a shell could have ended up in the middle of England. Wanting to go beyond the specimen as an isolated object, he realized that "[s]cience consists in grouping facts so that general laws or conclusions may be drawn from them."[8] Later that summer, Adam Sedgwick, one of Darwin's Cambridge professors, who was continuing his geological investigations of northern Wales, took Darwin along as an assistant. Sedgwick pointed out fossils and taught him how to investigate the geological history of a place.

Darwin could not have found a better mentor than Adam Sedgwick, who was one of England's pioneering modern geologists. An ordained Anglican clergyman, Sedgwick was a famous orator and preacher. Although his science lectures at Cambridge were not required as part of the curriculum, he attracted large crowds of students and other members of the faculty to his lecture hall. He spoke extemporaneously about basic principals as well as about his most recent fieldwork, illustrating both with maps and museum specimens. He also organized popular horseback field trips around Cambridge, and capped the day with dinner and exciting conversation at a local inn. It is no wonder he was regarded as one of the greatest university teachers of his day. His lectures and field excursions heightened Darwin's interest in geology and would provide models for his own investigations in the near future. As a clergyman-naturalist-professor, Sedgwick represented another model for Darwin to pursue. If he did not want to become a parish priest, the life of a university don in holy orders was another path open to him.[9]

Young Abraham Lincoln did not have a Cambridge professor to prepare him for a vocation, but he did find several educated men in New Salem who tutored him informally. In certain ways, New Salem became Lincoln's unofficial university, just as it was the setting for his "time out" from making decisions about his life. He moved to New Salem in late July of 1831, where he was already something of a local hero for having freed the boat from the milldam.

James Rutledge and John M. Cameron had founded New Salem just two years before.[10] They had built the dam and accompanying mill along the Sangamon River in the belief that there was enough water in the stream, at least during spring thaws, to make it navigable for flatboats all the way from New Salem to the Illinois River and from there to the Mississippi, making their village a center of trade and transportation for the surrounding countryside. They hired a surveyor and plotted lots on a ridge above the river—an area thick with trees that could be cut down for building materials, in contrast to the surrounding, treeless prairies.

Very quickly, about a hundred people settled in the village, building small but snug log houses with glass in the windows instead of the greased parchment typical of more isolated locations. Besides the mill, there were shops and stores, a tavern, two doctors, a cooper, blacksmith, wheelwright, hatter, and tanner. Lincoln biographer Benjamin P. Thomas described New Salem as a typical pioneer town: "Almost everything needed was produced in the village or the surrounding countryside. Cattle, sheep, and goats grazed on the hillsides. Hogs rooted in the woods and wallowed in the dust and mud of the road. Gardens were planted about the houses, and wheat, oats, corn, cotton, and tobacco grew in the surrounding fields."[11]

Lincoln's job was to run the mill, which had been rented by Denton Offutt, as well as to tend a general store that Offutt had built on a bluff along the path that led down to the river. He hired William G. Greene to assist Lincoln with both enterprises. The store had a front porch, where the two young men could lounge around and chew the fat. They slept in a small room behind the store and shared a bed so small that "when one turned over the other had to do likewise."[12]

The men ate their meals with local families, paying a dollar a week for whatever the woman of the house served up. This was a common practice for single men at the time and a way that women could supplement the household income. For Lincoln, boarding at various places around the village meant that he was never really alone, especially since conversation and warm friendship almost always came with the meals. With his ready supply of yarns, Lincoln was especially welcome to break bread. In the process, he widened his social contacts and learned about various personality types, experiences that would be very helpful in building a political career. His proclivity for telling humorous stories may also have been a way to avoid revealing too much of his inner self and of chasing away the blues.

Lincoln's easy conversational style and funny tales also became daily attractions at the store and mill. One of the stories told by Lincoln and recounted by Herndon concerned a backwoods Baptist preacher who began his sermon by saying, "I am the Christ, whom I shall represent today." At about this time, a blue lizard ran up beneath the preacher's baggy, homespun pants, and, not wanting to interrupt the flow of words, the preacher began slapping away at his legs in hopes of stopping the reptile. But it was no use; the lizard only climbed higher, at which point the preacher unloosened the only button that held his trousers together and kicked them off. By then, the lizard was "exploring that part of the preacher's anatomy which lay underneath the back of his shirt," causing him to unbutton it and throw it off. The congregation sat amazed for an instant until a woman shouted at the top of her lungs, "If you represent Christ then I'm done with the Bible."[13]

Making fun of preachers reflected Lincoln's own religious views. He still had not been baptized and did not belong to any church and he ridiculed such central beliefs as miracles, eternal damnation, the Virgin Birth, and the divinity of Christ. Lincoln carried a Bible around New Salem, reading passages aloud and questioning them, and even went so far as to put his doubts in writing. One fellow skeptic found the composition so extreme and so potentially damaging to Lincoln's reputation that he reportedly threw it into the fire.

In the course of his conversations with the other village doubters, Lincoln was introduced to and read Thomas Paine's *Age of Reason*, which openly attacked revealed religion as irrational. He may also have read *Ruins* by Constantin de Volney, a book that viewed morality as the only valid aspect of religion. Near the beginning of *Age of Reason*, Lincoln read Paine's own profession of faith: "I believe in one God, and no more. . . . I believe that religious duties consist in doing justice, loving mercy, and endeavoring to make our fellow creatures happy." Paine did not accept the creeds of any church, adding, "My own mind is my own church."[14] Most of what passed for biblical truth was little more than hearsay, according to Paine. Neither Mary nor Joseph, for example, had testified to the virgin birth of Jesus. The only true theology, he concluded, was what could be discovered in nature: "That which is now called natural philosophy, embracing the whole circle of science, of which astronomy occupies the chief place, is the study of the works of

God, and of the power and wisdom of God in His works, and is the true theology."[15] Lincoln would later take care not to connect publicly any of his own beliefs to the *Age of Reason*, but his views of religion throughout life remained very close to those of Thomas Paine.

Although the romantic era was well underway in the Western world during the 1830s when Lincoln was at New Salem and reading the religious criticisms of Thomas Paine, the Enlightenment had not yet come to the end of its long American twilight. What attracted Lincoln in particular was the Enlightenment belief in natural law, which could be interpreted as a doctrine of necessity, since inexorable and universal laws supposedly governed the universe and everything in it. In many ways, this was not unlike the Baptist doctrine of predestination with which Lincoln had grown up. By this point, he had become what might be called a predestinarian deist: God had created the universe and set it into operation according to certain natural laws that governed everything, including human behavior. While at different stages in their religious development, both Lincoln and Darwin were powerfully attracted to a sense of order and design in the world, whatever its cause. Although Darwin's sense of order would not ultimately sustain his belief in God, Lincoln's sense of order in the universe would strengthen his belief in an overarching Providence (or divine cause and direction).

Lincoln's self-education at New Salem went beyond the Enlightenment writers and criticism of the Bible. Knowing that his grammar was deficient, he turned for help to the village schoolmaster, Mentor Graham, who himself was largely self-educated. Graham told him that a farmer owned a copy of Samuel Kirkham's *English Grammar*, a standard text of the time, and Lincoln walked six miles to borrow it. He spent hours memorizing all the rules and examples and had his friends quiz him on them. Jack Kelso, described as the village philosopher, gave Lincoln an extensive introduction to Shakespeare as well as to Robert Burns. Lincoln memorized lines from Burns's poems and many Shakespearian passages and enjoyed reciting them for others. He was finally getting the education and mental stimulation he long craved. Fortunately, he had the imagination and good sense to reach out to the people and ideas he both wanted and needed.

Offutt, who liked to drink and was prone to boasting, claimed that Lincoln could "whip" any man in Sangamon County. A group of ruffians known as the Clary's Grove Boys took him up on the brag and designated their leader, Jack Armstrong, to represent them. Lincoln, who did not like fighting, hesitated at first but finally gave in. Standing six feet four and already renowned for his great strength, he was definitely a match for Armstrong. The results are unclear; some claimed that Armstrong won and others that Lincoln was the victor, but whatever happened, Lincoln gained even greater admiration in the village for his strength and courage in standing up to Armstrong, who himself became a friend and admirer.

Like Lincoln, Darwin was fortunate to meet people who respected him, recognized his talents, and shared their knowledge and skills. Darwin, too, remained uncertain about the direction he would take, and just as Lincoln had left his family to avoid becoming a farmer, Darwin was able to postpone parental expectations by leaving home. Possibilities for escape came in the form of a thick envelope in the mail on August 29, 1831. In it were letters from Professor Henslow and a Cambridge tutor named George Peacock that urged him to consider a round-the-world voyage on the HMS *Beagle*, originally slated to take about three years. Peacock had received a request from the captain, Robert FitzRoy, to find a gentleman companion who was scientifically inclined.

Darwin was not their first choice. Henslow himself thought of going but quickly dismissed the idea when he realized that the new baby at home would make the trip even more out of the question than the earlier proposed (and abandoned) expedition to Tenerife. Peacock then offered the spot to a Cambridge colleague named Leonard Jenyns, who turned it down after thinking about it for only a day, a decision he regretted for the rest of his life when he realized what the voyage had done for Darwin. Then, on Henslow's advice, Peacock wrote to Darwin. Despite Darwin's later insistence that he had learned little of any value at Cambridge, the contacts he had made there were offering him the opportunity of a lifetime. Darwin clearly fit FitzRoy's description, but chance had played an important role.

Although Charles could not know that he was not the first choice, he understood right away that a great gift had come his way. He knew that such a voyage would allow him to gather unique specimens to send back to England, with the potential to launch him into prominence as an up-and-coming naturalist. As Darwin biographer Janet Browne explained, "A natural history collection . . . possessed intrinsic social value as well as solid financial worth. It was an article of scientific commerce which an astute collector could use for furthering his status in scientific society." Such a collection would go "a long way towards helping [him] . . . join the community of British savants on their own terms."[16]

Darwin was not a mature, well-trained naturalist, but he had a grasp of basic geology, had been going on various collecting expeditions for years, and had read widely. In any case, he was not appointed as the official naturalist for the voyage, as has often been assumed. Instead, what most interested Captain Robert FitzRoy was having an acceptable young gentleman to dine with him and be an all-around companion.

FitzRoy was the grandson of the Duke of Grafton on his father's side and of the first Marquis of Londonderry on his mother's side, as well as a direct descendant of Charles II. His uncle had been Viscount Castlereagh, Britain's powerful foreign secretary at the end of the Napoleonic wars. FitzRoy's social standing was certainly higher than Darwin's, but the Darwins and Wedgwoods were very wealthy and more than respectable, and Charles was a well-mannered young man who had just received a degree from Cambridge. FitzRoy shared a strong interest in the natural sciences and the two were close enough in age: FitzRoy was twenty-six and Darwin twenty-two.

The only obstacle was Dr. Darwin's vehement objection to the whole idea (a problem that Lincoln, who had cut his ties to home, did not have to worry about). The voyage was far too dangerous, he believed, and it would keep Charles from preparing for the church. The last-minute request for him to join the *Beagle* also sounded suspicious, since it suggested that the vessel might not be seaworthy. Still wanting to accept the invitation but not wishing to disobey his father, Darwin wrote to turn down the offer. He visited his Wedgwood kin at Maer, where he could take out his frustrations shooting birds.

Charles carried along a note to Uncle Jos Wedgwood in which Dr. Darwin explained the invitation to join the *Beagle*, adding that if Wedgwood approved, he would agree to let Charles go. Uncle Jos did approve, and after writing his brother-in-law a long note to this effect, he and his nephew drove the thirty miles back to Shrewsbury to discuss the whole matter with Dr. Darwin, who finally consented. Luckily, Charles had decided to visit his uncle, which resulted in the exchange of letters. Without Wedgwood's intervention, Peacock would doubtless have selected yet another candidate to accompany FitzRoy. There is no reason to believe that his replacement (or for that matter Henslow or Jenyns, who had earlier walked away from the offer) would have gone on to accomplish what Darwin did, but it is impossible to imagine Darwin without the *Beagle*. Chance had certainly played a part, but Darwin's enthusiasm and persistence had also been essential for securing the opportunity, just as Lincoln's impressing Denton Offutt had led to his moving to New Salem.

With his father's permission to join the *Beagle*, Charles began a wild scramble to get ready for the voyage, which included an interview with FitzRoy in London. He later learned that FitzRoy almost turned him down because of the shape of his nose, since the captain believed that a facial profile foretold a person's character and that Charles's nose did not reveal "sufficient energy and determination for the voyage."[17] Reflecting back on the decision, Darwin wrote, "The voyage of the Beagle has been by far the most important event in my life and has determined my whole career; yet it depended on so small a circumstance as my uncle offering to drive me 30 miles to Shrewsbury, . . . and on such a trifle as the shape of my nose."[18]

The main goal of the *Beagle* voyage, sponsored by the British Admiralty, was a survey and mapping of the coast of South America, an area where Britain had increasing commercial interests. Especially important was the measuring and recording of various offshore ocean depths to help keep ships from running aground.

FitzRoy and Darwin spent two weeks in London rounding up supplies. Charles acquired a telescope, a rifle, some measuring equipment, writing materials, and a number of books, including the first volume of Sir Charles Lyell's recently published *Principles of Geology* (1830–1833). The book highlighted Lyell's "uniformitarian" thesis, which held that the earth's physical features had been shaped over long periods of time by gradual forces and uniform laws that are the same as those operating at present. The opposite school of thought, known as "catastrophism," held that geologic changes had taken place suddenly, such as in Noah's flood, and usually through some supernatural agency. Not all the books Darwin took with him were scientific. He also carried onboard the works of Shakespeare, which he continued to savor, and John Milton's *Paradise Lost*, a long poem about Adam and Eve's expulsion from the Garden of Eden and humankind's fall from grace.

Charles had to pay five hundred pounds (a huge sum when measured in early twenty-first century equivalents) for his passage on the *Beagle*, which he saw for the first time on September 11, 1831. He was shocked to discover that the vessel was an aging, three-mast, ten-gun brig, just 90 feet long and 24 feet amidships, a relatively small vessel that nevertheless carried 74 men. Although Darwin would have his meals in FitzRoy's cabin, he would share a sleeping cabin—the only other one aboard ship—with two senior officers. The place was tiny. Darwin had to sleep in a hammock stretched across the room at night and folded up in the daytime. The space contained a table, which Darwin used for writing and examining the specimens he collected. He had about as much room as Lincoln had in the small back room of Offutt's store, but without the freedom of getting up and walking down the street, unless they happened to be in port.

Delays in assembling equipment, last-minute repairs, and bad weather postponed their sailing until December 27. While waiting, there were massive demonstrations in London when Parliament failed to pass the reform bill that would have given a fairer share of seats in the House of Commons to the newer urban areas and extend the right to vote to the upper-middle class. This legislation would pass the following year when Darwin was away on his great adventure. Several years later, he would read Alexis de Tocqueville's *Democracy in America* and would come to conclude that extending the vote too widely could lead to what Tocqueville called the "tyranny of the majority." Years after that, the American Civil War would further erode Darwin's confidence in the wisdom of the masses.[19]

Almost immediately after they left port, Darwin was struck with terrible seasickness, which he would suffer in varying degrees throughout the entire trip. Their first stop was supposed to be Tenerife, but because cholera had broken out in England, the Spanish officials would not let them on shore unless they were quarantined for eleven days. FitzRoy decided not to wait and headed across the Atlantic. Darwin was very disappointed.

Soon after the voyage began, friction developed between Darwin and Robert McCormick, the ship's surgeon. Although neither McCormick nor Darwin had been officially appointed as the ship's official naturalist, it was traditional for the surgeon to take on the role of collecting specimens and sending them back to England. Like Darwin, McCormick was well aware of the potential for recognition back home if he amassed an impressive collection. But the elitist Captain FitzRoy deferred to Darwin in every way because he was a gentleman of means, even though McCormick's education was every bit as good as Darwin's. FitzRoy directed the crew to assist Darwin in any way they could and had Darwin's, rather than McCormick's, specimens sent back to England at the admiralty's expense.

Outraged over this treatment, McCormick left the ship just four months out of England. "He is no loss," Darwin sneered in a letter home to his sister Caroline. To Professor Henslow, he wrote, "Doctor [McCormick] has gone back to England,—as he chose to make himself disagreeable to the Captain." Throughout the whole affair, there is no evidence that Darwin did anything to put McCormick's case before FitzRoy or to arrange some sort of genuine cooperation with his rival. However Darwin may have treated McCormick, he was clearly ambitious to make a name for himself, as he later reflected: "I worked to the utmost during the voyage . . . to add a few facts to the great mass of facts in natural science. But I was also ambitious to make a fair place among scientific men."[20] On February 10, 1832, just two months into the voyage, Charles wrote to his father, "I shall be able to do some original work in Natural History.—I find there is so little known about many of the Tropical anima[ls]."[21] He said nothing about giving up a career in the church, but it was clear that his interests were shifting. In any case, making a mark in the world was already very important to him, as it was to Abraham Lincoln.

Meanwhile, Darwin had been keeping a journal, later revised and published as *The Voyage of the Beagle* (1839). In it he wrote about the overwhelming sensations of experiencing the Brazilian jungle for the first time: "The elegance of the grasses, the novelty of the parasitical plants, the beauty of the flowers, the glossy green of the foliage, but above all the general luxuriance of the vegetation, filled me with admiration. A most paradoxical mixture of sound and silence pervades the shady parts of the wood."[22] This was only one of the many paradoxes that he would confront over the next five years and that would set his mind to wondering about the origins and distribution of the many and astonishing varieties of life.

On February 28, 1832, the *Beagle* landed at All Saints Bay at Bahia (later Salvador), Brazil, where Darwin confronted the cruelties of slavery firsthand. His family had long opposed slavery, but actually seeing it in operation horrified Charles. In *The Voyage of the Beagle*, he asked readers to try to imagine the utter hopelessness they would feel: "What a cheerless prospect, with not even a hope of change! Picture to yourself the chance, ever hanging over you, of your wife and your little children—those objects which nature urges even the slave to call his own—being torn from you and sold like beasts to the highest bidder!" Especially infuriating was that the slave owners called themselves Christian gentlemen. Equally hypocritical were English and American masters who liked to boast about their heritage of liberty: "It makes one's blood boil, yet heart tremble, to think that we Englishmen and our American descendants, with their boastful cry of liberty, have been and are so guilty."[23]

Although horrified by slavery, Darwin did not believe that blacks and whites were equal, as he described an encounter with a slave aboard a ferry in Rio de Janeiro who dropped his hands to his side when he mistakenly supposed that Darwin was about to strike him in the face. Yet this sense of inferiority, Darwin thought, was the result of the terrible conditions under which the man had lived, "trained to a degradation lower than the slavery of the most helpless animal."[24] Here Darwin seems to be saying that blacks were inferior to whites because of the terrible conditions under which they were forced to live, rather than because of some innate deficiency. Still, he was not entirely clear in expressing this point. Later, Lincoln's stated opinions of race would also strike an ambivalent chord and open him to criticism by subsequent generations.

Darwin discovered that the South American colonial authorities were no kinder toward the Native American population than slave masters toward their bondsmen, since the authorities slaughtered Indians by the hundreds, captured their children, and sold them into slavery. Again, the cruelty and hypocrisy of an avowedly Christian people outraged him: "Who would believe in this age that such atrocities could be committed in a Christian civilized country?"[25] Perhaps John Milton's account of paradise lost offered Darwin some insight into this grievous sin amid such natural beauty. Yet there is no evidence that such hypocrisy had any effect on his still-conventional religious beliefs. Later he recalled "being heartily laughed at by several of the officers (though themselves orthodox) for quoting the Bible as an unanswerable authority on some point of morality."[26]

Darwin was delighted to hear from home that Parliament had voted in 1833 to abolish slavery throughout the British Empire, with financial compensation to the owners. When it looked as if this legislation was on the verge of passing, he wrote back to his sister Catherine, "I have watched how steadily the general feeling, as shown at elections, has been rising against Slavery.—What a proud thing for England, if she is the first European nation which utterly abolishes it!"[27]

FitzRoy, who was a conservative Tory, got into a terrible argument one evening with Darwin over slavery and became so angry with his companion that the two thought they "could not live any longer together."[28] FitzRoy cooled down after a few hours and apologized to Darwin, but these explosions of anger ("hot coffee" as the ship's crew called them behind their captain's back) were part of the violent mood swings he exhibited, suggesting that FitzRoy might have suffered from a bipolar mental illness. Although there was no such diagnosis at the time, FitzRoy was well aware of his condition, prompting biographers Michael White and John Gribbin to suppose that "FitzRoy had insisted on having an intelligent gentleman companion on board in the first place—to preserve his own sanity."[29] Like his uncle, Viscount Castlereagh, FitzRoy would later commit suicide.

In contrast, Darwin's spirits were generally high, though he continued to suffer from seasickness. Fortunately, he spent about 60 percent of the time carrying out expeditions on land while the ship sailed up and down coastal waters making soundings, freeing him from many more seasick hours. In fact, FizRoy's insistence on going back to particular spots to make additional surveys—or to check those he had already made—extended the voyage from three to nearly five years and caused Darwin to despair at times that he would never get back home. However, the extra time allowed him to take many more overland journeys than if FitzRoy had stuck to the original schedule.

Outfitting himself for these ambitious treks into the backcountry—buying supplies and hiring horses and guides—turned out to be very expensive, and Charles was forced to make large drafts against his father's letter of credit. Instead of writing to his father about the money, he confessed these withdrawals in letters to his sister Caroline, knowing she would relay the information to their father. In all of this correspondence, there is an unmistakable note of defensiveness, suggesting that Charles feared Dr. Darwin's disapproval of his seeming extravagance. In November 1833, for instance, he wrote to Caroline from Uruguay about his need for money: "I have drawn a bill for 50£.—I well know, that considering my outfit I have spent this year far more than I might do.—I should be very glad if my Father would make a real account against me, as he often says jokingly."[30] A year later, he wrote to Caroline from Valparaiso, "Tell my father I have kept my promise of being extravagant in Chili [sic]. I have drawn a bill of 100£."[31]

It is revealing that Darwin apparently wrote only two letters to his father during the entire *Beagle* voyage, and that there seems to be only one letter from Dr. Darwin to his son during this nearly five-year period. Of the seventy-six letters Charles exchanged with the family back at the Mount, nineteen were to or from his sister Susan, twenty-three were with his sister Catherine, and thirty-one, the largest number by far, were correspondence between Charles and his sister Caroline.[32] Of course, Charles understood that his letters would be read aloud to the whole family, and it may be that Dr. Darwin was more than happy to have his daughters handle the communications. One message that comes through very clearly in all the letters is the motherly concern that Caroline continued to feel toward her younger brother. In March 1833, she wrote to him, "Good bye My very dear Charles and God bless you[.] Sitting and writing in this old school room makes me feel so Motherly to you dear Tactus [her old pet name for Charles]."[33]

Other than the discomforts of seasickness, Charles enjoyed remarkably good health throughout most of the voyage. He had no trouble roughing it in the backcountry, with experiences not unlike those of Abraham Lincoln on the American frontier. Darwin hiked, rode, and climbed wherever he wanted to go and thoroughly enjoyed the hunts for fresh meat to supplement the food aboard ship. His one major illness came during an overland journey from Santiago to Valparaiso, Chile. It began with a violent stomachache, followed by exhaustion and loss of appetite. He was laid low for six weeks, and FitzRoy had to delay sailing until Darwin had recovered enough to leave Valparaiso.

Darwin was as well liked on the *Beagle* as Lincoln was in New Salem. The crew responded to the same friendliness, energy, and cheerfulness he had earlier exhibited at college by willingly helping him gather collections. Because of his education, they gave him the name "Philos," short for "Philosopher."

As the *Beagle* rounded the tip of South America—the notorious Tierra del Fuego, where so many ships had been swamped by storms or dashed on the sharp rocks—Darwin observed a group of natives that the English and other Europeans called the Fuegians. This inhospitable land made him think deeply about the tremendous contrasts in how people lived and about the ability of humans to endure almost any conditions on the planet. "Their country," he wrote, "is a broken mass of wild rocks, lofty hills, and useless forests: and these are viewed through mists and endless storms." He described the people as "the most abject and miserable creatures I anywhere beheld.... Viewing such men, one can hardly make one's self believe that they are fellow creatures, and inhabitants of the same world." Yet, "nature by making habit omnipotent, and its effects hereditary, has fitted the Fuegian to the climate and the productions of this miserable country."[34] This ability of people to adapt to such a harsh climate was just one of the many clues about human evolution that Darwin observed on the voyage.

Darwin wrote that, despite their living conditions, the Fuegians exhibited "more practiced habits of perception and keener senses, common to all men in a savage state, as compared with those long civilized."[35] He also had a chance to study three of these people up close, as there were three Fuegians onboard the *Beagle*—two men and a young girl whom Captain FitzRoy had captured three years before and taken back to England. FitzRoy regarded the Fuegians as an experiment and was curious to see if they could be civilized and then transfer their acquired European ways to their own people after returning home in the company of an English missionary named Richard Matthews, who would set up a mission station and spread the Gospel.

When the Fuegians were first seized, FitzRoy had named the two male captives Jemmy Button, age fifteen, and York Minister, in his midtwenties. He called the eleven-year-old girl Fuegia Basket. These made-up names were more appropriate for pets than for human beings and showed the condescending attitude that Englishmen (and other Europeans) generally exhibited toward native peoples. FitzRoy had named York Minister for an eight-hundred-foot-high rock promontory rising out of the sea that Captain James Cook had earlier named for the great cathedral in his native English city of York. The name Fuegia Basket came from a wickerlike craft that the *Beagle* crew had built, while Jemmy Button referred to his "purchase" with a single mother-of-pearl button.[36]

Darwin remarked that York Minister had a good intellect and that Jemmy Button was "remarkably sympathetic with any one in pain." Fuegia Basket was "very quick in learning anything, especially languages."[37] Although the three had lived in primitive conditions, Darwin seemed to be saying that they had just as much intellectual and emotional potential as any other human beings, including Europeans. But such potential was not enough to offset the ways of their fellow Fuegians, and as soon as they were put ashore again, members of their tribe stole everything they had brought with them, and soon the three were living exactly as they had before. Not surprisingly, the missionary project ended in disaster: the local inhabitants stole all the mission property and made Richard Matthews fear for his life. When the *Beagle* returned several weeks later to check on him, Matthews ran screaming in terror to the ship.

Besides these eye-opening experiences with the Fuegians, Darwin found fossils that would later play an important part in his thinking about evolution. At Punta Alta Bay in Brazil, he made his first major fossil finds when he came across the remains of a large extinct ground sloth called a *Megatherium*, which was already known to scientists, though there was just one complete specimen anywhere in Europe at the time. Later he found the remains of several extinct mammals that had not yet been discovered, including a large armadillolike creature (*Glyptotherium*), a large rodent (*Toxodon*), and a camellike mammal called *Macrauchenia*. He sent these specimens, along with others he had gathered, back to Professor Henslow at Cambridge, who had agreed to receive his collections. Significantly, Darwin realized that these extinct species were very similar anatomically to smaller mammals that presently inhabited the Pampas, a discovery that prompted him to conclude later that the latter-day forms were somehow descended from these predecessors.

The extinction of the South American horse in particular caused Darwin to reflect on the processes of biological distribution and on the irony that Europeans had reintroduced the horse to a continent where it had existed before: "Certainly it is a marvelous fact in the history of the Mammalia, that in South America a native horse should have lived and disappeared, to be succeeded in after-ages by the countless herds descended from the few introduced by the Spanish colonists!"[38] These finds gave further proof to Darwin, as well as those receiving his fossils back in England, that extinctions of many animals had taken place over time.

The existing animal population could be just as revealing for Darwin, and, in some cases, his means of discovery were unusual. In southern Argentina, he found a small species of rhea (a flightless South American bird) one evening while dining. At first he had assumed that it was just an immature specimen, but then he realized that it was really a smaller, separate species from the larger type of rhea that inhabited northern Argentina. He managed to salvage the head, neck, a wing, legs, and some feathers, which he shipped back to England and was rewarded by having the bird named *rhea darwinii*. But far more significant than having a newly discovered species named for him was his conjecture that closely related living species usually do not inhabit the same area, a conjecture that eventually led to the conclusion that each closely related type had evolved to exploit a different habitat.

Darwin's most important finds took place during five weeks in September and October of 1835 in the Galapagos Islands, located in the Pacific Ocean, some six hundred miles west of Ecuador. He described one of them, Chatham Island (San Cristobal to the Spanish), as utterly desolate and forlorn at first sight: "Nothing could be less inviting than the first appearance. A broken field of black basaltic lava, thrown into the most rugged waves, and crossed by great fissures, is everywhere covered by stunted, sunburnt brushwood, which shows little signs of life. The dry and parched surface, being heated by the noon-day sun, gave to the air a close and sultry feeling, like that from a stove."[39] In its own way, the island seemed as inhospitable to life as the Tierra del Fuego, yet plants and animals had exploited every niche that could support life.

Darwin marveled at the giant tortoises and the many finches. At first he accepted the prevailing opinion that sailors had put the tortoises on the islands as a future source of food. He discarded this view when he remembered that the Spanish governor of the Galapagos had told him that each island had distinct types of tortoises, which could be identified at a glance. He also realized only later that slight differences in the sizes and shapes of the finches' beaks allowed them to exploit different habitats or food supplies, and marked them as belonging to separate species. More than any other discovery, these finches would cause Darwin to ponder the causes of biological variation as the prime engine of evolution and the role of islands, as places of relative isolation, in the emergence of new types: "Most of the organic productions are aboriginal creations," he wrote, "found nowhere else; there is even a difference between the inhabitants of the different islands; yet all show a marked relationship with those of America, though separated from that continent by an open space of ocean, between 500 and 600 miles in width."[40] Later he would conclude that the distinct Galapagos species had diverged from animals originally from the mainland and that because of their isolation on the islands and their different habitats, they had developed into different species, which continued to bear similarities to their more distant ancestors on the continent. As yet, Darwin did not have a clue about the mechanisms of such divergence.

Still seeing himself as more of a geologist than anything else, Darwin was intensely interested in the geology of the many places he visited, and he found Lyell's *Principles* to be indispensable. In February 1835, a powerful earthquake in Chile demonstrated firsthand just how natural forces could shape the land. At Concepción, the quake had destroyed every building for miles around, and a huge tidal wave had washed away hundreds of people, livestock, and the remains of buildings. Darwin realized that the quake had also caused the land to rise by several feet when he saw exposed mussel beds lying well above high tide, the shellfish all dead. During his walk around Quinquina Island, he "observed that numerous fragments of rock, which, from the marine productions adhering to them, must recently have been lying in deep water, had been cast up high on the beach.... The most remarkable effect of this earthquake," Darwin wrote, "was the permanent elevation of the land.... There can be no doubt that the land round the Bay of Concepcion was upraised two or three feet."[41] Here was convincing proof of Lyell's uniformitarian theories, since the elevation of the land had resulted from the same natural forces in the present that had shaped the earth at earlier periods.

The most pleasant time at sea was the three thousand-mile voyage across the Pacific from the Galapagos Islands to Tahiti, a period of calm water and almost no seasickness, when Darwin "enjoyed bright and clear weather, while running along pleasantly at the rate of 150 or 160 miles a day before the steady trade wind."[42] From Tahiti they headed to New Zealand and Australia, where Darwin commented on the falling off of the aboriginal populations. He attributed this decline to the introduction of alcohol and European diseases (to which they had no immunities), as well as to the European destruction of wild animals on which the native population depended for food. He compared their fate to what had happened to native peoples everywhere upon contact with Europeans. His stark conclusion was that "the varieties of man seem to act on each other in the same way as different species of animals—the stronger always extirpating the weaker." These thoughts anticipated the concept of "survival of the fittest," a term later coined by Herbert Spencer and still later adopted by Darwin himself. Yet Darwin did not welcome such a fate for the aborigines: "It was melancholy at New Zealand to hear the fine energetic natives saying, that they knew the land was doomed to pass from their children."[43]

Despite his curiosity about the native peoples of Australia, Darwin's thoughts were turning more and more to home, and to English girls. He wrote to his sister Susan from Sidney in late January 1836: "There was such a bevy of pretty lady-like Australian girls, & so deliciously English-like the whole party looked, that one might have fancied myself actually in England."[44]

From Australia the *Beagle* sped across the Indian Ocean, stopping at Cape Town on the Horn of Africa. Darwin thought they would finally be homeward bound and was disheartened to find that FitzRoy had decided to go back to check a longitude measurement that he had made in Brazil.

Throughout the voyage, he had sent his family sections of his journal as he wrote them, which impressed and delighted the folks back home. In return, family members sent Charles new books, including novels by Walter Scott and the social reformer Harriet Martineau. Professor Henslow wrote to Darwin about the amazement that had greeted the collections he had shipped back, especially the large Megatherium bone, which had been displayed before the British Association for the Advancement of Science meeting at Cambridge.

Charles's sisters continued to comment in their letters on his becoming a clergymen, a prospect that Darwin did not contradict at the time, since he still had no idea of exactly what he wanted to do when he finally reached England. In July 1835, three and a half years into his voyage, he wrote to his cousin William Darwin Fox, "I do so earnestly desire to return, yet I dare hardly look forward to the future, for I do not know what will become of me."[45] By February 1836, even his family was uncertain what he would do and contemplated the possibility of an academic career for him. His sister Susan wrote, "Papa & we often cogitate over the fire what you will do when you return, as I fear there are but few hopes of your still going into the Church:—I think you must turn Professor at Cambridge."[46]

The *Beagle* finally reached England on October 2, 1836, almost five years after it had started on its epic voyage. Reflecting back on his odyssey four decades later, Darwin wrote, "I have always felt that I owe to the voyage the first real training or education of my mind."[47] The voyage of the *Beagle* was over, and Darwin's five-year moratorium from decision was nearing its end, though he probably did not know it at the time.

While not as dramatic as Darwin's voyage, Lincoln's continuing adventures at New Salem were equally important to him. By the spring of 1832, Offutt had overextended himself in business and, one by one, his enterprises collapsed, including the store kept for him by Lincoln and Greene. That fall, Lincoln went together with William F. Berry to buy another general store in the village, with Lincoln signing a promissory note for his share. Shortly thereafter, they bought the stock of yet another general store, and again signed notes. Business was poor, and the only item that brought any profit was whiskey, which Illinois law allowed them to sell but only by the jug or barrel. (Establishments designated as "groceries" could sell spirits by the drink.) In early 1833, the partners abandoned the business, and Berry died not long thereafter, leaving Lincoln liable for all their debts. According to Herndon, it took Lincoln years to make good on them, but he paid back every penny, a fact that helped to earn him the sobriquet of "Honest Abe."

Given Lincoln's limited finances, a moratorium from deciding on his life's work might seem foolish and irresponsible. But he was used to crude living conditions and to scraping by on whatever he could make from odd jobs and assignments. He was also single and did not have to worry about making a decent living for a wife and children. Just how he lived and what he did with his time were entirely up to him.

After closing the store at New Salem, Lincoln resorted again to day labor and also earned a little money as an election clerk and a juror. In the spring of 1833, his friends arranged for him to become the village postmaster, but fees brought him only about fifty dollars a year. One benefit of the job was the chance to read newspapers that came in the mail for subscribers. To supplement his postmaster's income, he applied to become the assistant county surveyor and went about teaching himself trigonometry and the surveyor's art. He learned quickly from books and on-the-job training and was soon highly respected for his accurate and meticulous work. With new roads being built and new properties being sold all over the area, he had plenty to do. His wide surveying also allowed him to meet and impress a good many men who would later vote for him.

Indeed, elective office was another way that Lincoln tried to make ends meet, taking advantage of his likeability and growing skills as a public speaker and debater. It was also a way to build up his self-esteem. His first election was a military one, when he was chosen captain of the militia during the so-called Black Hawk War in April 1832. The Sauk and Fox Indians had been tricked by a treaty into giving up their lands in northwestern Illinois. Forced to move west of the Mississippi River, Chief Black Hawk and about five hundred warriors came back to reclaim their tribal domain. Lincoln did his best to keep order among the men, assisted by Jack Armstrong, whom he made his first sergeant. The unit saw no action and was mustered out at the end of May after fulfilling their thirty-day enlistment. Lincoln then volunteered for two more stints, both times as a private in a cavalry unit, though he had to borrow a horse. His service finally came to an end on July 10; he had earned about $125 for a total of eighty days in the military. But it was his initial election as a militia captain, he wrote, "which gave him so much satisfaction."[48]

Lincoln's opportunity to meet and impress other men in the militia proved invaluable when he decided to run for the lower house of the Illinois legislature in August 1832. Well aware of the need for transportation improvements in the West, he agreed with Kentucky senator Henry Clay that governments on both the state and federal levels should fund such "internal improvements," and during the short campaign, Lincoln called for the clearing of snags in the local Sangamon River. He also spoke in favor of a national bank and protective tariffs, issues that would remain central to his political philosophy. In a field of thirteen candidates, he ran eighth, with the top four contenders winning seats in the legislature, but in New Salem he won 277 of the 300 ballots cast. Two years later, in August 1834, he ran again for the legislature and won with the second-highest number of votes. He had successfully waged a campaign of handshaking around the district and of attracting votes from both major political factions by carefully avoiding divisive issues. Lincoln had never owned a suit of clothes in his life and had to borrow $200 from wealthy New Salem resident Coleman Smoot to buy a new outfit, as well as to cover the other expenses of moving to the state capital, then at Vandalia.

Lincoln had been fascinated by the law for some time and had thought seriously about studying it in the year before his election to the legislature. Just after Lincoln's electoral victory, John T. Stuart, who had been an officer under Lincoln in the Black Hawk War and who had his own legal practice in Springfield, encouraged Lincoln to take up the law and he loaned Lincoln the books to prepare himself for the bar. He "studied with nobody," Lincoln later wrote, reading the arguments and rephrasing them several times until he had mastered them.[49] He plowed through William Blackstone's *Commentaries on the Common Law*, Chitty's *Pleadings*, Greenleaf's *Evidence*, and Joseph Story's *Equity Jurisprudence*. Lincoln's solo studies may have been unusual, but his failure to attend law school was not; at this time nearly all lawyers trained by "reading law," usually under the guidance of an established attorney.

Though New Salem was small, it provided Lincoln with a laboratory to experiment with possible lines of work—storekeeper, surveyor, soldier, postmaster, politician, and lawyer. It also offered a good transition from the pioneer life he had known and the more urban lifestyle that he would enjoy in just a few years. With a seat in the legislature, to which he was reelected in 1836, 1838, and 1840, and his determination to become a successful lawyer, Lincoln had finally hit on a plausible vocation. During these years he had also turned away from almost everything his father had stood for: he abandoned farming for the law, he rejected Tom Lincoln's Baptist faith in favor of deism and religious skepticism, and in politics he became a Whig instead of sticking with his father's devotion to the Democrats. He was determined to carve out a life of his own that would be very different from the one he had known as a child.

Darwin's distancing himself from his father's expectations differed from Lincoln's. Despite the fact that Dr. Darwin could be difficult and despite Charles's fears that he had disappointed his father, he loved and respected him. Dr. Darwin would also support Charles financially, so that he could have the leisure to become a gentleman naturalist.

Fortunately for each of them, young Darwin and young Lincoln had been able to put off decisions about who they were and where they wanted to go. In saying no to what was expected of them and in searching out their own avenues of meaning and satisfactory work, they provided themselves with an opportunity to think and act outside the boundaries of prevailing thought and action and later to lead revolts that changed the world.

NOTES

1. For a fascinating exploration of this view of change and opportunity, see Richard D. Brown, *Modernization: The Transformation of American Life, 1600–1865* (Prospect Heights, IL: Waveland Press, 1988).

2. William H. Herndon, *Herndon's Life of Lincoln* (New York: Da Capo Press, 1983), p. 64.

3. In his "Autobiographical Sketch," Lincoln writes that John Hanks had not accompanied them as far as New Orleans. See Roy P. Basler et al., ed., *The Collected Works of Abraham Lincoln* (New Brunswick, NJ: Rutgers University Press, 1953), 4:64.

4. Herndon, *Herndon's Life of Lincoln*, p. 64.

5. Nora Barlow, ed., *The Autobiography of Charles Darwin, 1809–1882* (New York: W. W. Norton, 1993), p. 59.

6. Ibid., p. 68.

7. Darwin to Caroline Darwin, April 28, 1831, *The Correspondence of Charles Darwin* (Cambridge: Cambridge University Press, 1985–[2005]), 1:12.

8. Barlow, *Autobiography of Charles Darwin*, p. 70.

9. On Sedgwick, see David Oldroyd, "Adam Sedgwick: A Confident Mind in Turmoil," in *Cambridge Scientific Minds*, edited by Peter Harman and Simon Mitton (Cambridge: Cambridge University Press, 2002), pp. 64–78.

10. For a good history of New Salem and Lincoln's time there, see Benjamin P. Thomas, *Lincoln's New Salem* (Carbondale: Southern Illinois University Press, 1954).

11. Ibid., p. 25.

12. Herndon, *Herndon's Life of Lincoln*, p. 68.

13. Ibid., pp. 67–68.

14. Philip S. Foner, ed., *The Complete Works of Thomas Paine* (New York: Citadel Press, 1945), 1:464.

15. Ibid., 1:487.

16. Janet Browne, *Charles Darwin: Voyaging* (Princeton, NJ: Princeton University Press, 1995), pp. 207–209.

17. Barlow, *Autobiography of Charles Darwin*, p. 72.

18. Ibid., pp. 76–77.

19. Darwin read Tocqueville in 1836. See *Correspondence of Charles Darwin*, vol. 4, appendix, pp. 4, 119, 226.

20. Ibid., pp. 80–81.

21. Darwin to his father, February 10, 1832, *Correspondence of Charles Darwin*, 1:206.

22. Charles Darwin, *Voyage of the Beagle* (New York: Barnes and Noble, 2004), p. 12.

23. Ibid., p. 527.

24. Ibid., p. 25.

25. Ibid., p. 105.

26. Barlow, *Autobiography of Charles Darwin*, p. 85.

27. Darwin to Charlotte Darwin, May 22, 1833, *Correspondence of Charles Darwin*, 1:312.

28. Barlow, *Autobiography of Charles Darwin*, p. 74.

29. Michael White and John Gribbin, *Darwin: A Life in Science* (New York: Dutton, 1995), p. 56.

30. Darwin to Caroline Darwin, November 13, 1833, *Correspondence of Charles Darwin*, 1:353–54.

31. Darwin to Caroline Darwin, November 8, 1834, *Correspondence of Charles Darwin*, 1:419.

32. These are the letters that appear in volume 1 of the comprehensive *Correspondence of Charles Darwin* being published by the Cambridge University Press. It is possible, of course, that some of the *Beagle* letters did not survive, but there is no reason to believe that if a few have been lost they would greatly tip the balance away from Caroline.

33. Caroline Darwin to Charles Darwin, March 7, 1833, *Correspondence of Charles Darwin*, 1:302.

34. Darwin, *Voyage of the Beagle*, pp. 220, 221, 223, 224.

35. Ibid., p. 213.

36. For more on this strange saga, see Peter Nichols, *Evolution's Captain: The Story of the Kidnapping that Led to Charles Darwin's Voyage Aboard the "Beagle"* (New York: HarperCollins, 2003).

37. Darwin, *Voyage of the Beagle*, p. 215.

38. Ibid., p. 134.

39. Ibid., p. 393.

40. Ibid., p. 397.

41. Ibid., pp. 317, 324.

42. Ibid., p. 423.

43. Ibid., p. 459.

44. Darwin to Susan Darwin, January 28, 1836, *Correspondence of Charles Darwin*, 1:483.

45. Darwin to William Darwin Fox, July 1, 1835, *Correspondence of Charles Darwin*, 1:460.

46. Susan Darwin to Darwin, February 12, 1836, *Correspondence of Charles Darwin*, 1:489.

47. Barlow, *Autobiography of Charles Darwin*, pp. 76–77.

48. Lincoln, "Autobiographical Sketch," *Collected Works of Abraham Lincoln*, 4:64.

49. Ibid., 4:65.

Chapter 3

LOVE AND WORK

Love and work are the cornerstones of our humanness.
—Sigmund Freud

he human need for love and work seems obvious, yet finding real love and satisfying work can be the most difficult tasks of a lifetime. Abraham Lincoln and Charles Darwin were no exceptions. Darwin was luckier in love than Lincoln, who endured the torments of the damned in finding a mate and then suffered through years of tumultuous domestic life. Both men chose work that promised success as well as difficulty. Despite the hazards, both had married and started careers by their early thirties.

The morning after the *Beagle* landed at Falmouth, England, Charles Darwin boarded a coach for home. The trip took successive teams of horses two full days at full speed to make Shrewsbury, and when Darwin reached The Mount on October 4, 1836, everyone had gone to bed. He crept in undetected and surprised the family when he showed up at breakfast the next morning. His father and sisters, well aware by now of what a significant contribution he was making to science, had given up on his entering the church. A flurry of letters from Charles to friends and extended family members showed an energy and confidence often absent in the past. He was now a man who had completed an epic journey and he knew that it had changed his life forever. At age twenty-seven, he had ended his years of searching and was about to begin his life's work.

Much as he reveled in being home, Charles was itching to discuss his great adventures and future plans with Professor Henslow, and after just a week at The Mount he was off to Cambridge. He also wanted advice about where to house his mass of collections, and Henslow, along with Professor Sedgwick, whom Darwin also visited at Cambridge, put him in touch with several naturalists and scientists in London who might help.

The family wanted Charles to stay with them at Shrewsbury, but after nearly five years at sea, he knew that he needed his independence. Despite the dirt and overcrowding in London with its two million people, he realized that it was the best place on earth to make contacts with the larger scientific community and with potential publishers for the several books he wanted to write. Living in London would also give him convenient access to his collections, and to his brother Eras, who had been living in the city for a decade and who could introduce him to leading writers, artists, and intellectuals.

Had Charles been the eldest son of a wealthy aristocratic family, he might have simply enjoyed the life of a country gentleman, managing his estate while riding, hunting, and dabbling in collections. He knew that he could depend on his father's financial support, but he also knew that his family would expect him to make something of himself, as Darwin and Wedgwood men had done over the generations. Having failed at medical studies and then having backed away from joining the clergy, Charles had to prove to his father that he could succeed at a time when naturalists could be hailed as scientific heroes. He could also show his father that he was worthy of love and support.

Charles traveled to London on October 20 and stayed with Eras on Great Marlborough Street, within easy walking distance of all the major natural science museums and institutions, including the Geological, Zoological, and Linnean societies, the British Museum, and the Royal College of Physicians. He was already a celebrity, since a number of his letters had been published and news about his specimens had impressed members of the scientific community, who were now eager to meet him. For several months, with frequent visits back to the family at Shrewsbury, Charles rented rooms just a few houses away from his brother. Although he loved Eras and appreciated his opening so many doors, Charles was dismayed that his brother had given up any serious thoughts of a career despite his medical training. It is unclear why Eras did not worry about disappointing their father, as Charles did. Perhaps as the younger son, Charles had been conditioned to trying out various ways to attract Dr. Darwin's attention and approval, while Eras had not felt compelled to do the same.

But like his brother, Charles did not have to worry about making a living, since his father gave him four hundred pounds a year upon returning from his travels, enough for a young, single gentleman to live comfortably. He could afford to hire servants and to pay for scientific specialists to help him sort and identify his mountain of specimens. Richard Owen of the Royal College of Physicians received the fossil mammals, museum curator George Waterhouse took the "living" mammal and insect collections, ornithologist John Gould had charge of the birds, and zoology professor Thomas Bell was tapped for the reptiles.

Charles also had plenty of time for general reading, and "took much delight in Wordsworth's and Coleridge's poetry."[1] He had several conversations with the prolific Whig novelist and social critic Harriet Martineau (1802–1876), with whom Eras was having a sporadic love affair. Martineau had just spent two years traveling extensively throughout the

United States and was in the process of writing her *Society in America* (1837), a groundbreaking description and analysis of the country's institutions—from slavery, the status of women, and prison reform to politics, education, and social class. Charles called on her, and although he was astonished to find her so ugly, he listened raptly to her talk of America. Martineau, for her part, found her visitor "simple, childlike, painstaking, effective."[2]

Whether or not Darwin read *Society in America* is uncertain, but he did admire Martineau's writing style, and there is every reason to think that he also paid careful attention to the book. Like virtually all the foreign observers who wrote about the new United States—Alexis de Tocqueville being the most famous—Martineau was fascinated by the country's great democratic experiment, and she was mostly a warm supporter of it. She nevertheless bored into the hypocrisies and inconsistencies of democracy and especially the growth of slavery in the United States, an observation that Darwin had made even though he had never visited the country. Yet Martineau believed that the conflict between the ideals of liberty and equality and the iniquity of slavery would eventually force the Americans to free their slaves. In fact, it was this very conflict between the real and the ideal that would increasingly plague Abraham Lincoln and legions of his countrymen.

The year that Martineau published her thoughts on America, Abraham Lincoln made a great step forward, which was, for him, as significant as Darwin's decision to become a naturalist at about the same time. On March 1, 1837, Lincoln was admitted to the Illinois bar. A little over a month later, he became the law partner of John T. Stuart, a man who had served with Lincoln in the Black Hawk War and who had originally encouraged his legal studies. Handsome, polished, well educated, and socially well connected, Stuart had a flourishing law practice in Springfield. On April 15, Lincoln left New Salem to enter a new life, riding into town on a borrowed horse.

Lincoln's Springfield was as different from Darwin's London as could be imagined. London was one of the oldest cities in Europe and probably the largest city in the world at the time, while Springfield was a raw boomtown of fifteen hundred people that had been founded only sixteen years before. This new state capital, a designation that Lincoln had helped to engineer as a member of the state legislature, still had unpaved streets, which became seas of sticky mud in wet weather and swirls of dust during dry summer months. Pigs roamed freely, and the stench from horse manure lying in the streets and piling up beside the livery stables was overpowering. Although there were some fine brick buildings, a number of log houses remained from the town's first years.[3] The great majority of earliest settlers in Springfield had hailed from the Upper South, and especially from Kentucky, but by the time Lincoln arrived, only about 28 percent were native Southerners, while 30 percent came from the Middle States, and 42 percent from New England, producing a cultural mix that would later help Lincoln to appreciate the growing sectional divisions in the country.[4]

Despite the vast differences between Darwin's London and Lincoln's small, newly founded Springfield, the fledgling lawyer found everything in town that he needed for success: professional opportunities, men with whom he could discuss and debate ideas and events, and powerful, well-connected individuals and families who were willing to help advance his related careers in politics and law. In fact, everywhere Lincoln turned, people bent over backward to help the tall, gaunt, and very likeable young attorney who seemed to exude every promise of success. Although social mobility was certainly possible in Darwin's England, the lack of a hereditary upper class in the United States and the more fluid social norms of frontier towns offered great opportunities for a bright and ambitious young man like Abraham Lincoln.

Lincoln found lodgings in Springfield without really trying when he stopped by A. Y. Ellis & Company, a general store located on the town square, to inquire about buying a mattress, sheets, and a pillow. Unable to afford $17 for the three items, he asked one of the proprietors, Joshua F. Speed, if he could have them on credit until the end of the year, adding that he was not sure he could pay him back even then. Speed, who had once heard Lincoln give a political speech and thought he had the makings of a fine lawyer, offered to share his own room above the store with the newcomer, where they both slept in one double bed.

Two centuries later, some have speculated that Lincoln and Speed might have entered into a homosexual relationship, since they slept in that same double bed for nearly five years. Yet two men sharing a bed was very common at the time.⁵ Friends, traveling business associates, or even strangers were often put into the same bed at inns and hotels. This was true of lawyers riding the judicial circuit from one town to the other. Still, Lincoln could well have afforded his own lodgings once he had established himself relatively quickly in the law. In truth, there is no reliable evidence one way or the other of a homosexual relationship between the two men, and there is likely never to be anything conclusive.

Lincoln, Speed, and a number of young friends spent winter evenings gathered around a large fireplace in the back room of the store. There they discussed politics, religion, literature, and current events, and read each others' essays and poems. As usual, Lincoln had a ready supply of stories to tell.

Lincoln was fortunate to join John Stuart's law office, since Stuart already had a prosperous practice. Thus Lincoln was spared the pain and uncertainty of having to start from scratch and hope that he could attract clients. Because Stuart was preoccupied with running for a seat in the US House of Representatives, he turned most of the work over to Lincoln from the very first days of their collaboration. When Stuart won the election and went off to Washington in November 1839, everything fell into Lincoln's lap. Fortunately, most of the cases were relatively simple civil suits, but Lincoln was assiduous about filing papers with the court for fear that a mistake might cause the case to be dismissed for lack of proper filing.

Despite having as much work as he wanted or could easily handle, Lincoln was hardly becoming rich on fees that commonly ranged from $2.50 to $10 a case—and this during a time when it was not unusual to be compensated in services, such as when an innkeeper paid him with $6 worth of meals. Exactly how much Lincoln earned in these early years is uncertain because he was a very sloppy bookkeeper who often neglected to record his fees. He had no regular filing system for legal papers in the office, which were usually spread all over tables and chairs in the office or stuffed into drawers at random. Lincoln also had the habit of sticking papers into his tall stovepipe hat. His slapdash method of dealing with records was a far cry from the more fastidious Charles Darwin.

Since there was not enough legal work in Springfield to support its attorneys, Lincoln and most of the other lawyers went from town to town in central Illinois, following the circuit judge as he made his rounds to hold court. Lincoln enjoyed the easy comradeship of the circuit, when the judge and all the attorneys rode together, putting up at the same lodging places and taking their meals together, only to face off against each other in court the following day, when some of them represented the plaintiffs and others the defendants. There were no hard feelings over these judicial contests when they all retired at the end of the day. Although Lincoln was a bona fide member of the bar, riding the circuit, observing the cases, and talking with his fellow circuit riders deepened as well as widened his knowledge of the law.

What a much later generation would call "networking" was also paying off for Darwin. On October 29, 1836, less than a month after arriving home from the *Beagle* adventure, he had dinner at the home of the great Charles Lyell, who already admired what Darwin had done and encouraged his further efforts. Several months later, Lyell wrote to Professor Sedgwick, "Darwin is a glorious addition to any society of geologists, and is working hard and making way, both in his book [about the *Beagle* voyage] and in our discussions."[6] Another guest during Darwin's first dinner with the Lyells was Richard Owen, a professor at the Royal College of Physicians, as well as a highly regarded zoologist and anatomist, who accepted Darwin's fossil specimens for the college's large and newly constructed museum and library. (Later Owen would become one of Darwin's fiercest critics.)

Darwin was fortunate to be so well connected, since Lyell was a great snob who frequently agonized with his wife over which dinner invitations were worthy of accepting. Their friendship would last until the end of Lyell's life, and although the geologist would continue to support Darwin, he would never completely accept his theory of natural selection. Yet Lyell's advice and approval placed Darwin at the center of a growing scientific network. Lyell and the other scientific men he met would be of incalculable value in helping him gain support for his most controversial conclusions.

What absorbed most of Darwin's energies at the time, however, was writing up the account of his voyage. Captain FitzRoy's idea was that Darwin's work should be one of three volumes, which included his own and one by Captain Philip King, who had headed an earlier South American survey while in command of the *Beagle*. Darwin's journal, which he had composed carefully aboard ship, needed only to be fleshed out and edited, and he completed the work in just seven months. Yet it was hard work, for as Darwin often admitted, he had difficulty writing anything in lucid, easily understood prose. For the rest of his life, he would struggle with smoothing out and simplifying his ponderous writing style, a problem that Lincoln, who had hardly any formal education, never had to face. Though Darwin agonized over his writing, the end product, after much editorial assistance, was compelling, easy to read, and very colorful in places. He rushed to complete his manuscript only to discover that FitzRoy was taking his time, a delay that held up publication for another eighteenth months.

While waiting for FitzRoy to finish, Darwin plunged into several other projects. He immediately started work on a book called *Zoology*, which was to contain reports by various experts on the collections he had sent back. Darwin used his social connections to secure a government grant of one thousand pounds to cover the cost of the hand-colored plates to illustrate the book. He also started a book titled *Coral Reefs*. In January 1837, he gave a paper before the Geological Society on coastal uplift in Chile. Shortly thereafter, he became a fellow of the society and became its secretary in February 1838, the same month that he agreed to serve as vice president of the Entomological Society. In June, under the sponsorship of Lyell, he was elected to the Athenaeum Club, a London social club, where he often dined and consorted with the most famous and socially prominent men of the day. Eleven months later, in January 1839, he was inducted into the prestigious Royal Society, where social standing counted as much if not more than any scholarly accomplishments, though Darwin was certainly worthy on both counts. As he approached his thirtieth birthday, he was well on his way to becoming a respected scientist.

At the same time, Darwin was starting to make some sense of what he had observed and collected during the *Beagle* voyage with the assistance of experts in several fields. He learned from John Gould, an accomplished ornithologist and taxidermist at the Zoological Society where he had deposited some four hundred and fifty stuffed birds, that those from the Galapagos Islands were all finches. Darwin had originally thought that some were finches, some wrens, and some blackbirds. In fact, the birds represented a dozen separate species of finches, varying mainly by sizes and shapes of beaks, some long and some short, some sharp and some blunt, among other characteristics. Unfortunately, he had not bothered to record the islands where he had collected each bird. Later, with the help of better records kept by Captain FitzRoy, he realized that each island had its distinctive species of finches, all of which resembled finches on the mainland of Ecuador. Just why this was true and how it had come about puzzled Darwin, and answering this puzzle would become one of the major building blocks of his evolutionary theory.

Meanwhile, at the College of Surgeons, Richard Owen was beginning to classify Darwin's fossils from Argentina. Among them were a giant ground sloth and a giant llama. Struck by the similarities between these large mammals and the smaller versions of the present-day that existed in the same general locations, Darwin again wondered if the modern types had somehow descended from the earlier ones, especially since he was noticing that other extinct forms usually had existed in the same general area as those that replaced them.

In July 1837, three months after Abraham Lincoln was admitted to the bar to practice law, Darwin began a series of small, pocket-sized notebooks in which he posed questions and formulated tentative answers to his ideas about the possible connections between fossils and later life forms, as well as the possible forces behind species differentiation. He called these jottings *Zoonomia*, a title borrowed from his grandfather Erasmus Darwin's speculations on evolution. He asked himself about the importance of sexual reproduction, answering that it was the only way to combine characteristics from two individuals and to enhance variety. He also wondered if the results from these combinations might allow certain members of a species to adapt to climate and other changes in the environment. He speculated further about the role that islands and the separations of larger landmasses by barriers such as mountain chains had played in creating new species. There would be many other questions to explore in the future: What part did extinction play in the emergence of new species? How did one species turn into another? Did the jump from inorganic matter to simple life forms occur only once, and if so, did that mean that all living beings could be traced to a single source and were therefore related? Was there an automatic, straight-line, progressive movement from simpler to more advanced life forms, or was biological development more multidirectional? Most importantly, what was the main cause of species change?

Unlike most of his fellow naturalists, who remained bound to conventional religious and philosophical beliefs, Darwin was open-minded about all these questions—a great strength for any scientist. Many of his answers were at first intuitive and based on the fragmentary evidence he had seen or collected, but he would go on to test these notions in every way he could think of. At the core of Darwin's method of investigation, according to Niles Eldredge, was always the question of "What would we expect to see if life had evolved?"[7] Eldredge also believes that Darwin had become convinced of evolution while still on the *Beagle*, but Darwin scholar David Quammen believes that this breakthrough occurred around March 1837, following Darwin's discussions with John Gould and Richard Owen about his specimens.[8] Darwin himself was less precise in his *Autobiography*, writing that he had become convinced "in the year 1837 or 1838" that "species were mutable productions."[9] In fact, it may be impossible to pinpoint the exact date of Darwin's "conversion" to evolution, though it is clear that what he had surmised on the *Beagle* and soon after his return were causing him to question the standard beliefs about species.

Darwin was far from the first person to ponder the origins and development of species. As far back as the ancient Greeks, twenty-five hundred years before, philosophers had asked the question and had put out a number of theories. Empedocles (495–435 BCE) proposed that plant life had originated first and that certain animal parts—arms, legs, heads, and so forth—had "budded" off from these plants, resulting in all sorts of monstrous forms. Eventually, the monstrosities died out, leaving only those animals whose various parts worked together harmoniously. Although this explanation now seems ludicrous, the belief that evolution had occurred through chance, rather than through design, was a conclusion that Darwin would also draw.

The great comprehensive philosopher Aristotle (384–322 BCE) believed that evolution could be compared to a ladder that led up though a hierarchy of life forms to the ultimate being: humankind. "Nature" seeking perfection, he said, was the vehicle of this progression from lowly animals to human beings. Disagreeing with Empedocles, Aristotle rejected the idea of chance variations in favor of purposeful design.

Several early Christian theologians, most notably Saint Augustine of Hippo (353–430 CE), embraced an evolutionary view of life. Augustine did not believe that the Genesis account of a six-day creation should be accepted literally but only as six units of time of indefinite length. God had created the potential for life, but the details had worked themselves out in accordance with laws set down by God. (In this sense, Augustine sounded remarkably like some Christians in the late nineteenth century who believed that Darwin's theory of evolution was just an explanation for laws that God had laid down and used to work out his creation.)

Twelve centuries after Augustine, as Protestant Reformers and the modern scientific revolution besieged the Roman Church, Catholic theologians were moving away from Augustine's philosophy to a concept called Special Creation. One theologian who embraced this view was Spanish Jesuit Francisco Suarez (1548–1617). He held that God had individually created each species and that each had remained unchanged over the ages. Interestingly, virtually all Protestant denominations likewise professed belief in the fixity of species, since it coincided with and supported the idea of an all-powerful, all-knowing, and unchanging God who had designed the universe and everything in it to fit together perfectly. These views would become a major stumbling block for anyone proposing a theory of evolution in the modern era.

The careful description and classification of plants did nothing to challenge beliefs in the fixity of species, since labeling each of them only seemed to confirm the permanence of life forms. The most famous of the modern classifiers was Carolus Linnaeus (1707–1778), who worked out a binomial system in which each plant or animal was given, in Latin, a genus and species name. In his *System of Nature* (1735), Linnaeus wrote that all seeds (or eggs) produced offspring resembling their parents and that they could not, as some believed at the time, produce creatures different from the parents. He also believed that each life form had descended from a single pair of ancestors, and that over time, their populations had merely grown larger but had not evolved. Although Linnaeus left no room for evolution, the idea of increasing populations over time would become an important element in Darwin's theory of natural selection.

Breaking with the insistence on species fixity was the Comte de Buffon (1707–1788). An independently wealthy man and the keeper of the Royal Garden in Paris, Buffon wrote a forty-four-volume work on the natural world, as well as the widely read *Natural History*. He concluded that the environment had the power to transform one species into another. Buffon was also interested in rudimentary organs and body parts that existed in various species where they performed no function. As an example, he pointed to the toe bones in pigs, which had cloven hooves and therefore had no need of toes. This insight suggested that evolution had occurred through a "trial and error" process that undercut the claim of either natural or divine perfection.

The single most important evolutionary thinker before Charles Darwin was Jean Baptiste Lamarck (1744–1829). Lamarck became best known for his assertions of acquired characteristics, claiming that parents could pass on traits that they had acquired during their own lifetimes. His most famous example was of succeeding generations of giraffes stretching their necks to reach leaves higher in the trees and of passing these longer necks on to their babies. Although this theory would later be discredited, Lamarck believed wholeheartedly in "transmutation"—that species were not fixed and that one species could develop into another. He also rejected the familiar image of a progressive ladder of life in favor of a branching pattern that Charles Darwin would also adopt. For many years Darwin, like Lamarck, would use the word *transmutation* rather than *evolution*, since *evolution* was then understood to mean any type of gradual change and was not a term that those in the life sciences generally used at the time.

There was also the mounting fossil record to which Darwin had contributed himself. As early as the eleventh century, Arabic scholars had observed the remains of sea creatures embedded in rocks on mountainsides, far from the sea where they had originated. The invention of the microscope in the seventeenth century allowed scientists to make detailed observations of these and other fossils and to confirm that they were the remains of once-living organisms. In the late eighteenth century, an English surveyor and canal builder named William "Strata" Smith (1769–1839) noticed that the excavations for canals revealed distinctive layers of rock, each of which contained characteristic fossil types. He also saw that the lower layers contained only simple life forms, while the higher ones had successively more complex forms, graduating from fish, to reptiles, to mammals.

In the early nineteenth century, dinosaur fossils were correctly identified for the first time as the remains of large extinct reptiles. The disappearance of these and other life forms, along with the layering of fossil remains, undermined the belief in a single act of divine creation and the associated belief that species had remained unchanged over the ages. Even if one accepted that God had created all living things, it seemed clear that creation was an ongoing process over an exceedingly long period of time. And if some plants and animals had become extinct, one might have to conclude that God, believed to be all-powerful, all-knowing, and perfect had, in fact, made a number of "mistakes" and been forced to start over again.

To explain evolution though natural causes was the goal Darwin set out for himself. In his *Autobiography*, he recalled an insight in the fall of 1838 while reading the sixth edition of Thomas Malthus's *Essay on Pop-*

ulation, first published in 1798. Malthus (1766–1834), an Anglican priest and widely known as Parson Malthus, was struck by the recent, rapid increases in human populations in various parts of the world, including Great Britain and the United States. Under optimum conditions, he believed, their numbers could double every twenty-five years. Unfortunately, the food supply could not keep up with this relentless onslaught of more and more people. Or, as Malthus explained it, population increased geometrically (1-2-4-8), while the food supply increased arithmetically (1-2-3-4). The only "natural" forces standing in the way of disastrous overpopulation were disease, war, and famine. In later editions of the book, Malthus suggested immigration, late marriage, and sexual abstinence as ways to avoid catastrophe.

Malthus's views had a large impact on economic theory and political ideology during the nineteenth century. Laissez-faire economists, who wanted government to sanction free enterprise and refrain from economic regulation, extolled competition. Malthus contributed to these arguments by opposing any kind of state assistance to the poor, since it would only allow them to marry early and to have more children, thereby contributing to overpopulation. The Whig Party, to which Darwin and his family belonged, used this Malthusian argument to campaign against the country's Poor Laws, which gave relief to the poor through Church of England parishes. For years the poor had received assistance (known as "outdoor relief") while living in their own homes, but in 1834 the Whig government, arguing that those on relief were simply too lazy to work, passed legislation that ended outdoor relief and forced people on assistance to live in workhouses, where they would have to labor for their meager subsistence. Darwin was well aware of these arguments. Harriet Martineau subscribed to them completely and often discussed Malthusian concepts at social gatherings that Darwin attended in London. As a result, some Darwin scholars have questioned whether his reading of the *Essay on Population* in the fall of 1838 was quite the revelation that he remembered, especially since he already knew about the tendencies for overpopulation among virtually all life forms. If so, the essay may have been more a confirmation of his own thinking than it was a sudden flash of insight.

Whatever the case, Darwin's dramatic account of a Malthusian revelation in the *Autobiography* bears repeating, if only because it underlines the importance of population pressures in his thinking about the transmutation (or evolution) of species:

> In October 1838, that is, fifteen months after I had begun my systematic enquiry [in the *Zoonomia* notebooks], I happened to read for amusement Malthus on *Population*, and being well prepared to appreciate the struggle for existence which everywhere goes on from long-continued observation of the habits of animals and plants, it at once struck me that under these circumstances favorable variations would tend to be preserved, and unfavorable ones to be destroyed. The result of this would be the formation of new species. Here, then, I at last got a theory by which to work.[10]

Darwin went on to call this theory "natural selection." He saw it as a natural law, but one that had nothing to do with Paley's ideas of benign design. As he explained, again in the *Autobiography*,

> The old argument of design in nature, as given by Paley, which formerly seemed to me so conclusive, fails, now that the law of natural selection has been discovered. We can no longer argue that, for instance, the beautiful hinge of a bivalve shell must have been made by an intelligent being, like the hinge of a door by man. There seems to be no more design in the variability of organic beings and in the action of natural selection, than in the course which the wind blows. Everything in nature is the result of fixed laws.[11]

This statement clearly left the Judeo-Christian God out of the picture. Up to the time of his return from the *Beagle*, Darwin had been orthodox in his beliefs, even though he had had reservations about the Thirty-Nine Articles of the Church of England ever since college days. But his wide reading and thinking about species development led him to some very serious doubts about the Old Testament: "During these two years [after returning home] I was led to think much about religion. . . . I had gradually come . . . to see that the Old Testament from its manifestly false history of the world, with the Tower of Babel, the rainbow as a sign, . . . and from its attributing to God the feelings of a vengeful tyrant, was no more to be trusted than the sacred books of the Hindoos, or the beliefs of any barbarian." Nor could he accept the miracles of the New Testament: "The more we know of the fixed laws of nature the more incredible do miracles become,—that the men at that time were ignorant and credulous to a degree almost incomprehensible to us."[12] He also recognized that the Gospels differed greatly in their details and even contradicted one another. Still, he daydreamed about the possible discovery of some old Roman records, perhaps unearthed at Pompeii, which might provide an independent confirmation of the Gospels. In time he came to wonder how anyone could wish Christianity to be true, since it condemned all skeptics to the everlasting torments of hell, including his father, his brother, and most of his best friends. (Eternal damnation along with unbelievable miracles and numerous contradictions and inconsistencies in the Bible had already affected the young Abraham Lincoln.)

The endless pain and suffering in nature also undermined Darwin's beliefs in a benign creator, as he confessed in an 1842 sketch of his ideas about natural selection:

It is derogatory that the Creator of countless systems of worlds, should have created each of the myriads of creeping parasites and [slimy] worms which have swarmed each day of life on land and water on [this] one globe. We cease being astonished, however much we may deplore, that a group of animals should have been created to lay their eggs in bowels and flesh of other[s] [parasitic wasps]—that some organisms should delight in cruelty. . . . From death, famine, rapine, and the concealed war of nature we can see that the . . . creation of the higher animals has directly come.[13]

Darwin's religious faith was ebbing, but he would cling to aspects of belief for many years to come.

Although Darwin was increasingly confident about the process of species development, he was afraid to share his ideas with others. The reasons were obvious: The scientific establishment continued to hold fast to Paley's argument for an intelligent designer, and to question this widely held idea would have meant ostracism by the very people whose help and good opinions he both needed and desired. He also hesitated to disappoint or alienate his old Cambridge professors, who were ordained clergy in the Church of England and who had done so much to advance his career. Finally, Darwin did not want to give intellectual ammunition to the more radical groups in Britain who were challenging the whole social and political establishment, since denying a divine order of things could easily be interpreted to mean that both the government and the established church were simply arbitrary human creations that could and should be overturned. If the world were constantly in flux, as a broader view of evolution seemed to suggest, then there was no reason why the class structure and aristocratic government might not be challenged and successfully changed.

In the late 1830s and 1840s, the most worrisome of these antiestablishment groups were the Chartists, so called because they supported the People's Charter, drawn up in 1838. The charter called for universal male suffrage, vote by ballot (as opposed to voice votes), abolition of property qualifications for members of Parliament, equal electoral districts, parliamentary sessions every year, and pay for members of Parliament (so that persons of modest means could afford to serve). These reforms would seem very modest to later generations, but at the time, they appeared radical and dangerous to the ruling classes. Despite the Chartists' submission of massive petitions containing millions of signatures, Parliament refused their demands in 1839, 1842, and 1848.

At the head of Britain's government, if increasingly a symbolic head, was the young Queen Victoria, who at age eighteen in 1837 inherited the throne from her uncle, William IV. Reigning for more than sixty-three years, Victoria would give her name to a cluster of attitudes, tastes, and moral bearings and to the apex of Britain's power and influence in the world. In many ways, too, Charles Darwin would come to personify Victorian England, with his devotion to home and family, hard work, and assumptions of English and European superiority. His reaching out over the globe for specimens to bolster his research and, paradoxically, his questioning long-held views about religion and humanity's place in the universe were also part of the Victorian world, as power, wealth, and optimism were inextricably linked to rapid change and doubts about old certainties.

Lincoln's United States was still much weaker than Darwin's Great Britain, but its rapid population growth and territorial expansion were also producing a heady optimism. The two countries continued to share a common heritage and some common political principles. This was particularly true of the Whig Party in Great Britain and Lincoln's Whig Party in the United States, though there were no formal or official ties between the two. Both parties traced their ideas back to the Glorious Revolution of 1689 and its resistance to unchecked executive authority—in England the monarch, and in the United States the president. The English Whigs were also weary of the power of the Church of England, and many of them were religious dissenters. In the United States, the Whigs had their largest support among New England Protestants and British immigrants and their descendants. Both Whig parties stressed individual responsibility and the belief that individuals could reshape themselves and the world around them through sheer willpower. These bourgeois values were especially prevalent in the business community on both sides of the Atlantic, where there was a strong emphasis on hard work, thrift, self-restraint, and moral rectitude. They were also standards of Victorian morality in both countries. Although individual rights were very important to both English and American Whigs, each group tended to stress duties more than rights. They both also liked to emphasize reason over emotion.[14]

Both American and English Whigs held an organic view of history. Countries and their institutions in particular had developed slowly over time and had unfolded according to a pattern, perhaps ordained by God. In the Anglo-American world, this historical pattern had produced an ordered liberty, grounded in reason and Protestant principles. Progress, to be real and sustained, had to be gradual and orderly. The law and respect for the law were therefore all-important for a stable, safe, and prosperous society. History was an important storehouse of lessons, and Whigs typically began any discussion of an issue by starting with its history. Lincoln adopted this historical approach in all his important speeches, and even Darwin, with his emphasis on the gradual unfolding of biological evolution according to the laws of natural selection, practiced what might be called a Whiggish approach to science.

In the United States, the Whig Party had emerged in response to President Andrew Jackson (1829–1837), whom the Whigs denounced as "King Andrew I" for his energetic and expanded use of executive authority. Ironically, while opposing the dangers of executive power, the Whigs generally supported strong government at both the state and national level, so long as the legislative branch exercised this power. One of their chief platforms was support for a central banking system, which had been destroyed when Jackson vetoed the bill to renew the charter of the Second Bank of the United States. The Whigs attracted many lawyers, clergymen, doctors, and well-educated men who despised Jackson's coarse frontier manners and his attraction to the common person.

Jackson had alienated business interests by opposing federal spending for transportation projects such as roads and canals, arguing that such projects violated states' rights and benefited the moneyed interests at the expense of farmers, laborers, and small businessmen. Although Lincoln was from a humble background, he was very much a "man on the make," who believed that internal improvements and sound money would help him and others like him to rise further. Ironically, given the Whigs' opposition to strong executive authority, Lincoln would later become the most powerful president the United States had ever seen and would be denounced by his political opponents as a dangerous tyrant. This disparity between his earlier views of executive authority and his actions as president would also trouble Lincoln himself and would eventually force him to come up with a rationale that involved divine providence and predestination.

As a Whig state legislator, Lincoln championed a variety of internal improvements, such as canals, an elaborate railroad network, and river dredging and he joined other legislators in vigorously supporting the Illinois State Bank. Lincoln also gave a speech about government to Springfield's Young Men's Lyceum on January 27, 1838, titled "The Perpetuation of Our Political Institutions." In it, he spoke about the rapid changes that were transforming their world—better transportation systems and new wealth, a bourgeoning population, increasing immigration, growing sectionalism, mounting arguments over slavery, and a fraying political consensus.

True to Whig principles, what most disturbed him, he told his audience, were the mobs "who substitute [their] wild and furious passions, in lieu of the sober judgment of Courts."[15] As an example, he pointed to the vigilantes in Mississippi who started hanging gamblers, even though gambling was legal in their state, then moved on to hanging "Negroes" who were suspected of plotting an insurrection. These outrages continued, "till, dead men were seen literally dangling from the boughs of trees upon every road side."[16] He also referred to a lynch mob in St. Louis who seized a free biracial man, dragged him through the streets, chained him to a tree at the edge of town, and burned him to death for allegedly murdering a prominent local resident. Surprisingly, he spoke only indirectly of the recent murder in nearby Alton, Illinois, of abolitionist editor Elijah Lovejoy by an inflamed mob that had objected to Lovejoy's outcries against slavery. This may have been because Lincoln rejected the law-breaking tactics of the abolitionists almost as much as Lovejoy's murder revolted him. His simple solution was for every lover of liberty to swear never to break the law:

> Let every American, every lover of liberty . . . swear by the blood of the Revolution, never to violate in the least particular, the laws of the country. . . . Let reverence for the laws, be breathed by every American mother, to the lisping babe, that prattles on her lap;—let it be taught in schools, in seminaries, and in colleges;—let it be written in Primmers [*sic*], spelling books, and in Almanacs;—let it be preached from the pulpit, proclaimed in legislative halls, and enforced in courts of justice. . . . In short, let it become the *political religion* of the nation.[17]

Just as dangerous as the mob, Lincoln warned his audience, was the individual of great ambition who, like men seeking glory in other countries, might try to become an American Napoleon, Caesar, or Alexander. Such a man would not be satisfied to merely support and maintain a political system that had been built by others. He would see "*no distinction* in adding story to story, upon the monuments of fame, erected to the memory of others."[18] It was unreasonable not to expect that "some man possessed of the loftiest genius, coupled with ambition, sufficient to push it to its utmost stretch, will at some time, spring up among us[.]"[19] And the question of slavery, Lincoln believed, offered a great opportunity for exploitation by this genius: "It will have it, whether at the expense of emancipating slaves, or enslaving freemen."[20] A quarter century later, with the nation plunged into bloody civil war, Lincoln's opponents would see him as just such an evil and ambitious man.

Lincoln ended his speech with a call for reason over passion. Although passion had been necessary to win independence from Great Britain, it could no longer help the nation: "It will in future be our enemy. Reason, cold, calculating, unimpassioned reason, must furnish all the materials for our future support and defense."[21]

Lincoln's cosponsorship of an anti-abolitionist protest before the Illinois state legislature a year earlier reflected these pleas for reason and moderation. At the time, many of the Southern state legislatures were passing resolutions demanding the suppression of abolitionist societies, citing the US constitutional protections of slavery. Illinois, which had a large percentage of its population coming originally from the Upper South, passed a similar resolution by a vote of 77–6. At the very end of the legislative session, Lincoln joined fellow representative Daniel Stone, a native Vermonter, in submitting a written protest against the resolution, but only after bills for internal improvements and the removal of the capital to Springfield were safely passed. This calculated delay showed Lincoln's political shrewdness, as did the careful wording of the protest. It began by saying that the institution of slavery was "founded on both injustice and bad policy," but quickly added that "the promulgation of abolition doctrines tends rather to increase than to abate its evils."[22] In other words, Lincoln again condemned both slavery and the abolitionists, a middle-of-the-road position that he would hold until later events forced (or allowed) him to change course.

Lincoln's views on what to do about the abuse of alcohol were equally moderate and well balanced and paralleled his opinions about the abolitionists of the time: "Too much denunciation against dram sellers and dram-drinkers was indulged in," he told the audience in an address to the Springfield Washingtonian Temperance Society on Washington's Birthday, February 22, 1842. "This, I think, was both impolitic and unjust."[23] He insisted that "thundering tones of anathema and denunciation" would do nothing to end drunkenness. A far better approach would be "unassuming persuasion."[24]

But Lincoln, like so many young men, did not always practice what he preached. He could be emotional on the floor of the legislature and hurl sarcastic verbal attacks against his political opponents. He was even more out of control in the anonymous letters he wrote to the *Sangamo Journal*, whose Whig editor opened the pages of his newspaper to Lincoln whenever he cared to contribute anything. When the Illinois state bank was forced to close in 1842 because of the Democrats' opposition to it, he hurled especially sharp words at James Shields, the state auditor and a fiercely partisan Democrat. In a letter to the newspaper, he called Shields a fool, a braggart, and a liar. The hot-tempered and excitable Shields then demanded to know the identity of the writer and, after being informed by the editor, challenged Lincoln to a duel.

Dueling was illegal in Illinois, so the men and their seconds agreed to fight across the Mississippi River in Missouri. Since Lincoln had been the one challenged, he had the right to select the weapons and he chose broadswords, reasoning that with his longer arms he would have a distinct advantage over the shorter Shields, though he promised himself not to hurt Shields except in self-defense. Fortunately, a mutual acquaintance intervened to stop the potentially deadly contest by persuading Shields to withdraw the insulting note he had sent to Lincoln, and by having Lincoln swear that he had never intended to question Shields's personal or private character and that he had written the criticisms only for "political effect." The two men then shook hands and went back across the river to Illinois. For a man who had advocated obedience to law and cold, pure reason as the twin solutions to his country's most serious problems, the preempted duel was utterly hypocritical, and Lincoln retained painful memories of it for the rest of his life.

In England, Charles Darwin would have agreed with the young Springfield lawyer's advice for the need for caution and moderation. By the early winter of 1838, just six months after beginning his transmutation notebooks, Darwin was so worried about the potentially subversive nature of his religious doubts and his nascent theory of natural selection that he was laid low with severe headaches, stomach cramps, vomiting, and muscle aches, combined with a generally depressed mood. Biographers have noted that these symptoms tended to appear at times of stress throughout the remainder of Darwin's life. Besides this stress factor, some investigators have proposed that his illnesses resulted from strong, multiple allergenic reactions to certain foods, preservative fluids, and the terrible air pollution in London, at least while he remained in the capital. One researcher has suggested that Darwin was bitten by the *benchuca* bug while in South America, which caused him to come down with Chagas disease, though the nature and timing of his symptoms would seem to rule this out. Still another idea is that he suffered from myalgic encephalomyelitis, caused by a breakdown of the immune system. Biographers Michael White and John Gribbin assert that a variety of diagnoses might have some merit and that several factors may have worked together to cause Darwin's illnesses.[25]

The fact that Darwin had to cope with symptoms that went well beyond the lassitude and mental suffering experienced by depressed persons is another indication that his illnesses probably stemmed from multiple factors that might have reinforced and exacerbated one another. It also seems clear that his depression was unipolar, since he did not experience extreme mood swings that indicated any sort of manic phase. Instead, he would experience periods when he felt better—even "normal"—only to become ill again. In the end, it is impossible to come up with a definitive diagnosis of Darwin's illnesses.

In any case, living alone in London and not feeling well much of the time made Charles start to think seriously about marriage in the spring of 1838, and he sat down to list the advantages and disadvantages of matrimonial life. If he stayed single, he could travel as much as he wanted—to the European continent or perhaps to the United States (which he never did), like so many others who were intrigued by the political and cultural experiments of this young society. He could spend his days working hard on his science while socializing in the evenings. Marriage, on the other hand, might force him to work for a living, and children might keep him from his research and writing. By the summer, he had overcome most of his reservations: Remaining single would give him the freedom to do whatever he wanted, but he would be lonely and have none of the charms of home life. A good wife could be a constant companion, and children would give him something to live and work for.

Charles discussed the prospect of marriage with his father, and it was only then that he discovered how wealthy his sometimes intimidating father was and how generous he was willing to be with a marriage settlement. Dr. Darwin heartily agreed that it would be a good thing for Charles to marry and also agreed that Charles's first cousin Emma Wedgwood, the youngest daughter of Uncle Jos, would be an excellent choice. Charles began making frequent visits to Maer to see Emma, who was a year older than he, all the while concerned that she might find him too unattractive. Emma had no trouble with Charles's looks, but she did worry about his religious doubts, fearing that he would be condemned to hell and that the two of them would not meet again in the afterlife— a fear that would be shared by Mary Lincoln about her husband. Dr. Darwin had warned his son not to share his religious doubts with Emma, a problem, he knew well from friends and patients, that had caused difficulties between many husbands and wives, but Charles had been unable to hold himself back. He was touched by Emma's concern and told her so, while she remained hopeful that somehow, some day, her husband might regain his faith.

Financially, the couple was well set. Emma's father gave her a dowry of five thousand pounds, along with an income of four hundred a year, and Dr. Darwin gave his son ten thousand pounds to invest. The couple wed on January 29, 1839, just two weeks before Charles's thirtieth birthday, at St. Peter's Church in an Anglican ceremony performed by their common cousin, John Allen Wedgwood. The service dispensed with certain Anglican forms so that the Unitarian members of the family would not be offended. In the marriage ceremony, as in his scientific work up to this point, Charles chose outward conformity.

Lincoln's approach to marriage was far more confused and painful than Darwin's.

Lincoln biographers now generally agree that his first real feelings of love were for Ann Rutledge back in his New Salem days. There is also a consensus that Lincoln was not only in love with Ann but that they had become engaged.[26] It was Herndon, who, based on conversations with former residents of New Salem in the years after Lincoln's death, first picked up the story and reported it.

According to Herndon, Ann was the daughter of James Rutledge, one of the two founders of New Salem and the proprietor of the local tavern where Lincoln boarded in 1833. His sources reported that Ann was pretty if slightly plump. She was also described as charming, sympathetic, and intelligent, with a "womanly skill" in the domestic arts. Unfortunately for Lincoln, Ann was already engaged to a man named John McNeil, whose real name turned out to be John McNamar, an alias, he later explained, to keep his impoverished family back in New York from discovering his whereabouts and asking him for money before he had had a chance to establish himself. McNamar finally did go back to New York and kept Ann waiting for months. Hearing nothing from him, according to the stories, she and Lincoln began courting.

In the summer of 1835, Ann came down with a fatal fever (probably typhoid) and died on August 25. Lincoln was devastated, according to Herndon: "He had fits of great mental depression, and wandered up and down the river and into the woods woefully abstracted—at times in the deepest distress."[27] A prolonged period of rain and gloomy weather after her death only worsened his grief, and he reported to friends that he could not stand the idea of the rain falling on Ann's grave. They feared that he might take his life and watched over him with special vigilance. Psycho-biographer Charles Strozier believes that Ann's death reawakened the trauma that he had felt over the loss of his mother.[28] Whatever the causes, Lincoln's friends became so alarmed that they asked Bowling and Nancy Greene, who lived in a secluded spot south of New Salem, to take him in. Lincoln stayed with the Greenes for several weeks and gradually regained his emotional balance.

Lincoln's second romantic adventure is well documented. His intended was Mary Owen, who first came to New Salem from Kentucky in 1833 to visit her sister. Her father was one of the wealthiest men in his part of the state. Mary had been well educated and was a good conversationalist. That Mary was considerably overweight did not bother Lincoln initially, who seemed to prefer plump women—at least to a point. After her first visit to New Salem, Lincoln supposedly said that if Mary ever returned he would marry her, a declaration that was supposed to have inspired her second visit to New Salem in 1836.

By the time Lincoln left for Springfield in the spring of 1837, the two had some kind of understanding that they would marry, but both had reservations. She resented his lack of proper attention to her, writing to Herndon many years later that when they had gone out riding one day and she fell behind, he did not look back to see how she was getting along. When she finally did catch up and asked if he did not care whether her "neck was broken or not," he laughingly replied that he thought she was smart enough to take care of herself.

Lincoln's doubts were less specific. He worried that her willingness to come back to New Salem to see him showed her a little too desperate to find a husband, and he began finding fault in her appearance. In a letter to Mrs. Orville H. Browning, whom he had met in Vandalia, the former state capital, he wrote, "I knew she was over-size, but she now appeared a fair match for Falstaff." No doubt exaggerating the case to amuse Mrs. Browning, but also to convince himself that he no longer wanted her, Lincoln continued with his negative descriptions: "I knew she was called an 'old maid,' and I felt no doubt of the truth of at least half of the appellation; but now, when I beheld her, I could not for my life avoid thinking of my [step]mother; and this, not from withered features, for her skin was too full of fat, to permit of its contracting in to wrinkles; but from her want of teeth, [and] weather-beaten appearance in general."[29] He ended the letter by saying he would never again think of marrying, since he could never be "satisfied with any one who would be block-head enough to have me."[30]

Lincoln then instigated a correspondence with Mary, with the aim of getting her to call off the engagement. Soon after arriving in Springfield, he wrote to tell her how dull life was in the new capital, adding that she would probably not like to live there and have to share his poverty. In August he wrote that she might have been mistaken about his true feelings toward her and said that he would release her from their engagement, adding that she did not need to answer him if that suited her best. As he hoped, she did not write back, yet he felt "mortified almost beyond endurance" at being rejected and even began to think that he had really been in love with her. Whatever his feelings might have been, they did not match the intense emotions he had reportedly cherished for Ann Rutledge.

Not quite a year after breaking off with Mary Owen, Lincoln met Mary Todd, the sister of Elizabeth Edwards, whose husband Ninian W. Edwards was wealthy, socially prominent, and one of the leading Whigs in Springfield. Though Lincoln was unrefined and often crudely dressed, Edwards, a fellow member of the state legislature, recognized his value to the Whig Party and began inviting him to gatherings at his home. Springfield society was far more fluid than the highly stratified class system in Darwin's England. Many families in Illinois were themselves only a generation or two removed from obscurity, and they were often willing to recognize and embrace merit wherever they found it.

Lincoln first met Mary Todd at one of the Edwards's entertainments in June 1839. She was the daughter of Robert S. Todd, a prosperous merchant, banker, and slave owner in Lexington, Kentucky. She was also a cousin of Lincoln's first law partner, John Todd Stuart. Mary had been educated in the best private schools, spoke fluent French, and from a young age had been fascinated by politics. Her father frequently entertained top Whig politicians, including Kentucky's Henry Clay. Mary was graceful, witty, charming, and a wonderful conversationalist who attracted the attention of many of Springfield's bachelors, including Stephen A. Douglas, who would later become Lincoln's greatest political rival. She more than made up for Lincoln's reticence around women by carrying on much of the conversation herself, and they soon discovered their keen mutual interests in politics. They were both from Kentucky, both were ardent Whigs, and both liked the poetry of Robert Burns.

Mary had come to live with her sister and brother-in-law in Springfield partly because she could not get along with her stepmother. Both Abraham and Mary had lost their mothers in childhood, but while Lincoln's stepmother had been a salvation, Mary came to despise her stepmother. Possibly as a strategy for getting attention from her father, who was forever discussing politics with his powerful friends, Mary developed a strong interest in politics herself and was allowed as a young girl to sit at dinner with many of the political figures of the time, overhearing all the gossip and electioneering schemes.

Mary had also grown up in the city and in a society where violence, honor, and revenge, even for small or imagined slights, were a way of life. As her biographer Jean H. Baker has written, "In Mary Todd's youth both rich and poor used violence as a means of enhancing status and reputation."[31] Mary herself would always be sensitive to slights and was ever ready to seek some kind of revenge, against real or imagined perpetrators, including her future husband. Her fighting spirit would also cause her, at times, to reject the Presbyterian teachings with which she had grown up, which emphasized Christian resignation and an acceptance of God's plan for her and her family.

The Edwards were initially all in favor of her proposed marriage, since they believed that Lincoln was bound for success, as did Mary, who had once supposedly said that she was going to marry a man who would become president of the United States. Since she could not enter politics as a woman, the next best thing would be to marry a successful politician. She may have also been attracted to Lincoln's fatherly demeanor. Even as a youth, those around Lincoln had often commented on how he seemed already old, with a paternal concern for others. The fact that he was ten years older than Mary could only have reinforced this image in her mind. If true, Lincoln may have represented a father figure for her, someone who would give her the attention she so craved but had infrequently received from her father after his remarriage.

Psychologists and marriage counselors some decades later might describe this as a "jailbreak" marriage, at least on Mary's part, since marrying Lincoln allowed her to escape her childhood home for good. Individuals in such circumstances will often marry someone who is even more domineering than the parent they wish to flee, or someone they think they can control. In the Lincolns' case, Mary may have seen Abraham as a kindly parental figure whom she could control and in that way become fulfilled. Such marriages are seldom happy: either the domineering spouse becomes abusive or the spouse who is the object of control will find ways to revolt, or at least to escape from its demands whenever possible.[32] By contrast, Emma Wedgwood had enjoyed a happy home life and had no need to escape into marriage, an obvious circumstance for all to see, including her future husband, Charles Darwin.

Lincoln, for his part, may have been attracted to the idea of caring for a child-wife. An added dividend would have been the social clout and political influence wielded by her extended family of Todds, Edwardses, and Stuarts. In their own way and in their own part of the world, these allied families were nearly as influential as the Darwin-Wedgwoods in England and would more than make up for the obscurity of his Lincoln-Hanks relations.

Whatever their different motives, Abraham and Mary became engaged at the end of 1839, but Lincoln almost immediately began to second-guess the decision. According to his friend Orville Browning, Lincoln had meanwhile fallen in love with Mary's cousin, Matilda Edwards, a pretty eighteen-year-old (who ultimately rejected his proposal of marriage). Under the circumstances, Lincoln thought it would be a great wrong to wed Mary Todd. Or it may be that Lincoln sensed that his marriage would not be a happy one. In any case, he called at the Edwards residence in early 1841 and told Mary that he did not love her, and she burst into tears. After he left, she wrote him a letter releasing him from the engagement, but added that she had not changed her mind and would leave her own commitment open. As with Mary Owen, Lincoln immediately regretted his decision to break the engagement, but this time the emotional toll was far worse. Consumed with guilt and remorse for making Mary unhappy and castigating himself for his inconsistency and inability to stick to his resolves, he became deeply depressed and took to his bed. Again some of his associates feared he might commit suicide and Speed, his friend and roommate, removed all razors, knives, or other dangerous objects from their room to keep him from hurting himself.

Lincoln was so miserable that he sought out Dr. Henry Anson, a Springfield physician, and for a week spent several hours every day receiving treatments. The doctor's diagnosis was "hypochondradriasis" (or "the hypo" for short), defined as a form of melancholia. It was not a complete madness but severe enough to require treatment so that the patient did not slip into insanity or attempt suicide. There is no actual record of the treatment for Lincoln, but the medical textbooks of the day called for what amounted to a vigorous assault on the body to shock it back into balance, an approach based on the ancient idea that illness was caused by an imbalance of bodily "humors." If Dr. Anson followed such a theory and used the prescribed treatments of the day, he probably drew many ounces of blood from Lincoln, induced vomiting and diarrhea, required him to fast for several days, and may have blistered him by applying small heated glass cups to the temples, behind the ears, or around the nape of the neck in a technique known as "cupping," to bring the blood to the surface.[33] Understandably, Lincoln emerged from this ordeal worse than before he started the treatments. According to a local lawyer named James Conkling, who saw him at the end of his time with Dr. Anson, Lincoln appeared "reduced and emaciated in appearance and seems scarcely to possess enough strength to speak above a whisper."[34]

Joshua Wolf Shenk, who has investigated Lincoln's lifelong struggle with depression—or melancholia, as Lincoln and his contemporaries would have called it—agrees that he had a second major emotional breakdown during the first part of 1841, the first having occurred nearly five years before, following the death of Ann Rutledge. In both instances, Shenk believes that a combination of factors led to depression. The earlier event had involved both Ann's death and a protracted period of dark, rainy weather. Lincoln had also been at an age—twenty-six—when unipolar depression typically manifests itself for the first time.

The second and more severe episode, Shenk points out, was probably triggered by several events besides the breakup with Mary Todd. A nationwide economic depression had affected Illinois very badly. The state was now unable even to pay the interest on the bonds it had floated for the massive internal improvements that Lincoln and his Whig allies had sponsored a few years before. Just as the economic crisis was beginning to unfold, Joshua Speed, Lincoln's closest friend since coming to Springfield, left town and moved back to Kentucky. Lincoln's legal partnership with John T. Stuart also came to an end in January 1841, when Stuart won a second term in Congress and decided to discontinue his practice back in Springfield. It was Stuart who had first proposed a legal career to Lincoln and who then became a mentor and confidante. In addition, the winter of 1840–41 was particularly severe, with record wind and cold that swept in from the gray skies and the flat, snow-covered prairies surrounding the town. The fact that Lincoln did not love

Mary Todd, combined with the usual worries of a man who knew he would have to work even harder to support a wife and children, only added to his stress.[35]

Unlike Charles Darwin, Lincoln had had few chances in childhood and early adulthood to interact with girls around his own age. Darwin, in contrast, was frequently in the company of female cousins and a wide circle of family friends who had daughters. Both consciously and unconsciously, Darwin had learned to interact with young women By marrying Emma Wedgwood, his first cousin and a person he had known since she was born, he had a very good idea what Emma would be like as a wife. Lincoln, on the other hand, had known too few young women to figure out who might be compatible, and he actually knew very little about Mary Todd's background and overall demeanor at the time he married her.

Lincoln's keen recognition of the challenges surrounding his life at this time, including his own culpability for the state's debt, the great responsibilities if he became a husband and father, and the departure of his friend Speed all pointed to a sensitive and realistic assessment of his situation. This mixture of realism and pessimism, according to Shenk and some other modern psychologists, is a leading cause of depression. When these feelings do not completely overwhelm the individual, they can lead to deep insights and to a sense of the many complexities and contradictions in the human condition. A determination to manage the negative consequences of these insights by channeling them into creative work can also be of great help to the individual sufferer, as well as to society at large, which can also benefit from the creativity. In contrast, the person with a generally sunny, optimistic temperament is often unaware of problems or minimizes their significance and is unlikely to spend the time and energy necessary for tackling them. In the struggle to get well, and then to manage his depression, Lincoln would throw himself into the responsibilities of family and work and ultimately into taking on his country's most complex and intractable problems.

Shenk also believes that Lincoln's sadness and emotional vulnerabilities, often seen in the romantic nineteenth century as signs of sensitivity and creativity, attracted others to him. Instead of repelling friends and acquaintances, Lincoln's melancholia only confirmed their belief that he was an especially sensitive and intelligent individual. His black moods also made others feel sorry for him and wish to help, especially if they had come to like him already. Lincoln's humor, which was another way that he fought back the blues, also attracted people to him, who gladly stepped forward to help when he relapsed into melancholia.

In August 1841, while Lincoln was still feeling out of sorts, Speed invited him to visit his plantation near Louisville, Kentucky, where the family did everything to make him comfortable, including—ironic for a man who would later abolish slavery—providing a personal house slave to attend his every need. He befriended Speed's half-sister Mary, as well as his brother James, a lawyer who loaned him books from his law library. Speed's mother tried to help Lincoln by giving him a Bible and urging him to read it regularly. Michael Burlingame has suggested that Mrs. Speed, like Nancy Greene in the aftermath of Lincoln's earlier collapse following Ann Rutledge's death, became a surrogate mother, who through sincere maternal affection and care helped her son's friend regain a measure of emotional health.[36] Indeed, by the time Lincoln headed home, he reported feeling much better, and in his lighthearted mood he even managed to convince himself that the dozen chained slaves he saw onboard the steamboat were cheerful despite their circumstances. He described the scene in a letter to Mary Speed:

> A gentleman had purchased twelve negroes in different parts of Kentucky and was taking them to a farm in the South. They were chained six and six together, . . . so that the negroes were strung together precisely like so many fish upon a trot-line. In this condition they were being separated forever from the scenes of their childhood, their friends, their fathers and mothers, and brothers and sisters, and many of them, from their wives and children, and going into perpetual

slavery where the lash of the master is proverbially more ruthless and unrelenting than any other where; and yet amid all these distressing circumstances, as we would think them, they were the most cheerful and apparently happy creatures on board.[37]

Besides allowing his own mood to color the scene, Lincoln may have misinterpreted as cheerfulness the bondsmen's attempts to endure by simply refusing to give into despair. He may have also been the victim of mistaken beliefs that Africans were naturally lighthearted and did not experience the same strong family bonds as white people, though he would later conclude otherwise.

While in Kentucky, Lincoln discovered that Speed himself had become engaged. When Speed confessed his own doubts about this crucial step, Lincoln did his best to still his friend's fears and encouraged him to pursue the marriage, doubtless talking to himself as much as to Speed. When Speed did marry and report to Lincoln how happy he was, Lincoln decided to renew his courtship with Mary Todd. The two were married, on only a day's notice, at the Edwards home on November 4, 1842, with the service performed by the minister of the local Episcopal church. Just before the ceremony, Lincoln seemed terrified. One friend said that the groom looked "as pale and trembling as if being driven to slaughter," and when his landlord's son noticed him getting all dressed up and asked him where he was going, Lincoln answered, "To hell, I suppose."[38] He was still not sure that he was making the right decision, and the fact that the Edwards had changed their minds about Lincoln and were not enthusiastic about the match could not have helped.

Lincoln would turn thirty-three a little over three months after his marriage, and he must have felt that it was high time to settle down. Whether he had come to love Mary Todd is uncertain, but he did decide to take on the responsibilities of a family. If not exactly going to hell, he was undoubtedly frightened by the real hazards that can befall any marriage; and because of the courting restraints within the proper society of the time, which did not allow young couples to be alone together, there was no good way of finding out what a potential mate was really like. Once married, it was both disgraceful and almost impossible to obtain a divorce. In this regard, Charles Darwin was far more fortunate. He had known his cousin Emma and her immediate family all his life and had every reason to believe that the two of them and their families would be compatible. Though Lincoln's and Darwin's marriages would turn out very differently, tying the matrimonial knot marked a passage for both men into the full-fledged adulthood of hoped-for love and promising careers.

NOTES

1. Nora Barlow, ed., *The Autobiography of Charles Darwin, 1809–1882* (New York: W. W. Norton, 1993), p. 85.

2. Quoted in Adrian Desmond and James Moore, *Darwin: The Life of a Tormented Evolutionist* (New York: Warner Books, 1991), p. 206.

3. For a full account of the town, see Paul M. Angle, *Here I Have Lived: A History of Lincoln's Springfield* (1935; repr., Chicago: Abraham Lincoln Book Shop, 1971).

4. These figures are from Kenneth J. Winkle, *The Young Eagle: The Rise of Abraham Lincoln* (Dallas: Taylor Trade Publishing, 2001), p. 159.

5. The question of Lincoln's homosexuality is explored in C. A. Tripp, *The Intimate World of Abraham Lincoln* (New York: Free Press, 2005). Despite any direct evidence, Tripp believes that Lincoln was in fact bisexual and that he did engage in several homosexual relationships during his life.

6. Quoted in Ronald W. Clark, *The Survival of Charles Darwin* (New York: Random House, 1984), p. 44.

7. Niles Eldredge, *Darwin: Discovering the Tree of Life* (New York: W. W. Norton Company, 2005), p. 58.

8. Ibid., pp. 2, 44; David Quammen, *The Reluctant Mr. Darwin* (New York: W. W. Norton, 2006), p. 27.

9. Barlow, *Autobiography of Charles Darwin*, p. 130.

10. Ibid., p. 120.

11. Ibid., p. 87.

12. Ibid., pp. 85, 86.

13. Darwin, "Summer Notebooks," 1842, quoted in Desmond and Moore, *Darwin*, pp. 293–94.

14. On the Whig tradition in both England and the United States, see Daniel Walker Howe, *The Political Culture of the American Whigs* (Chicago: University of Chicago Press, 1979).

15. Lincoln, "Address Before the Young Men's Lyceum of Springfield, Illinois" (January 27, 1838), *The Collected Works of Abraham Lincoln*, edited by Roy P. Basler et al. (New Brunswick, NJ: Rutgers University Press, 1953), 1:109.

16. Ibid., p. 110.

17. Ibid., p. 114.

18. Ibid.

19. Ibid.

20. Ibid.

21. Ibid., p. 115.

22. Lincoln, "Protest in Illinois Legislature on Slavery," *Collected Works of Abraham Lincoln*, 1:75.

23. Lincoln, "An Address Delivered Before the Springfield Washington Temperance Society" (February 22, 1842), *Collected Works of Abraham Lincoln*, 1:272.

24. Ibid., p. 273.

25. Michael White and John Gribbin, *Darwin: A Life in Science* (New York: Dutton, 1995), pp. 109–12.

26. Historian James G. Randall and his wife, Ruth Painter Randall, who wrote a laudatory biography of Mary Todd Lincoln, were particularly critical of the Ann Rutledge story and attacked Herndon as unreliable in many areas. In 1993, historian John Evangeline Welsh in his book *The Shadows Rise*, believed that the preponderance of evidence points to the basic truth of the Ann Rutledge romance.

27. William H. Herndon, *Herndon's Life of Lincoln* (New York: Da Capo Press, 1983), p. 113.

28. Charles B. Strozier, *Lincoln's Quest for Union* (Philadelphia: Paul Dry Books, 2001), p. 42.

29. Lincoln to Mrs. Orville H. Browning, April 1, 1838, *Collected Works of Abraham Lincoln*, 1:118.

30. Ibid., p. 119.

31. Jean H. Baker, *Mary Todd Lincoln: A Biography* (New York: W. W. Norton, 1987), p. 65.

32. A novel that brilliantly treats the subject of "jailbreak marriage" is Helen Scully, *In the Hope of Rising Again* (New York: Penguin Press, 2004).

33. Joshua Wolf Shenk, *Lincoln's Melancholy: How Depression Challenged a President and Fueled His Greatness* (New York: Houghton Mifflin, 2005), pp. 57–59.

34. James Conkling to Mercy Levering, January 24, 1841, in Carl Sandburg and Paul M. Angle, *Mary Lincoln, Wife and Widow* (New York: Harcourt, Brace, 1932), p. 179.

35. Shenk, *Lincoln's Melancholy*, pp. 22–13, 51–57.

36. Michael Burlingame, *The Inner World of Abraham Lincoln* (Urbana: University of Illinois Press, 1994) pp. 101–102.

37. Lincoln to Mary Speed, September 27, 1841, *Collected Works of Abraham Lincoln*, 1:260.

38. Herndon, *Herndon's Life of Lincoln*, p. 180.

Chapter 4

CAREER AND FAMILY

A single Man has not nearly the Value he would have in that State of
Union. He is an incomplete Animal. He resembles the odd Half of a
Pair of Scissars. If you get a prudent healthy Wife, your Industry in
your Profession, with her good Economy, will be a Fortune sufficient.

—Benjamin Franklin,
"Advice to a Young Man on the Choice of a Mistress"

When Benjamin Franklin wrote a humorous letter of advice to a
young friend in the 1740s, he characterized marriage as more of a
practical arrangement than a romantic love match. A century later,
romance was a highly desirable aspect of matrimony, but it remained no
less practical, and both Abraham Lincoln and Charles Darwin drew
many benefits from married life, though Darwin's personal experience as
a husband was far more pleasant than Lincoln's.

Lincoln and Darwin had ended their bachelor days within three
years of each other. Both soon became fathers and moved to larger and
better quarters as families grew in size and as their work allowed or
demanded. Solidifying their careers in the next decade, they became even

more ambitious to succeed. Both sharpened their skills at building wide networks among the men who could help them achieve their goals. The deaths of young children were sore trials for both, and both buried themselves in work to chase away the blues. They also lost their fathers during this time of life, an event that was far harder on Darwin than on Lincoln. The late 1840s and early 1850s also represent lulls for both men, when the promises of earlier years seemed to fade. As it turned out, these lulls were fortunate, since the time was not right for either of them. Conditions were not yet ripe in England for Darwin to publish his shocking conclusions, and the crisis over slavery and states' rights had not yet entered a critical enough phase for Lincoln to seek the presidency.

After their marriage in November 1842, Abraham and Mary Lincoln moved into the Globe Tavern, a thirty-room hotel that catered mainly to visitors but that also kept a few rooms for boarders, a common arrangement in towns like Springfield. Their eight-by-fourteen-foot accommodations cost them $4.00 a week. It was better than any of Lincoln's previous lodgings, but for Mary, who had grown up in large houses with plenty of slaves, their lodgings were a real comedown in living standards.

When their first child, Robert, was born in August 1843, Abraham and Mary rented a small house, and a year later purchased a dwelling on the corner of Eighth and Jackson streets for $1,200. Mary had to do much of the housework herself, with the help of a "hired girl" whom she paid out of a $120 annual income from her father. The birth of a second child, Edward, in March 1846, only added to her domestic cares.

The Eighth and Jackson Street house was initially quite modest, with three rooms downstairs and two bedrooms upstairs under a sloping ceiling that was so low Lincoln could stand erect only in the center of the rooms. The residence was a brisk five-minute walk from the center of town, where Lincoln had his law office and where Mary could go shopping.

And shop Mary did—for the latest fashions in clothes and household furnishings, especially as Lincoln prospered in the law. By 1856 his income, supplemented with $1,200 from the sale of eighty acres of land that Mary Lincoln's father had given her eight years before, was enough for them to enlarge their house in Springfield. They raised the cramped one-and-a-half-story structure to two full floors, with Greek Revival details on the exterior. On the new first floor there was a large sitting room, parlor, and back parlor that Lincoln used as an office. Upstairs there were four large bedrooms, with separate, connecting rooms for Abraham and Mary. It was no mansion even by midwestern standards, but it was a respectable upper-middle-class dwelling and certainly one of the better residences in Springfield.[1] To the early twenty-first-century visitor, the interior presents a quintessential scene of mid-Victorian appointments. Every room seems stuffed with chairs, tables, sofas, and draperies that look as if they had all been purchased at about the same time with an eye toward matching everything in their elaborate textures and muted colors.

As Abraham and Mary Lincoln were establishing a family, Charles and Emma Darwin were doing the same. Following their marriage, they moved into a row of houses on Upper Gower Street near the Bloomsbury section of London. They dubbed the place "Macaw Cottage" because of the garish color scheme inside—yellow curtains, blue walls, and plush red upholstered furniture. Like the Lincolns, they did not wait long to start a family. Within three months of their wedding, Emma was pregnant, and on December 29, 1839, she gave birth to a son they named William Erasmus. Still squeamish at the slightest hint of pain in others, Charles was shaken by the birth ordeal, as he wrote to his cousin, William Darwin Fox: "What an awful affair a confinement is; it knocked me up, almost as it did Emma herself."[2] However difficult both of them might have found the experience, it did nothing to delay the birth of a second child, Ann Elizabeth (Annie), a little more than fourteen months later on March 2, 1841.

Although Charles had found London, with its museums, scientific societies, and fellow naturalists a convenient location for his work, he had never lost his love for country life and thought the city was no place to bring up children. While visiting his father at The Mount during the summer of 1842, he persuaded Dr. Darwin to buy them a country house somewhere south of London. He started the house hunting in August, and if he had any lingering doubts about leaving the city, a violent general strike and the sight of Chartist rioters streaming by the front of their house made both Charles and Emma count the days until they could leave town for good.

Luckily Charles had found a house in the village of Downe, some sixteen miles from London. The house that he, Emma, and the two children occupied in mid-September 1842 was called Down House, without the final *e*. That same year the British government had added the *e* to the village name so that it would not be confused with County Down in Ireland, but Darwin saw no need to change the spelling of their residence.

Down House, once inhabited by the vicar of the local Anglican church, stood about a quarter of a mile up a hill from the village. Fittingly, the one thing that Charles had once liked about entering the church was the country living that came with a rural parish. Now he was living in a country parson's house, but without the doctrinal requirements and pastoral duties. Though within easy reach of the teeming capital, Charles reveled in the attractive countryside and his family's isolation from the world. To cousin Fox he wrote, "The scenery is moderately pretty: its chief merit is its extreme rurality; I think I was never in a more perfectly quiet country; Three miles South of us the great chalk escarpment quite cuts us off from the low country of Kent, & between us & the escarpment, there is not a village or a gents house, but only great woods & arable fields, . . . so that we are absolutely at the extreme verge of the world."[3]

The couple concluded soon after moving in that they needed to enlarge and remodel the house, but they decided to wait until Emma delivered their third child, who was born in late September. Named Mary Eleanor, she was tiny and weak and lived only three weeks. Both parents were deeply saddened, but three months later Emma was pregnant again. The promise of another baby and the decision to go ahead with the work on the house helped both of them to recover. The Darwins added a new bedroom and schoolroom, greatly altered the existing bedrooms, and expanded the kitchen. Outside they had the house stuccoed and built a large bow window extending up three stories, which became covered by a tangle of creepers. Because the dwelling was so close to the road, they had the lane moved out from the front of the house, lowered it by two feet, and built a brick and flint wall along the part that ran past their garden, so it could not be seen from the house. Accompanying the house were eighteen acres of land, giving them plenty of space to plant a small orchard. On the south side of the house, the property included a pleasant, twelve-acre field, scattered with fair-sized oaks and ashes. Besides paying for the house and property, Charles's father covered the cost of the renovations—some three hundred pounds—as a charge against his inheritance.

Although the house was spacious, it was more comfortable than it was grand. The same could be said for the gardens, however pleasant. To one side of the garden were the greenhouses where Darwin experimented on exotic plants that could not withstand the English winter. Large beds beyond the flower gardens provided vegetables for the family table, as well as space for other plant experiments.

At the far end of the garden, Darwin laid out his sandwalk, so called because the quarter-mile path that led around this rectangular acre-and-a-half lot was covered with sand and small pieces of gravel. On one side there was a low hedge over which he could see "a quiet little valley losing itself in the upland country."[4] Filled with scrub and oaks when he bought the piece of land from his neighbor, Darwin improved and extended the little woods by planting hazel, alder, lime, hornbean, birch, privet, and dogwood. Emma ornamented the ground layer with bluebells, anemones, cowslips, primroses, and wild ivy. Several times a day, Charles took his constitutionals around the sandwalk, marking count by kicking a stone into the path at the end of each turn. Unable to work out some knotty problem inside, an answer often came to him while walking. At one corner of the sandwalk there was a small wooden shelter with a built-in bench, where the nurse would sit and knit while the children played in the woods. Darwin's dog usually accompanied him on these walks; in later years a rough white fox terrier named Polly. As a pet lover, Darwin was a regular contributor to the Royal Society for the Prevention of Cruelty to Animals.

Darwin soon became the village squire. He was the treasurer of the parish's Coal and Clothing Club, which assisted the poor of the community, and he founded the Downe Friendly Society, a cooperative insurance fund for the local working class. He also served as a justice of the peace, adjudicating minor disputes from his dining room table.

A visit to Down House today does much to demystify Darwin while taking nothing away from his greatness. Although the house and grounds were spacious, it was clearly not one of England's grand country estates. Inside, the furniture was a mixture of inherited or handed-down pieces, combined with some new items that were generally simple in style. There was none of the elaborately carved high-Victorian furniture bought to match, as found in the Lincoln's stiff and formal parlor in Springfield. In fact, the Darwins had no parlor at all, just a drawing room, where the informal furnishings had been chosen and arranged for comfort rather than for the formal entertaining of guests. The same could be said of the Darwins' dining room. The chairs and table did not match, and there was a long, plain, well-worn sofa at one side where Charles could lie down and rest after a meal. The overall effect is one of sparseness in contrast to the overstuffed feeling of the Lincolns' dining room. Unlike the insecure Mary Lincoln, Emma Wedgwood Darwin had nothing to prove to anyone.

Emma was fortunate to have a strong constitution, plenty of money, and a battery of servants to help her with both the children and the household. They had Charles's manservant, Joseph Parslow, who came with them from London and headed up the domestic staff. The Darwins considered him to be an ideal servant, and he considered them to be ideal employers. In fact, Charles looked on Parslow as a loyal friend as much as a servant. Besides Parslow, the Darwins had a footman, a coachman, a cook, a gardener, two nurses for the children, and several housemaids—compared to Mary Lincoln' one hired girl. They also engaged a wet nurse on at least one occasion and perhaps for all the babies. The possibility that Emma did little breast-feeding may also help to explain her many and closely spaced pregnancies.

Down House not only sheltered the family, it was also Charles's workplace. His old study, where he wrote his most important works, was cluttered with papers, books, shelves, and chests with small drawers. And contrary to the popular image of scientists with tubes, coils, beakers, and white lab coats, what the modern visitor finds in Darwin's study are a simple microscope, small tools for cutting, scraping, and dissecting, a few glass bottles with dried powders, and the dark woolen cloak that Darwin wore on his walks about the property or down to the village. A small dog basket lined with a plaid blanket sits near the fireplace, ready for one of Darwin's beloved pets, possibly his fox terrier, Polly.

Lincoln's workplace was different. He also worked in his study at home, especially in the evenings, but for the most part, he used his office downtown when he was not in court or out on the judicial circuit—a necessity, given the nature of his profession, and a godsend during times of marital discord. To support his family, Lincoln threw himself into the law as never before. His first partnership had ended when John T. Stuart won a second term in the US House of Representatives, and in April 1841, Lincoln teamed up with Stephen T. Logan, a very skilled Springfield attorney and the undisputed leader of the local bar. Unfortunately for Lincoln, who had split all fees fifty-fifty with Stuart, his share of the new firm's income was set at only one-third. This partnership ended in the autumn of 1844, when Logan decided to take his son David into the practice with him. At this point, Lincoln asked William Herndon, a man nine years his junior who was then reading law with Logan, to become his partner, even though Herndon was not yet admitted to the bar.

Lincoln could have resumed his old arrangement with Stuart, who was now back from Washington, or he could have teamed up with another, more seasoned attorney in town. Understandably, Herndon was both surprised and flattered by the offer, but he was dubious about accepting until Lincoln remarked, "Billy, I can trust you, if you can trust me."[5] Besides liking and trusting Herndon, the book-loving Lincoln was probably impressed by Herndon's extensive private library, including works by Kant, Renan, Fichte, Buckle, Emerson, Froude—and Darwin (most probably the *Journey of the Beagle*).[6] He also valued his partner's leadership of the younger Whigs in Springfield, a great asset if he wanted to run for elective office again. Then, too, Herndon's relative youth and inexperience meant that Lincoln would be the senior member of the firm, a status reflected by the fact that Herndon invariably addressed his partner as "Mr. Lincoln," while Lincoln always called Herndon "Billy." Even so, Lincoln insisted on splitting all fees fifty-fifty.

In his early years as a lawyer, Lincoln had relied mainly on his common sense, knowledge of the common law, and ability to convince juries. Impressed by Stephen Logan's learning, he now began reading up on legal procedures and precedents and spent many evenings in the nearby law library of the Illinois Supreme Court researching cases he would have to argue. Later, the more scholarly Herndon researched the case law while Lincoln interviewed the clients and advocated in court. Herndon also kept track of their finances. John H. Littlefield, a former student in their firm left an account of the small and unimpressive office of Lincoln and Herndon, located in a brick building across the square from the courthouse: "There was one long table in the center of the room, and a shorter one running in the opposite direction, forming a T, and both were covered with green baize. There were two windows[,] which looked out into the back yard. In one corner was an old-fashioned secretary with pigeon-holes and a drawer, and here Mr. Lincoln and his partner kept their law papers. There was also a book-case containing about 200 volumes of law as well as miscellaneous books."[7] The place was seldom swept and there was no system for filing papers, which often meant that the partners had to waste immense amounts of time looking for lost documents.

Herndon vividly described Lincoln's usual posture in the office, along with his irritating habit of reading out loud: "When he reached the office, about nine o'clock in the morning, the first thing he did was to pick up a newspaper, spread himself out on an old sofa, one leg on a chair, and read aloud, much to my discomfort." Exasperated, Herndon once asked his partner why he did this. Lincoln explained, "When I read aloud two senses catch the idea: first, I see what I read; second, I hear it, and therefore I can remember it better."[8]

Herndon could also be exasperated when Lincoln spent an entire morning telling stories, but he admitted that they were sometimes clever ways of avoiding certain subjects without seeming to do so: "If a man came to see him for the purpose of finding out something, which he did not care to let him know and at the same time did not want to refuse him, he was very adroit. In such cases Lincoln would do most of the talking, swinging around what he suspected was the vital point, but never nearing it, interlarding his answers with a seemingly endless supply of stories and jokes."[9] The man would leave in good humor, only to realize a little later that Lincoln had told him nothing he had wanted to know.

Lincoln and Herndon took on all sorts of clients, both plaintiffs and defendants, with cases ranging from property disputes, debt collection, theft, and embezzlement to assault and divorce. Believing that everyone deserved legal representation, Lincoln did not let his own scruples stand in the way of doing his best for a client, including arguing for one Robert Matson who was trying to recover runaway slaves in Coles County, Illinois. In this case, Lincoln maintained that Matson had never intended to hold slaves permanently in the free state of Illinois but was merely exercising his right of transit—that is, transporting his slaves through a free state, a right that the courts had upheld many times. Lincoln lost the case, and Matson reportedly left immediately for Kentucky without paying his attorney fees. Most interesting is Lincoln's willingness to uphold the law even when it involved a practice that he abhorred, a law and order stance that he would maintain toward slavery until well after the Civil War had begun.

Lincoln was usually more successful in persuading juries than he had been in the Matson case. A fellow Springfield lawyer called him "wise as a serpent" in the courtroom and gave as an example the way Lincoln frequently lulled the opposition into thinking he would not fight hard. He would seldom object to evidence or statements made by the opposition, and when the judge did rule against him, he would typically say, "Well, I reckon I must be wrong." In fact, he was giving away points he could not have carried anyway, only to stand firm when he was likely to prevail: "By giving away six points and carrying the seventh he carried his case.... Any man who took Lincoln for a simple-minded man would very soon wake up with his back in a ditch."[10]

Lincoln was also very good with juries, especially in his closing statements, where he had an ability to explain everything in a clear, straightforward way that they could easily understand, and that made him seem like an honest, down-to-earth fellow rather than some slick lawyer. Opposing lawyers also feared the unconventional and surprising methods that Lincoln would spring on juries, which his adversaries were unprepared to oppose or answer. According to Herndon, "He brushed aside all rules, and very often resorted to some strange and strategic performance which invariably broke his opponent down or exercised some peculiar influence over the jury."[11] One surprise that he pulled over on the prosecution was in a murder trial of one William Armstrong, whom Lincoln was defending. A crucial witness testified that he had seen Armstrong deliver the fatal blow by moonlight, only to have Lincoln produce an almanac showing that the moon had gone down by the time the witness reported being at the scene of the crime. This was enough for the jury to acquit.

Lincoln was the most successful in court, Herndon believed, when he had plenty of time to prepare: "He thought slowly and acted slowly; he must . . . have time to analyze all the facts in a case and wind them into a connected story."[12] For this reason, Lincoln was most adept in the cases he argued before the Illinois Supreme Court, where the lawyers always had plenty of time to prepare. A steady and deliberate gathering of facts and putting together a story were habits that Abraham Lincoln and Charles Darwin shared and that helped them to prevail with great success in such different fields.

The fees that Lincoln and Herndon charged were modest, commonly $10 to $20 per case. Once when a client sent him a check for $25, Lincoln thought it excessive and returned $10 of it. At most, he earned $2,000 a year during the 1840s from the partnership, a respectable middle-class living for which he had to work incessantly. This meant riding the Eighth Judicial Circuit for more than four months every year. At first Lincoln rode horseback, later he drove a small buggy, and still later he made use of the railroads as they appeared on the scene. He enjoyed these times on the circuit—the shared meals with the judge and other attorneys and in the evenings swapping stories around the fireplace, despite the often bad food and crowded sleeping conditions at the inns and hotels where he invariably shared a bed with one of the other men. Lincoln never complained of these rough conditions. "If every other fellow grumbled at the bill-of-fare which greeted us at many of the dingy taverns," recalled Judge David Davis, "Lincoln said nothing."[13]

Unlike many of the other lawyers, Lincoln generally did not go home over the weekends while on the circuit, and some folks back in Springfield as well as Judge Davis speculated that the main reason for this was his difficult wife. In fact, as time went on, and the marital strife became more difficult for Lincoln to bear, he spent increasing amounts of time on the circuit without going home.[14] Neighbors and others who knew the Lincolns said that Mary would fly off the handle unpredictably, reportedly hitting her husband with a piece of firewood, throwing hot coffee in his face, hurling potatoes at him, and chasing him down the street with a broomstick (or butcher knife, according to one source). She also quarreled with the help and had a hard time keeping any of them for long. She once slapped the hired girl across the face, and when her uncle came over to the house to see about it, Mary gave him a severe tongue lashing and hit him in the face with a broom. The man then went downtown to demand some sort of explanation from Lincoln, who answered in a calm and mournful voice, "*Friend* . . . can't you endure this one wrong done to you . . . without much complaint for old friendship's sake while I have had to bear it without complaint and without a murmur for lo these last fifteen years[?]"[15]

Lincoln tried to ignore his wife's eruptions, sometimes laughing at them and often escaping to his office, strategies that further fueled her fury. During the most difficult altercations, he would arrive uncommonly early in the morning and stay well into the evening, sometimes even sleeping at the office on a long sofa he kept there. Herndon, who never liked Mary Lincoln, wrote that his partner was sometimes so depressed over troubles at home that he would find him, "lying on the lounge looking skyward, or doubled up in a chair with his feet resting on the sill of a back window," so miserable that he could not even manage to say, "Good morning."[16] Generally speaking, Lincoln "was a sad-looking man," Herndon wrote of his law partner: "His melancholy dripped from him as he walked. . . . Lincoln's melancholy never failed to impress any man who ever saw him. The perpetual look of sadness was his most prominent feature."[17]

Lincoln never confided in anyone about these black moods, but Herndon associated them with the problems at home. Although Lincoln's domestic situation doubtless added to his overall melancholy, he may also have been depressed for other reasons, including the weather, political disappointments, or worries over money. Since he had suffered from depression long before his marriage, the turmoil with Mary could not have been the only reason for the black moods that Herndon observed.

Biographer David Donald has speculated that Mary Lincoln suffered from some form of mental instability, which had afflicted other members of her family.[18] Charles Strozier believes that Mary's mental state was rooted in her mother's death, the loss of her father's attention when he remarried, and her impossible dependency on Lincoln to compensate for these losses. Lincoln was not a demonstrative man, and in order to escape from his wife's emotional demands, he would spend increasingly long periods away from home, first as a lawyer riding the judicial circuit and then in political campaigns. But the more time he spent away from home, the more Mary felt ignored and craved his attentions. Lincoln could not have compensated for all of his wife's needs and insecurities no matter how attentive he might strive to be, but his avoidance only seemed to stoke the worst fears and to fuel her anger.[19]

Herndon had little sympathy for Mary's behavior, but he did pass on a close relative's explanation that one cause of her outbursts may have been Lincoln's lack of what his wife considered proper manners, such as when he would answer the front door in his shirtsleeves or persist in dipping his own table knife into the butter dish instead of using the "silver-handled one intended for that purpose."[20] However, Herndon's main speculation about Mary Lincoln concerned her desire for revenge. He insisted that Lincoln had married her to save his honor after promising her and then breaking off the engagement. Humiliated at this rejection despite their eventual marriage, Mary had spent the rest of her life spiraling down into bouts of angry revenge, leading her husband on "a wild and merry dance."[21]

Although Lincoln's legal work was very time-consuming, this was not the reason why he decided, for the time being, to hold off seeking further elective office. In 1840, he declined to run again for the state legislature because of hostility to the internal improvement projects that he and other Whigs had sponsored just as the United States was falling into a deep economic depression and state revenues were shrinking alarmingly. Although he might have won another term, he also knew he could do little to advance any legislative agenda in the face of growing strength for the Democrats in Illinois. By not running for office himself, he had plenty of time to campaign vigorously for Whig candidate William Henry Harrison in the 1840 presidential election. Harrison won nationally but failed to carry Springfield and surrounding Sangamon County, where Lincoln had concentrated his efforts.

Lincoln by no means gave up on running for office again, but he decided to bide his time until the political atmosphere seemed more promising—just as Darwin was biding his time in England until social and intellectual conditions were more favorable. The right timing was a factor that both men understood very well and that contributed greatly to their successes.

Marriage was proving far more pleasant for Charles Darwin than for Lincoln. His wife, Emma, could not have been more different from Mary Lincoln. Ever calm, she seemed to manage her growing household without effort. Eight children were born at Down House: Mary Eleanor (1842), who died in infancy; Henrietta (1843); George Howard (1845); Elizabeth (1847); Francis (1848); Leonard (1850); Horace (1851); and Charles Waring (1856). With ten children born during a seventeen-year period between 1839 and 1856 (including William Erasmus and Annie, who had been born in London), the Darwins were clearly doing nothing to limit the size of their family.

Charles delighted in the children, and from the beginning he observed them closely and took careful notes on their behavior.[22] After William's birth, he looked for the first facial expressions of anger, fear, and pleasure, and compared the baby's reaction to seeing himself in a mirror with that of Jenny, the orangutan, whom he had seen in the London Zoo just the year before. While Jenny never tired of looking at herself and was "astonished beyond measure," baby William realized by the time he was seven months old that his image in the looking glass was not real and would turn away from it as soon as anyone distracted his attention. Though humans soon outstripped orangutans and other apes in their understandings of the world, Darwin still marveled at the similarities in expressions between his children and these most humanlike animals. Years later he reflected, "The appearance of dejection in young orangs and chimpanzees, when out of health, is as plain and almost as pathetic as in the case of our own children. The state of mind and body is shown by their listless movements, fallen countenances, dull eyes, and changed complexions."[23]

The Darwin children had very fond memories of their father, recalling him "as the most delightful play-fellow."[24] They loved the stories he told about his childhood and about his adventures on the *Beagle*. He also good-humoredly put up with their "raids" into his study, even when he was hard at work, to find "sticking-plaster, string, pins, scissors, stamps, foot-rule, or hammer."[25]

Darwin had virtually everything he needed or wanted at home and went to London infrequently, even though it was only two hours away. He depended increasingly on the mail to communicate with other naturalists and collectors, and his correspondence with those in the far corners of the world was made possible by the great reach and efficiency of the British mail service. A new, lifelong friendship also helped him to keep in touch with the scientific world and provided him with a sounding board for his research and speculations. This friend was Joseph Dalton Hooker (1817–1911). Eight years younger than Darwin (approximately the same age difference as between Lincoln and William Herndon), Hooker had studied medicine at Edinburgh and then had taken part in an Antarctic expedition headed by Sir James Ross. Darwin heard of Hooker's work as a naturalist through Joseph's father, Sir William Hooker, who was director of the Royal Botanic Gardens at Kew, a position that the younger man assumed following his father's death. Soon after Hooker returned from an expedition to the Antarctic, Darwin offered him all the plant specimens from the *Beagle* voyage, which the younger man immediately realized would make an impressive addition to his collections. Hooker soon began making frequent visits to Down House, sometimes staying for several weeks at a time. He was also generous in sharing his extensive knowledge of plant distribution around the world, information that Darwin would find essential to working out his theory of natural selection.

As their friendship grew and Darwin came to trust Hooker, he let him in on his big secret, the still-germinating theory of species transmutation through natural selection. Hooker's initial skepticism and pointed questions convinced Darwin that he needed to put his views into more organized form, and during the spring of 1844 he began writing what turned out to be a 189-page manuscript, which grew to 231 pages once Darwin had it copied in "fair hand" by the village schoolmaster. It was an expansion of the thirteen-page pencil sketch that he had written two years earlier.

The first person to read the 1844 manuscript was Emma, who made some stylistic corrections and posed a few questions for clarification, but remained noncommittal about her husband's central thesis, which clearly contradicted her religious faith. He was still not ready for publication, in large part because of unsettled political conditions at home and abroad. Chartist demonstrations continued in London throughout the decade, and in 1848, bloody revolutions erupted on the European Continent, both of which made the British establishment fearful of any radical ideas. At the same time, Darwin wanted to accumulate even more evidence of his theory, fearing ridicule by the scientific community. Although he would hold back, Darwin wanted to make sure that the treatise would be published in case he died prematurely. In a testamentary letter to Emma, he directed her to find an appropriate person to complete, improve, and edit the work, to offer him all his books and notes, and to pay the person four hundred pounds. If she could not find anyone to do the work at that fee, she should then offer five hundred pounds. He went on to suggest several colleagues to complete his work, including Lyell, Hooker, and old Professor Henslow at Cambridge, despite his orthodox religious beliefs. If no one would take on the project, Emma was to have the 1844 manuscript published as it was.

By taking Hooker into his confidence about the manuscript, Darwin also hoped to win him over to his views and eventually to help pave the way to have those views accepted by leading scientists, many of whom respected Hooker's work as a botanist. Darwin, like Lincoln, who had decided not to seek elective office again until the time was ripe, would bide his time. In his own quiet way, Darwin was as good a "politician" as the up-and-coming lawyer from Springfield, Illinois. It also seems apparent that Darwin was bursting to tell someone about his thoughts, even if he was not willing to go public with them As a way of conveying just how controversial he feared his theory would be to others, he wrote to Hooker that it "is like confessing a murder."[26]

The correspondence with Hooker about a sensational new book also revealed something of why Darwin believed he could not go public yet with his theory: The book was *Vestiges of the Natural History of Creation*. Published anonymously, its author was later revealed to be Robert Chambers, an unusually gifted and compelling Scottish writer and publisher. Chambers was a generalist with no scientific training, but he proposed a concept of evolution that included everything from the stars and planets to the earth's crust, plants and animals, and eventually humans. He had no proof for all of this and relied on the works of others, but his book was widely read and discussed—and ridiculed by the scientific establishment.

One of the most caustic reviews came from Darwin's old geology professor, Adam Sedgwick. Hooker found the book delightful, but Darwin did not: the author's geology was terrible and his zoology was worse. Besides being slightly envious of the success of *Vestiges*, he was alarmed that the book had given naturalists a splendid chance to lacerate the whole idea of transmutation. *Vestiges* might have made for fascinating reading, but it certainly was not respectable, and Darwin was not about to stick his neck out until he had a mountain of evidence to back up his theory.

Besides collecting additional evidence, Darwin believed that he needed to establish his credentials as a biologist. His publication of *Geological Observations on South America* in 1846, along with several of his earlier writings, had made his reputation in geology but not in the life sciences. To correct this, he set to work on what turned out to be a massive study of barnacles. His initial idea was to study and write up his own barnacle collections, but he soon discovered that there was much confusion about the genus as a whole, so he decided to study the entire category. The project demanded painstaking research using a microscope to view these tiny creatures that attached themselves to a seemingly infinite number of objects, both natural and manmade. The project took eight painstaking years. The publication of this work (1851–54) not only established Darwin's reputation as a biologist, but as a result of his studies, he discovered that barnacles represented a transitional stage between hermaphroditism (individuals with both male and female sex organs) and full-blown sexual differentiation and the possibility of sexual reproduction. This strengthened an important insight Darwin had already made and that he would continue to emphasize: that sexual reproduction was essential to variation in species, since this was the only way that the different characteristics of two individuals could be joined and passed along to their offspring. Without sexual reproduction, in other words, succeeding generations would simply be more or less exact copies (or clones) of their ancestors. Still, in comparison to the excitement of the late 1830s into the mid-1840s, when Darwin was formulating his basic theory of evolution, the barnacle years have been called "Darwin's delay" by a number of scholars.

Even though Darwin's life at Down House gave him everything he required (or had even imagined), he was, in fact, frequently very ill there. The headaches, nausea, exhaustion, and depression became worse than ever, and he was often able to work only a few hours each day. Emma, despite her duties of running a household and mothering a growing family, albeit with plenty of help from servants and nannies, showered Charles with love and attention, according to their son Francis: "For all the later years of his life she never left him for a night; and her days were so planned that all his resting hours might be shared with her. She shielded him from every avoidable annoyance, and omitted nothing that might save him trouble or prevent him from becoming overtired, or that might alleviate the many discomforts of his ill-health."[27]

Laying Darwin low were often circumstances over which neither he nor the rest of the family had any control, as when he received the news in April 1847 that his dear friend Hooker, to whom he had given a copy of his manuscript on evolution to read, was planning to embark on what turned out to be a three-and-a-half-year expedition to the Himalayas. He confessed in an almost plaintive letter to Hooker, "You will hardly believe how deeply I regret for *myself* your present prospects—I had looked forward to [our] seeing much of each other during our lives. It is a heavy disappointment; & in a more selfish point of view, as aiding me in my work, your loss is indeed irreparable."[28] Like Lincoln's reaction to the loss of his friend Speed when he moved back to Kentucky, Darwin was greatly depressed by Hooker's departure.

Perhaps even more than Darwin, Lincoln tried to keep depression at bay through work. Despite the tempestuous times at home and Lincoln's decision in the early 1840s to put off standing for election, Mary Lincoln remained intensely interested in politics and ambitious to share in her husband's electoral glory, ever encouraging his party activities and efforts to win office.

Lincoln's driving ambition for political success and the public recognition that it brought was very evident to Herndon: "That man who thinks Lincoln calmly sat down and gathered his robes about him, waiting for people to call him, has a very erroneous knowledge of Lincoln. He was always calculating, and always planning ahead. His ambition was a little engine that knew no rest."[29] Herndon does not say what drove Lincoln in politics, but his humble background and the shame he felt about his father's lack of success may well have been important factors in his ceaseless efforts for political honors.

Joshua Shenk would add that Lincoln's desire for office was part of his drive to manage his by now chronic depression. At the time of his breakdown in January 1841, Lincoln wrote to John T. Stuart, then his law partner and Mary Todd's cousin, that he was "now the most miserable man living. . . . Whether I shall ever be better I can not tell. . . . To remain as I am is impossible: I must die or be better."[30] If he decided to live, his friend Speed added, it was because he wanted to "connect his name with the events transpiring in his generation, and so impress himself upon them as to link his name with something that would redound to the interest of his fellow-men." That "was what he desired to live for;" that was what would make his suffering worthwhile.[31] Later, this powerful ambition would haunt Lincoln as he sent thousands of men to their deaths during the Civil War.

Whatever the motivational mix, Lincoln's convoluted efforts to be elected to the US House of Representatives demonstrated his political skill and tenacity. Because of the Democrats' considerable majorities in Illinois, Lincoln reasoned that he had little chance of winning statewide office and concluded that his best opportunity lay in running for Congress from the Seventh Congressional District, one that included Springfield and much of the judicial circuit where he was well known as a lawyer, as well as an area where the Whigs enjoyed consistent majorities. He became more active in Whig Party affairs, attending meetings and making speeches. Although he failed to secure his party's nomination for the 1844 election to Congress, the Whigs had committed themselves to rotation in office, meaning that the person elected would step down after just one term, opening the way for Lincoln two years later.

Although Lincoln was elected to Congress in the fall of 1846, the next session did not begin until the end of 1847 at a time when the national legislature commonly met for only a few months each year—from early December until late winter or early spring of the ensuing year. The entire Lincoln family arrived in Washington on December 2 and soon moved into Mrs. Ann G. Sprigg's boardinghouse, located just east of the Capitol building on a site now covered by the Library of Congress complex. Eight other Whig congressmen boarded at Mrs. Sprigg's, and Lincoln became immediately popular among them with his amusing store of anecdotes and political sagacity, but Mary Lincoln was soon dissatisfied. Few other congressmen had brought their wives and families with them, which left her feeling isolated without female friends and with a husband who was too busy to spend much time with her and their children. Being cooped up in one room with two boys whose normal noisiness irritated the other boarders was also a trial for her. By May she had had enough and temporarily moved with the children to her father's house in Lexington, Kentucky.

Lincoln plunged into his legislative work with great enthusiasm, missing only 13 of the 456 roll calls during his term in the House. He became a member of two committees: Post Offices and Post Roads and Expenditures in the War Department. He continued to be very active in Whig politics and joined other members of his party in discussing their seemingly dismal prospects for the presidency in 1848, in view of the recent great success of the incumbent Democrat James K. Polk in winning a war with Mexico and the prospect of soon annexing California and the rest of the Southwest. Under the circumstances, Lincoln and other Whigs thought that Polk and the Democrats were vulnerable only in the way they had taken the United States to war with Mexico. Polk had insisted to Congress in his war message that Mexican troops had invaded the United States and shed blood on American soil. In fact, the Mexicans had moved into a disputed territory between the Rio Grande and Nueces rivers that was claimed by both countries.

Lincoln tried to embarrass Polk by introducing a resolution on December 22 requiring the president to give Congress "a full knowledge of all the facts which go to establish whether the particular spot of soil on which the blood of our *citizens* was so shed, was, or was not, *our own soil*, at that time."[32] Early in the new year, the Whig representatives, in caucus, voted to support the resolution, and on January 12, Lincoln made a blistering attack from the House floor against Polk, calling particular attention to the many gaps in the president's evidence and logic, as if the chief executive were on trial and Lincoln were the prosecuting attorney. Polk ignored both the speech and what has come to be known as Lincoln's "Spot Resolution," and the House as a body neither debated nor voted on the measure.

Lincoln's attack on Polk turned out to be one of the few blunders of his political life. The Mexican War was very popular in Illinois, and Lincoln made himself look both unpatriotic and foolish. Predictably, the Democratic newspapers back home ridiculed him, but many of the Whig papers found fault with him too. He also received critical letters from Illinois Whigs, including Herndon. Lincoln shot back, saying, "Allow the President to invade a neighboring nation whenever *he* shall deem it necessary to repel an invasion, and you allow him to do so *whenever he may choose to say* he deems it necessary for such purpose—and you allow him to make war at pleasure, ... and [place] our President where kings have always stood."[33] Such arguments did him no good, and it would take him a long time to live down his derisive nickname of "Spotty Lincoln." Paradoxically, Lincoln's political opponents during the Civil War would accuse him of acting like a king in going to war with the South when Congress was in recess and then riding roughshod over the civil liberties of his critics.

Lincoln stayed in Washington after the legislative session ended and spent the summer of 1848 helping to make Whig Zachary Taylor the nation's next president, in spite of earlier doubts that a Whig could be elected. Ironically, Taylor succeeded in large part because he was a general and one of the heroes of the Mexican War. Although the Whigs had been critical of the war, political expediency dictated their move to nominate "Old Rough and Ready," as supporters called Taylor.

Lincoln's letters during that hot summer in the capital show a lonely man who missed Mary and the boys very much. He invited them to join him on a campaign tour of New England, where he gave speeches for Taylor in a number of towns. On the way back to Illinois, the family visited Niagara Falls, which moved him to write, "Niagara is strong, and fresh to-day as ten thousand years ago. The Mammoth and the Mastodon—now so long dead, that fragments of their monstrous bones, alone testify, that they ever lived, have gazed on Niagara."[34] Lincoln was impressed by both the ancient majesty of the falls and the now-extinct large mammals that once roamed about them. He clearly shared Charles Darwin's rejection of the widely held assertion that the earth was only six thousand years old.

When Lincoln returned to Washington in early December of 1848, the hottest items on the legislative agenda concerned the extension of slavery into the territories recently won from Mexico. The Wilmot Proviso, introduced by Congressman David Wilmot of Pennsylvania, would forbid slavery in these new territories. Lincoln took no part in the heated debates over Wilmot's proposal—partly because he did not want to anger Southern Whigs—but when he had to vote directly or indirectly on the issue, he voted for the proviso, which itself never became law. Principle mixed with practicality continued to inform his decisions.

Lincoln took a more active role in legislative efforts to end slavery in Washington, DC. Slavery in the Federal District was an affront to

Northerners who were against it and a scandal to members of the foreign diplomatic corps whose own countries had abolished the institution and who could—and often did—point out the hypocrisy of the United States for proclaiming liberty and democracy while upholding human bondage. The slave markets in the city, where buyers inspected men and women as they would horses or cattle, were a particular affront. Lincoln worked out a compromise bill that would compensate owners in Washington who freed their slaves and that would guarantee the right of owners to hunt down and retrieve fugitive slaves in the District while abolishing slavery in Washington itself. So long as the bill was being discussed quietly, Lincoln thought he had enough support to get it through the House, but once it became public, many Northern representatives denounced the idea of paying owners for their slaves, and Southerners rejected the attempt to end slavery in the capital as a grave insult to their way of life. Sensing sure defeat, Lincoln did not even introduce the bill.

Before leaving Washington, Lincoln attended the inauguration of President Taylor and was admitted to practice before the US Supreme Court. He also applied for and obtained a patent for an invention to buoy vessels over shoals, a move clearly influenced by his success many years before in easing Denton Offutt's flatboat over the milldam at New Salem. The spring of 1849 found Lincoln back at his law practice in Illinois. The next half dozen years would roughly correspond with Darwin's hesitation to publish his evolutionary studies.

Over the years, Lincoln had occasionally visited his father, stepmother, and stepbrother, John D. Johnson, at their farm in Coles County, Illinois, especially when his circuit riding took him to that part of the state. Given his feelings about his father, he may have made these visits mainly to see his stepmother, Sarah, and simply put up with his father as a price he had to pay for the visits. He also gave them varying amounts of money from time to time to relieve their incessant financial distresses, both out of a sense of duty and no doubt to spare Sarah undue hardship.

Shortly after returning from Washington, he received a letter from Johnson saying that Tom Lincoln was dying and wanted to see his only son one last time. Although actively campaigning for an appointment to head the General Land Office in Illinois (a post he did not get), Lincoln rushed off to see his father, only to find him much improved. The next January, Lincoln received additional letters predicting his father's imminent demise and at first assumed that they, too, were false alarms. When another letter finally convinced him that the end was near, he wrote back to Johnson to tell his father, "Say to him that if we could meet now, it is doubtful whether it would not be more painful than pleasant; but that if it be his lot to go now, he will soon have a joyous [meeting] with many loved ones gone before; and where [the rest] of us, through the help of God, hope ere-long [to join] them."[35]

Given Lincoln's skeptical views, he could not have believed a word about joining loved ones in heaven, and he probably asked Johnson to pass these sentiments along as soothing thoughts. When Tom Lincoln finally died on January 17, 1851, his son did not attend the funeral. The two of them had parted ways long before, and Lincoln clearly had no great affection for his father. Besides, Mary Lincoln was still recovering from the birth of their third child, and a round-trip by horse and buggy to Coles County would have taken six days. In any case, Tom Lincoln would have been buried long before Lincoln arrived, since in those days before modern embalming, the interment would have taken place as soon as possible.

The Lincolns' new baby, a son named William Wallace, called Willie, was born in December 1850, just ten and a half months after the death of their son Edward, who was not quite four years old. The cause of little Eddie's death was probably pulmonary tuberculosis, and after struggling for fifty-one days, he died on February 1, 1850. Both parents were devastated, but Lincoln said little and buried himself in his work, by now a technique that he used to ward off the worst episodes of depression. The more emotional Mary could not accept the idea that their son's untimely death was somehow part of God's plan, to be accepted on faith. Within weeks, Mary was pregnant with Willie, an obvious move to replace the lost child. So that Willie would have a playmate, the Lincolns had another child, named Thomas, born on April 4, 1853. Because of his large head and small body at birth, Lincoln called him "Little Tadpole," later shortened to "Tad." It seems odd that they would have named this last child after his paternal grandfather, given Lincoln's feelings toward Tom Lincoln. Charles Strozier has speculated that Lincoln may have done so out of guilt, believing deep down that he had not treated his aging father properly.[36]

The spacing of the Lincoln children's births suggests that the parents were practicing birth control. There were just over two and a half years separating Robert and Eddie and just under two and a half years between Willie and Tad—and nearly five years between Eddie and Willie. That Mary Lincoln intentionally became pregnant so soon after Eddie's death adds to the idea that the Lincolns practiced some sort of family planning. Mary Lincoln's biographer, Jean Baker, indicates that middle-class women in Springfield were well aware that they were not as likely to become pregnant while breast-feeding and that some purposely held off weaning their children, as did Mary Lincoln, in order to prevent conception. Baker adds that some men and women at the time also used coitus interruptus (or the withdrawal method) as another form of birth control.[37]

Lincoln felt closer to Willie and Tad than he ever had toward his oldest son, Robert, perhaps because he had so often been away on the judicial circuit while Robert was little. Now with enough lucrative practice in Springfield, he was more often at home during the early and middle 1850s. He hauled the boys around the neighborhood in a little wagon and later walked them downtown, the youngsters holding onto his hands or maybe onto a coattail. If one of them complained of being too tired to walk home, he would hoist the boy over his shoulders for a ride back. On Sunday mornings, when their mother went to church, Lincoln often took them down to the law office.

Ever indulgent with Willie and Tad, he let them run wild in the office. As Herndon described the scene, "The boys were absolutely unrestrained in their amusement. If they pulled down all the books from the shelves, bent the points of all the pens, overturned ink-stands, scattered law-papers over the floor, or threw the pencils into the spittoon, it never disturbed the serenity of their father's good-nature."[38] Charles Darwin was also a kindly and indulgent father, but he hardly would have tolerated such behavior from any of his children. Lincoln's lenient attitude may have been an overreaction to his father's rough treatment of him or it may have been his ability to lose himself in his own musings, as suggested by Herndon: "Frequently absorbed in thought, [Lincoln] never observed their mischievous but destructive pranks . . . [and] said nothing—and, even if brought to his attention, he virtually encouraged their repetition by declining to show any substantial evidence of parental disapproval."[39]

Darwin also lost his father as he was moving into middle age. All during 1848, he made long and frequent visits to his childhood home at The Mount, where he spent much of the time in bed or resting on a sofa, seemingly little better off than his dying father. Charles had returned to Emma and the family when he received news of Dr. Darwin's death on November 13. Although they had sometimes been at odds, and Charles had found his father's criticisms and censorious tone difficult to take at times, he loved his father deeply, had always turned to Dr. Darwin for valued advice, and knew very well that his freedom to pursue the life of a gentleman naturalist had depended on his father's financial successes and generosity. Certainly Dr. Darwin had every reason to be proud of Charles, who had already published several books and made a name for himself in the scientific community, especially since his brother Erasmus had continued as a bon vivant in London with nothing solid to show for it. The contrast between these attitudes and Abraham Lincoln's feelings at the time of his father's death a little over two years later could not have been greater: If Robert Darwin had not been a precise vocational model for Charles, he had been a helpful guide and had offered practical support for all his son's life. Lincoln's need to rise so much farther than his father may have been another factor in the emotional distance between the two of them, whereas Darwin's father was a wealthy and highly successful physician that the son could admire.

Although relations between father and son were more than satisfactory at the time of Dr. Darwin's death, Charles waited for several days before starting off to Shrewsbury and arrived at The Mount shortly after the funeral procession had left the house. Instead of hurrying to catch up with it, he remained at the house and missed the graveside service. Perhaps he was sick, as he usually was at times of strain, and may have welcomed the excuse of being late. In any case, Robert Darwin's death sent Charles into a physical and emotional collapse. In March 1849 he described his symptoms to Hooker, who was still in India: "Indeed all this winter I have been bad enough, with dreadful vomiting every week & my nervous system began to be affected, so that my hands trembled & head was often swimming. I was not able to do anything one day out of three, & was altogether too dispirited to write to you or to do anything but what I was compelled.—I thought I was rapidly going the way of all flesh."[40]

Charles's health was so bad by early 1849 that the few visitors who saw him became alarmed. One of them was an old friend from *Beagle* days, who recommended Dr. James Gully's Water Cure Establishment at Malvern. Hydrotherapy, which involved all sorts of immersions and scrubbings—including seaside bathing at some establishments—was quite common at the time in both England and on the Continent. Darwin was very skeptical at first but was so sick that he was willing to try almost anything. He read Dr. Gully's book, *The Water Cure in Chronic Disease*, and on March 8 he and the entire family left for Malvern, where Gully diagnosed his illness as nervous disorder brought on by excessive metal exertion. Dr. Gully believed that this condition resulted from a congestion of blood in the vessels around the stomach and that his treatments with cold water and friction would draw the blood to the body's extremities and away from the stomach.

For nearly four months, Darwin began each day wrapped in blankets and sitting on a chair warmed by a spirit lamp until he was sweating profusely, then plunged into a cold shower or bath. He next drank a tumbler of cold water and walked for twenty minutes. Throughout the day, he kept a cold compress on his forehead, and Dr. Gully prescribed various homeopathic medicines in addition to forbidding sugar, salt, bacon, alcohol, or other stimulants. He was not allowed to do any of his scientific work and was banned from reading anything except the newspapers. Although the treatment was rigorous and surely unpleasant in many respects, it was both mild and benign compared to the brutal assault on his system that Lincoln had endured at the hands of his doctor in Springfield. In any case, Darwin's treatment apparently worked: the headaches were less severe, he no longer felt nauseous, and he even forgot about his blasted barnacles. If nothing else, the successful treatment seems to suggest that Darwin's illness was partly stress related, since his work and worries about his work may have been major reasons for his illness.

Determined to continue Dr. Gully's regimen at home, Darwin had his carpenter build him a "church-shaped" hut in the yard outside his study, where he installed a chair and spirit lamp. He described his home treatment to Hooker: "I have built a douche & am to go on through all the winter, frost or no frost. My treatment now is lamp five times per week & shallow bath for five minutes afterwards; douche daily for 5 minutes & dripping sheet daily. The treatment is wonderfully tonic, & I have had more better consecutive days this month, than on any previous ones."41 He was now allowed to work two and a half hours a day, but he was so exhausted by evening that he had to go to bed at eight. Work was a double-edged sword. However exhausting, it provided Darwin an escape from his troubles and gave him a reason to press on, as work did for Lincoln.

Although Darwin was feeling better, Annie, his favorite daughter was not well, and in the summer of 1850 she became gravely ill with stomachaches, exhaustion, and severe depression, often crying for no apparent reason. She improved somewhat in the winter, but by March 1851, she was so sick that Charles took her for a stay at Dr. Gully's, where she showed some improvement at first and then relapsed alarmingly. With Emma eight months pregnant and in no shape to travel, Charles hurried off to Malvern and was by Annie's bedside when she died on April 23. The cause may have been a breakdown in her immune system, similar perhaps to one of the conditions that had plagued her father for so many years but that had never been severe enough to kill him. Darwin's great-great-grandson, Randall Keynes, after placing her symptoms before several medical historians, concluded that Annie probably suffered from tuberculosis. If so, the cold-water treatments at Malvern were about the worst possible actions, though her parents could not have known that.

By now Charles was exhausted and ill himself and was encouraged to return home at once by his sister-in-law Fanny Wedgwood, who had joined him in Malvern for the death vigil. Fanny and her husband, Hensleigh (Emma's brother), took care of burying Annie the next day in the Priory Churchyard at Malvern.[42] Once again, Darwin took the opportunity to avoid a stressful situation that he knew would make him sick. In addition to his grief and exhaustion, it may be that he simply could not have stood hearing some clergyman intone about the promise of Annie's resurrection, when he could not believe a word of it himself.

Exactly a week after Annie's death, Charles did manage to write down his impressions of her, so that "in after years . . . the impressions now put down will recall more vividly her chief characteristics." The main feature of her disposition, he recalled, was "her buoyant joyousness . . . and her strong affection." He remembered, too, how "she would at almost any time spend half an hour in arranging my hair, 'making it,' as she called it, 'beautiful,' or in smoothing . . . my collar or cuffs." "We have lost the joy of the household, and the solace of our old age."[43]

Emma tried very hard to submit to "God's will" and to believe that Annie was now in a better place and that she could look forward to the day when they would be united in the afterlife. For Charles, the death of this beautiful, kind, and beloved child was the last blow to any faith he had in God. How could a supposedly good and just God design a world in which a beautiful and beloved child was allowed to suffer and die? From then on Charles was a total, self-avowed unbeliever.

During the first decade of their respective married lives, both Darwin and Lincoln had experienced the loss of their fathers and of young children. Darwin's health deteriorated badly during the same time that Lincoln faced serious marital difficulties and continued to fight to keep his depression at bay. Both sought solace in their work, Darwin as a respected scientist and Lincoln as a successful lawyer and rising politician. Both also experienced lulls in their careers, Lincoln in his limited success at being elected to public office and Darwin in his decision not to publish his theory. In the long run, these lulls turned out to be beneficial, since the time had not yet come for either of these men to launch their main efforts.

NOTES

1. Jean H. Baker, *Mary Todd Lincoln: A Biography* (New York: W. W. Norton, 1987), p. 116.

2. Darwin to William Darwin Fox, June 7, 1840, *The Correspondence of Charles Darwin* (Cambridge: Cambridge University Press, 1985–[2005]), 2:270.

3. Darwin to William Darwin Fox, March 25, 1843, *Correspondence of Charles Darwin*, 2:352.

4. Ibid., p. 93.

5. William H. Herndon, *Herndon's Life of Lincoln* (New York: Da Capo Press, 1983), p. 211.

6. Herndon also had works by Charles Lyell and Herbert Spencer in his library. See Henry Steele Commager, "Introduction to the Da Capo Edition," *Herndon's Life of Lincoln*, p. vii.

7. Quoted in ibid., p. 255.

8. Ibid., p. 268.

9. Ibid., p. 269.

10. Leonard Swett, quoted in ibid., pp. 269–70.

11. Ibid., p. 287.

12. Ibid., p. 272.

13. Quoted in ibid., p. 280.

14. On this point, see Charles B. Strozier, *Lincoln's Quest for Union* (Philadelphia: Paul Dry Books, 2001), pp. 146–50.

15. Quoted in Michael Burlingame, *The Inner World of Abraham Lincoln* (Urbana: University of Illinois Press, 1994), p. 277.

16. Herndon, *Herndon's Life of Lincoln*, p. 348.

17. Ibid., p. 473.

18. David Herbert Donald, *Lincoln* (New York: Quadrangle Books, 1995), p. 158.

19. Strozier, *Lincoln's Quest*, pp. 94–103.

20. Quoted in Herndon, *Herndon's Life of Lincoln*, p. 345.

21. Ibid., p. 182.

22. The best account of Darwin's relations with his children is Randall Keynes, *Annie's Box: Darwin, His Daughter and Human Evolution* (New York: Riverhead Books, 2002).

23. Quoted in ibid., p. 55.

24. Ibid., p. 101.

25. Francis Darwin, "Reminiscences of My Father's Everyday Life," in *The Life and Letters of Charles Darwin*, edited by Francis Darwin (New York: D. Appleton and Company, 1896), p. 113.

26. Quoted in Adrian Desmond and James Moore, *Darwin: The Life of a Tormented Evolutionist* (New York: Warner Books, 1991), p. 314.

27. Francis Darwin, "Reminiscences," p. 135.

28. Darwin to J. D. Hooker, February 10, 1845, *Correspondence of Charles Darwin*, 3:139.

29. Herndon, *Herndon's Life of Lincoln*, p. 304.

30. Lincoln to John T. Stuart, *The Collected Works of Abraham Lincoln*, edited by Roy P. Basler et al. (New Brunswick, NJ: Rutgers University Press, 1953), 1:229.

31. Joshua F. Speed to Herndon, February 9, 1866, quoted in Herndon, *Herndon's Life of Lincoln*, p. 172.

32. Lincoln, "'Spot Resolutions' in United States House of Representatives" (December 22, 1847), *Collected Works of Abraham Lincoln*, 1:421.

33. Lincoln to William H. Herndon, *Collected Works of Abraham Lincoln*, 1:451–52.

34. Quoted in Donald, *Lincoln*, p. 132.

35. Lincoln to John D. Johnson, *Collected Works of Abraham Lincoln*, 2:97.

36. Strozier, *Lincoln's Quest*, p. 73.

37. See Baker, *Mary Todd Lincoln*, pp. 128–29.

38. Herndon, *Herndon's Life of Lincoln*, p. 344.

39. Ibid.

40. Darwin to Hooker, March 28, 1849, *Correspondence of Charles Darwin*, 4:227.

41. Darwin to Hooker, October 12, 1849, *Correspondence of Charles Darwin*, 4:269.

42. Fanny Wedgwood was the wife of Emma's brother Hensleigh.

43. Quoted in Francis Darwin, "My Father's Everyday Life," in *Life and Letters*, pp. 110–11.

Chapter 5

TIME AND PLACE

A magnifying of the theatre till life itself is turned into a stage, for which it is our duty to study our parts well, and conduct with propriety and precision.

—Henry David Thoreau,
A Week on the Concord and Merrimack Rivers

By the 1850s, Abraham Lincoln and Charles Darwin were no longer young men. Now in their forties, both sensed that the time had come for major accomplishments. After several years of seeming delay during the late 1840s and early 1850s, when Lincoln waited for new political opportunities to open up and Darwin absorbed himself in his barnacle studies, both men pushed forward again. Success was not assured, but their own circumstances, combined with wider events, set the stage for greatness, and this sense of timing became apparent to both.

In England, the combination of growing prosperity, intellectual criticism of the old order, and a mounting faith in economic competition and personal exertion convinced Darwin that it was safe to unleash his controversial theory of evolution through natural selection. In the United States, on the contrary, it was not optimism and contentment but fierce and sometimes violent clashes over the nature of the American Union and the future of slavery that gave Lincoln the opening he needed. Strikingly, both men stepped forward in 1854, only to experience seemingly fatal setbacks four years later in 1858: Lincoln failed to win a seat in the United States Senate against archrival Stephen A. Douglas, and Darwin's claims to discovery appeared smashed when Alfred Russel Wallace came up with a theory of evolution very similar to his own.

Several circumstances in Britain produced a sense of well-being and optimism: the end of the Chartist disturbances of the 1840s, the country's escape from the revolutions that swept the Continent at the end of that decade, and the industrial and imperial dominance of the British Isles. The most impressive symbol of the new mood was the 1851 Crystal Palace Exhibition in London, the first of the great world's fairs, where Britain showcased its scientific, technological, and industrial accomplishments. The exhibit hall itself, a gigantic greenhouse made of prefabricated iron, wood, and glass and designed by Joseph Paxton, was a marvel to the millions of visitors who poured through it between May and October.

The Darwins did not manage to visit the Crystal Palace until July, after Emma had recovered from the birth of Horace, their ninth child, who was born on May 13—less than a month after Annie's death. Charles also wanted to finish his latest volume on barnacles so he could deliver the manuscript in person to his publisher while in London for the exhibition. Finally, on July 30, they arrived at brother Erasmus's house in Mayfair, which was only a short distance from the exposition grounds. Darwin marveled at the huge steam engines, the intricate machinery for making an unbelievable array of goods, and the products imported from all over the world.

Returning to Down House, Darwin continued to labor over his barnacle studies, with periodic lapses into the old illness because of overexertion, but also possibly because of an allergic reaction to the chemicals that he used to preserve his specimens. He would then return to his water treatments, either at home in his specially built shed or at some treatment establishment such as one near Farnham, but not to Dr. Gully's because of its sad associations with Annie's death.

Darwin's son Leonard left a detailed description of his father's daily life at home. He typically got up early and took a short walk before breakfast at 7:45, and then busied himself in the study, believing that the hour and a half between 8:00 and 9:30 to be "one of his best working times."[1] He then went into the drawing room for the mail, where Emma read any family letters aloud while he lay on the sofa. After this, Emma read to him from a novel until about 10:30, when he went back to work until 12:00 or 12:15. At that point he considered the bulk of his work done for the day, and would often exclaim in a satisfied voice, "*I've* done a good day's work."[2]

Darwin then went outside, stopping first at the greenhouse to check on any germinating seeds or experimental plants. After that he took his daily constitutional, either a stroll through the immediate neighborhood or around the sandwalk. Luncheon, the main meal of the day, came when the walk was finished, after which Darwin rested on the sofa in the drawing room, where he read the newspaper. This was the only material, besides scientific journals, that he read silently to himself. Then he settled into a large horsehair chair by the fireplace in his study to write letters on a board supported by the arms of the chair, sometimes dictating the longer letters from rough drafts that he had made. He was very conscientious about answering every letter, even the hostile ones, and felt guilty when he fell behind.

At 3:00, when the letter writing was over, Darwin rested in his bedroom by lying on a sofa and smoking a cigarette while Emma read from a novel or some other nonscientific book. (Besides smoking, he also took snuff during working hours as a stimulant, a habit he had picked up while a student at Edinburgh.) The reading upstairs often put him to sleep, causing him to complain later about missing some crucial part of a story. At four o'clock he went downstairs for a few more turns around the sandwalk, and at 4:30 he returned for another hour's work in the study. It was back to the drawing room for an idle half hour and then upstairs for another cigarette, Emma's reading aloud, and rest. Supper was at 7:30, after which he and Emma played two games of backgammon every night. Then Darwin read a scientific book or article to himself, followed by Emma's playing on the Broadwood grand piano (the make preferred by Beethoven). Emma was an accomplished pianist and for a brief period had taken lessons from Chopin while her family was traveling on the Continent. Then came another session of reading aloud, before Charles went to bed around 10:30. He often had trouble sleeping or awoke in the middle of the night, roused "by the activity of his thoughts" or upset because he had not answered "some troublesome person's letter."[3]

In order to keep such a predictable and rigid daily schedule, the household had to revolve around Darwin's needs, with the greatest burden falling on Emma, who nevertheless could afford to spare the necessary time and energy because she had a large household staff. She willingly shouldered the burden because she had learned through long experience that a daily structure reduced the stress on her husband and helped to keep him from becoming ill. He also found that playing billiards helped to take his mind off his worries, and he bought a billiard table and had it installed in the large room next to his study. Sometimes when he found himself unnerved, he would call his butler Parslow to play billiards. The billiard table sometimes served as a handy spillover for Darwin to lay out papers or experiments.

The predictable order at home, along with occasional water cures, left Darwin feeling particularly well by 1854. He had also finished his eight-year barnacle research and believed it was time to return to his

"Species Theory," as he was now calling his work on evolution. On September 9 of that year he began sorting through the many notes he had accumulated on the subject, but he was not yet ready to publish, not until he had made additional inquiries and carried out a number of his own experiments. He was especially curious about plant and animal dispersal, especially over seemingly insurmountable barriers such as hundreds of miles of ocean. So he soaked various kinds of seeds in salt water for varying periods to see if they would still germinate, and found that some did after many days and even months. He floated a dead pigeon in salt water to see if seeds in their crops would sprout after thirty days: They did. He carried out other experiments that proved lizard eggs could float in salt water for long periods and still hatch. Other small eggs, he demonstrated to himself, could attach to the feet of ducks and "hitch rides" to completely new but hospitable habitats. His experiments suggested that fresh-water snails could cling to duck feet and survive for flights of up to six hundred miles. As Darwin biographer David Quammen mused, "If there was no special creation, there was no special delivery."[4] If plants and animals had been dispersed around the globe, then there had to be some natural means of dispersal.

Darwin even created a printed request form that he sent out to hundreds of individuals all over the world who might send him information on plant and animal specimens. Nearer to home, he acquired young animals for the purposes of comparative anatomy. Some of the birds he requested came alive, and he had to kill them with ether or chloroform, boil them, and then strip off the flesh, a sickening process that often made him vomit. He was also keen to collect as much information as he could from animal breeders, since he wanted to make analogies between the selective breeding of domestic species and natural selection. Knowing that pigeons had been bred in England for centuries, he went to pigeon breeders' shows and even joined the Borough pigeon breeders club in London. He also took to breeding and raising pigeons in his own aviary at Down House.

The year 1854 was also a turning point year for Lincoln, but not because of calmer waters, as in Darwin's England. On the contrary, the Kansas-Nebraska Act of 1854 was the first in a series of explosive events that historians have seen as prime causes for the Civil War and that gave Lincoln new outlets for his surging political ambitions. Yet as the 1850s began, Lincoln was struggling to find some way back into political prominence. His one term in the US Congress had been less than stellar, and his opposition to the Mexican War had lost him considerable support at home. If this were not enough, his Whig Party appeared to be disintegrating before his eyes.

Most men, but not Lincoln, could take great satisfaction from an increasingly lucrative law practice. Lincoln and Herndon's most important case during this period was in defense of the Illinois Central Railroad, which McClean County had sued for payment of back property taxes, even though the state legislature had granted the railroad immunity from such levies. The case went all the way to the Illinois Supreme Court, where Lincoln and Herndon finally won in 1855. Another lucrative case, argued in 1857, involved claims of patent infringements by the McCormick Reaper Company. Although McCormick hired a lawyer from Philadelphia to be its main counsel, Lincoln was initially chosen as a local defender at a time when the trial's likely location was Chicago. Lincoln prepared himself assiduously, only to learn that the trial would be held before the US Circuit Court in Cincinnati and that the defense team had engaged Edwin M. Stanton, then a resident of Pittsburgh, to replace him. Lincoln was hurt by the slight, vowed never to set foot in Cincinnati again, and complained to Herndon about being "roughly handled by that man Stanton."[5] (Ever the pragmatist, Lincoln would later appoint Stanton as his secretary of war.)

Although Lincoln must have felt some pride in his newly enlarged house, he was still preoccupied by a yearning for higher political office and making a bigger name for himself. "Oh how hard it is," he exclaimed to Herndon, "to die and leave one's Country no better than if one had never lived for it."[6] During these frustrating years, Herndon continued to notice his partner's bouts of depression. Lincoln might come to the office in a cheerful mood and then for no apparent reason he would succumb to "a sad and terribly gloomy state." He might pick up a pen and write a few lines, only to put it down and stare into space or gaze vacantly out a window for hours at a time. He also had terrible nightmares during this period. One lawyer traveling with Lincoln remembered seeing him "sitting up in bed, his figure dimly visible by the ghostly firelight, and talking the wildest and most incoherent nonsense all to himself." Suddenly Lincoln jumped out of bed, threw some wood on the fire and sat there in front of it, "in a most somber and gloomy spell" until breakfast.[7]

Besides blaming these dark moods on Lincoln's marital situation, Herndon believed that overwork was another source of his partner's afflictions: "Lincoln thought . . . that there were no limitations to the endurance of his mental and vital forces" and he would pitch himself into legal cases "with a severe, persistent, continuous, and terrible" concentration of effort that resulted in "physical and mental exhaustion, a nervous morbidity and spectral illusions, irritability, melancholy, and despair."[8] Like Darwin, Lincoln would throw himself into work to promote his own fame and success as well as to escape from melancholic thoughts. But too much work and worry for both men could also touch off another round of gloom, in what became a vicious cycle of depression, overwork, and more depression.

Despite the quarrels at home, which probably contributed to Lincoln's dark moods, Mary Lincoln, like Emma Darwin, contributed significantly to her husband's accomplishments. She ran an orderly household, where Lincoln could depend on regular meals and all the physical comforts of a prosperous middle-class life. Mary was also as ambitious for political success as her husband and had lost none of her fascination for politics, though she showed little interest in his law practice. Political conversation had gotten her father's attention, and Mary may have used a similar tactic, consciously or unconsciously, to gain attention from her husband. In any case, Mary helped Lincoln to compile a number of small notebooks on the likelihood of support from other politicians in his campaigns, and she reviewed political editorials for him. She also kept after him to dress well and observe proper manners, believing that both would help in the political arena, at the same time keeping him from embarrassing her and the rest of the family.[9]

What reopened the door to political success was an inflammation of the slavery issue, beginning with passage of the Kansas-Nebraska Act in May 1854. The law's principal author was Democrat Stephen A. Douglas, a US senator for Illinois. His main goal was to organize the middle part of the Louisiana Territory so that the nation's first transcontinental railroad could be built through it, with its eastern terminus at Chicago. As a director of the Illinois Central Railroad and as an Illinois land speculator, Douglas stood to profit from such a route. However, both the Kansas and Nebraska territories lay north of the parallel, 36 degrees, 30 minutes, where the Missouri Compromise, passed by Congress back in 1820, had forbidden slavery. To win the support of Southerners, who wanted the transcontinental line to take a southern route, Douglas agreed to have the Missouri Compromise repealed as part of the Kansas-Nebraska Act and to deal with the question of slavery in the new territories in accordance with what he called "popular sovereignty." That meant leaving the question of slavery up to the people living there.

The repeal of the Missouri Compromise unleashed a maelstrom of protest in the North, causing many who had taken a moderate stance on slavery to denounce the machinations of the "slave power" in bringing about the repeal. The Kansas-Nebraska Act turned out to be the opening salvo in a series of events that would lead the nation into secession and civil war, though no one could know that at the time.

When elections for a territorial legislature in Kansas took place in

March 1855, thousands of "border ruffians" crossed over from Missouri (a slave state), voted illegally, and elected a proslavery legislature located in Lecompton, which promptly authorized slavery and a slave code to protect it. Antislavery settlers refused to recognize this government and elected their own legislature, which met in Topeka. A mini civil war then erupted in Kansas between the two factions. Among the fighters was the fanatic abolitionist John Brown, who with four sons and two other supporters dragged five unsuspecting proslavery men out of their cabins and slaughtered them with broadswords. The violence even spilled onto the floor of the US Senate, when Representative Preston Brooks of South Carolina decided to exact revenge over a speech that Senator Charles Sumner of Massachusetts had made criticizing proslavery actions in Kansas and verbally attacking Brooks's uncle, Senator Andrew P. Butler of South Carolina. Brooks crept up behind Sumner's desk on a day when the Senate chamber was nearly empty and began beating the Massachusetts senator over the head and shoulders, nearly killing him. Members of both the House and Senate began carrying pistols and knives into the chambers for self-protection.

Adding fuel to the fire was the US Supreme Court case of *Dred Scott v. Sanford*, handed down on March 6, 1857, just two days after the presidential inauguration of Democrat James Buchanan. Scott was a slave who had traveled into both Illinois (a free state) and the Wisconsin Territory (also free) with his master, who was a surgeon in the US Army, later returning with him to Missouri. With the help of a friendly lawyer, Scott sued for his liberty, claiming that his having lived in both a free state and a free territory made him free. The Supreme Court ruled that Scott could not sue in a federal court since he was not a citizen and that he had not gained his liberty by living in Illinois, since its laws no longer applied to him once he had returned to Missouri. Not stopping there, the court also held that the Missouri Compromise itself was unconstitutional, because it deprived slave owners of their property without "due process of law," contrary to the Fifth Article of the Bill of Rights.

Slavery opponents were outraged that the court had used the Bill of Rights to justify enslavement and that the court's decision appeared to make slavery legal everywhere in the United States unless state laws specifically forbade it. The Dred Scott decision also nullified Stephen Douglas's principle of popular sovereignty, since neither Congress nor the inhabitants of a territory now had the right to decide on whether or not there would be slavery during the prestatehood period. Northerners became even more convinced that the Southern slave power would stop at nothing to advance its interests. Interestingly, many Northerners were far from high-minded in their opposition to the spread of slavery and wanted to keep slaves out of the territories mainly because they believed blacks to be racially inferior to whites and a threat to free (white) labor.

Lincoln did not respond immediately to the Kansas-Nebraska Act, partly because he was preoccupied with the Illinois Central Railroad case and partly because he was not a public official or seeking elective office at the time. But in August 1854, just a month before Charles Darwin resumed work on his theory of natural selection, he entered the fray by campaigning for fellow Whigs. Lincoln also decided to take on Stephen Douglas himself, who was giving speeches around the state to justify his position on popular sovereignty in the territories. Douglas's argument (in the pre–*Dred Scott* period) was that leaving the question up to the people in each territory was the most democratic solution and one that would speed up the process of settlement and statehood, as it would avoid long, drawn-out disputes over slavery in the Congress. Besides, Douglas argued, in the months before a territorial legislature had been elected in Kansas, slavery was not likely to be adopted in an area so far north. A perennial optimist, the ebullient Douglas may well not have anticipated the mayhem that could result from his idea of popular sovereignty, as opposed to a more pessimistic realist like Abraham Lincoln.

Lincoln spent weeks preparing for combat with Douglas by going over to the state library, located in the capitol building directly across the street from his law office. He read everything he could find that would help him counter Douglas's arguments, including pamphlets, various laws, census reports, and congressional speeches. Douglas refused to debate him. However, after Douglas had spoken at length on October 3 at the Illinois State Fair, Lincoln called out from a stairway to the exiting crowd that he would answer Douglas the next day. It was hot and humid when Lincoln got up to speak the following afternoon, and he walked up to the platform without a jacket, tie, or collar. Douglas was present and responded at the end of Lincoln's three-hour presentation. A newspaper editorial the next day, anonymously written by Herndon, declared that it was the best speech Lincoln had ever given up to that time: "He felt upon his soul the truths burn which he uttered, and all present felt that he was true to his own soul. . . . He quivered with emotion. The whole house was as still as death."[10]

There was no transcription made of Lincoln's state fair speech, and he did not write it out for publication, but he delivered essentially the same address on October 16 at Peoria, Illinois. This time Lincoln gave a written copy to the *Sangamo Journal*, which published it in full. He began, in traditional Whig fashion, with a history of congressional action to prohibit slavery from various territories—from the Northwest Ordinance of 1787, which forbade slavery north of the Ohio River, down to the recent Compromise of 1850, which admitted California as a free state, with the question of slavery in the New Mexico and Utah territories to be left to their eventual state constitutions. Zeroing in on the Missouri Compromise, recently overturned by the Kansas-Nebraska Act, Lincoln lamented that this arrangement, which had worked so well for a quarter of a century, had been repealed: "[It has] received the sanction and approbation of men of all parties in every section of the Union. It [has] allayed all sectional jealousies and irritations growing out of this vexed question, and harmonized and tranquilized the whole country."[11]

Lincoln then went on to attack all of Douglas's main arguments. His specific points are not important one hundred and fifty years later, but one of the most telling things about them was his conciliatory attitude toward the South (an attitude that he would hold until the outbreak of civil war and one to which he would return as the war was coming to an end): "I think I have no prejudice against the Southern people. They are just what we would be in their situation. If slavery did not now exist among them, they would not introduce it. If it did now exist among us, we should not instantly give it up."[12] Nor did he have any quarrel with the Fugitive Slave clause of the Constitution and the laws passed to enforce it, which allowed owners to reclaim and recapture slaves who had run away into the free states and territories.

Lincoln was no radical abolitionist and he agreed with the South that slavery would be very difficult "to get rid of . . . in any satisfactory way." Even if "all earthly power" were given to him, he added, "I should not know what to do, as to the existing institution." His first impulse would be to return the slaves to Liberia, but sending them all at once to that fledgling African country would be a disaster, and they "would all perish in the next ten days." Some system of "gradual emancipation" would make more sense, he thought, but believed it would prove impossible to make former slaves politically and socially equal to whites: "My own feelings will not admit this; and if mine would, we well know that those of the great mass of white people will not."[13] Having been born in the border state of Kentucky and having lived all his adult life in a part of Illinois largely settled by people from the Upper South in its early days, Lincoln was closely attuned to public opinion about racial equality. He was also an astute enough politician to reassure his listeners that he had no sympathy with claims of "Negro equality." In the end, it is impossible to tell if Lincoln was just being a political opportunist or if his own views of race conveniently paralleled public opinion in his region. In all likelihood, it was a bit of both.

Despite what he said about the inequality of the races, Lincoln argued that slavery was wrong and that it made no sense to allow this evil practice to spread: "Slavery is founded on the selfishness of man's nature—opposition to it is [in] his love of justice. . . . Repeal the Missouri Compromise—repeal all compromises . . . , you still cannot repeal human nature. It still will be the abundance of man's heart, that slavery extension is wrong; and out of the abundance of his heart, his mouth will continue to speak."[14]

Lincoln had been nominated by the Whigs for the state legislature in 1854 and won the election, but he refused to take the seat, knowing that the legislative rules would not allow him to seek a higher prize, a seat in the US Senate later that year. He went on to campaign hard as an anti-Nebraska candidate, but he failed to win in the Illinois legislature, which continued to elect the state's members of the US Senate until the Seventeenth Amendment in 1913 provided for the direct election of senators by the people.

Lincoln lost because the Democrats enjoyed a majority in the legislature and also because his own Whig Party was dying as its antislavery faction (the so-called Conscience Whigs) quarreled with Southern members of the party (the Cotton Whigs). The old Whig platform of federally sponsored internal improvements as a way of stimulating the economy also failed to appeal in a time of expansion and prosperity. Entering this political vacuum was the new Republican Party, made up of various groups that opposed the spread of slavery, as well as abolitionists, although in a distinct minority, who wanted to abolish slavery completely.

It made sense for Lincoln to throw his lot with the Republicans, but he had no patience for the anti-Catholic Know Nothing Party, which was becoming part of the Republican coalition. He shared these misgivings in an August 1855 letter to his old friend Joshua Speed, who had long ago moved back to Kentucky:

I am not a Know-Nothing. That is certain. How could I be? How can any one who abhors the oppression of negroes, be in favor of degrading classes of white people . . . ? As a nation, we began by declaring that "*all men are created equal.*" . . . When the Know-Nothings get control, it will read "all men are created equal, except negroes *and foreigners and Catholics.*" When it comes to this I should prefer emigrating to some country where they make no pretense of loving liberty—to Russia, for instance, where despotism can be taken pure, and without the base alloy of hypocrisy. [15]

By the spring of 1856, Lincoln had decided to join the Republicans and attended their founding meeting in Illinois, held at Bloomington on May 29. The Republicans called on Lincoln to make the closing speech. The delivery was extemporaneous and went unrecorded. Herndon, who was there, later wrote that it was "full of fire and energy and force; it was logic; it was pathos; it was enthusiasm; it was justice, equity, truth, and right set ablaze by the divine fires of a soul maddened by the wrong; it was hard, heavy, knotty, gnarly, backed with wrath." [16]

Herndon was far more extreme than Lincoln on the subject of slavery and had close contacts with Illinois abolitionists. From time to time, Lincoln tried to soften his partner's radical tendencies and worried that his close association with Herndon might hurt him politically, just as Charles Darwin would worry that his young protégé Thomas Huxley was much too radical and potentially hurtful to his cause. Herndon carried on an extensive correspondence with leading Republicans in the east, writing angrily to Horace Greeley, editor of the *New York Tribune*, who thought Illinois Republicans should support Douglas rather than Lincoln, despite Lincoln's joining the Republican fold. Then in early 1858, Herndon took the train to New York and Boston where he met with all the leaders of the party on Lincoln's behalf and returned home with the good news of their support. Herndon also brought back several pamphlets and sermons denouncing slavery, and he continued to point out newspaper articles and other printed materials that he thought Lincoln should read. Lincoln was grateful for Herndon's help, but unlike Darwin, who shied away from public appearances and was more than happy to have others do all or most of the speaking for him, Lincoln craved attention from audiences and thrived on the political stump.

Darwin wanted recognition as much as Lincoln, but he preferred to enjoy it quietly at home, while others fought his battles for him.

By the early 1850s, cultural changes in England were providing Darwin with a more congenial climate to publish his evolutionary theory. Part of the new atmosphere came from widespread recognition of change as the one seeming constant in modern society, with both winners and losers, especially in an all-out economic competition. Chief among the spokespersons of this view was Herbert Spencer (1820–1903), a native of Derby and the product of a dissenting religious background (like Darwin), with a strong emphasis on hard work and moral restraint. Spencer believed that society would grow better and better through ruthless competition resulting in "survival of the fittest." Social welfare programs were therefore counterproductive, since they would allow the unfit to survive and reproduce their own kind. This argument became a basic tenet of nineteenth-century liberalism, as well as the so-called and often mislabeled social Darwinism, which so many economists, sociologists, and political thinkers—depending on their point of view—would find either seductive or repugnant in the years ahead.

A new crop of scientists was also emerging, and they, unlike those a generation or two before, were not necessarily wealthy gentlemen naturalists or academics from the Oxford-Cambridge establishment. Thomas Henry Huxley (1825–1895) was an outspoken example of this new breed (as well as the grandfather of novelist Aldous Huxley and biologist Julian Huxley). The son of a lower-middle-class schoolteacher, Thomas Huxley had obtained a scholarship to Charing Cross Medical School. He had nothing but contempt for the university dons and believed that scientists should be hired as civil servants, well paid by the government, and respected for their merit. Although Huxley was at first skeptical of Darwin's concept of natural selection, he would eventually become his most outspoken champion and come to be known as "Darwin's bulldog."

Even Charles Lyell, who feared the religious implications of Darwin's ideas, began encouraging him to publish his "species book." Despite misgivings, Lyell respected Darwin as a scientist and feared that someone else might come up with basically the same idea and beat him into publication and scientific precedence. Lyell accordingly urged his friend to get his ideas out as quickly as possible by publishing a sketch of his ideas, a suggestion that threw Darwin into a terrible quandary. As he wrote to Lyell in May 1856:

> With respect to your suggestion of a sketch of my view; I hardly know what to think, but will reflect on it; but it goes against my prejudices. To give a fair sketch would be absolutely impossible, for every proposition requires such an array of facts. If I were to do anything it could only refer to the main agency of change,—selection—& perhaps point out a very few of the leading features which countenance such a view, & some of the main difficulties. But I do not know what to think: I rather hate the idea of writing for priority, yet I certainly shd be vexed if any one were to publish my doctrines before me.[17]

However modestly he seemed to express himself, Darwin clearly wanted the credit due to him.

Although worried about priority and the possibility of a competitor, Darwin decided to produce a long work. He had actually started on the sketch that Lyell had proposed, but confessed to his cousin Fox, "I found it such unsatisfactory work that I have desisted & am now drawing up my work as perfect as my materials of 19 years collecting suffice. . . . I find to my sorrow it will run to quite a big book."[18] It was very painstaking work, as he had written to Joseph Hooker: "After describing a set of forms, as distinct species; tearing up my MS., and making them one again (which has happened to me) I have gnashed my teeth, cursed species, & asked what sin I had committed to be punished."[19]

While struggling with his research and writing, Darwin began to worry about the next generation. He wanted his children to live comfortably, but he knew that only a substantial inheritance and good professional careers for his sons would ensure them a decent level of prosperity. They would, in fact, come into a goodly inheritance: both Charles and Emma had received large estates from their parents, and Charles worked hard and generally successfully to make sound investments that would increase both income and capital. In 1854 their annual income was £4,600—probably worth well over a half a million dollars one hundred and fifty years later—half of which they reinvested for greater returns in the years ahead.

Darwin also worried constantly about the children's health. Etty and George were often ill with symptoms similar to his own. Elizabeth had trouble learning and seemed abnormally quiet. Then in December 1856, a forty-eight-year-old Emma gave birth to their tenth child and sixth son. They named him Charles Waring, but it soon became clear that he was "slow," possibly suffering from Down syndrome. Because of what Darwin had learned about the magnification of certain characteristics through inbreeding, he worried that one cause of so much sickness among his children had resulted from his marrying a first cousin. Then when Charles Waring was just two and a half, he contracted scarlet fever and died on June 28, 1858. As Darwin wrote to Hooker, the grief over his son's death was mixed with the thought that it had come as something of a blessing: "Thank God he will never suffer more in this world."[20]

Just ten days before Charles Waring's death, on June 18, Darwin received a letter that seemed to destroy all possibility of his being the first to publish a plausible theory of evolution that would stand up to scientific scrutiny. The letter was from Alfred Russel Wallace (1823–1913), just thirty-five years old and a self-trained English botanist then living in Malaya, who had eked out a living gathering and selling specimens from various parts of the world. Enclosed with the letter was a paper on evolution that Wallace asked Darwin to forward to Lyell for review.

Actually, Darwin had been corresponding with Wallace for more than a year and had even bought some specimens from him. Wallace had also presented some of his own thoughts about evolution to Darwin in an effort to find out if he were on the right track. Back in 1856 none other than Lyell had read one of Wallace's published papers and, fearing that he was moving toward a theory very similar to Darwin's own, had warned his friend about it. Since Wallace had cloaked his views in this article in religious language, Darwin had been led to believe that the younger man posed no threat. Although there were some differences in their two theories, Wallace's adoption of natural selection as the main cause of evolution was identical to Darwin's.[21]

Overwhelmed on reading Wallace's letter, Darwin immediately decided that he had no choice but to cede the credit for discovery. He was so upset that he wrote at once to Lyell, saying that he could not cope with the matter and turned all responsibility over to him and Hooker. His feelings of desperation and foolishness at not heeding earlier warnings were evident in the letter to Lyell: "Your words have come through with a vengeance—that I shd. be forestalled.... I never saw a more striking coincidence, if Wallace had my M.S. sketch written out in 1842 he could not have made a better short abstract. Even his terms now stand as Heads of my Chapters.... So all my originality, whatever it may amount to, will be smashed."[22] He clearly wanted to go down as the discoverer of natural selection, but, like Lincoln, he could not bear the thought of behaving dishonorably.

Wallace had been influenced by many of the same authors as Darwin. He had read Humboldt's great travel narratives of South America, Lyell's *Principles of Geology*, and, uncannily, Darwin's *Voyage of the Beagle*. The message of Malthus's *Essay on Population* had also resonated powerfully for Wallace. Such coincidences showed how the various intellectual pieces were coming together to nudge someone toward formulating a plausible theory of evolution. In much the same way, the need to describe moving objects in mathematical form had earlier caused Newton and Leibniz to come up with calculus completely independent of each other—and Joseph Priestly and Antoine Lavoisier to "discover" oxygen at about the same time. In the twentieth century, physicists in Great Britain, the United States, and Japan would all "invent" radar within a few years of each other. In the case of Darwin and Wallace, the evidence for evolution was available to any naturalist who wanted to recognize it. Sooner or later, someone—if not Darwin or Wallace—would have postulated ideas very similar to theirs, though this in no way detracts from their hard work and original conclusions. Some experts have held that without Darwin's copious evidence, acceptance of evolution among most scientists might have been delayed for decades.

Knowledge of such coincidences in science would have been cold comfort to Darwin, who wrote to Lyell a week later, asking whether he now dared to publish anything on evolution after receiving Wallace's "sketch," even though Wallace had not asked him to present the paper for publication. Tormented by ethical scruples, Darwin asked, "Do you not think his having sent me this sketch ties my hands?" He added, "I would far rather burn my whole book than that he or any other man should think that I have behaved in a paltry spirit."[23]

Fortunately, Darwin had given his 1844 sketch on evolution to Hooker to read, and just a year before, he had sent Lyell an abstract of his theory. He had also discussed his ideas in several long letters to American botanist Asa Gray, a professor at Harvard College, who would become one of his champions in the United States. All these factors, Darwin finally realized, could allow him to claim precedence over Wallace, but he graciously insisted on sharing the credit. The solution, as worked out by Lyell and Hooker, was to hold a reading before the Linnean Society in London. The reading consisted of a brief distillation of Darwin's 1844 sketch, an excerpt from one of his letters to Gray, and Wallace's paper—in that order. The event took place on July 1, at the last meeting of the society before recessing for the summer. Because of little Charles Waring's death just three days before, and the illnesses of several other members of the family, Darwin did not attend the meeting.

Given Darwin's sensitivity to any kind of stress and his distaste for entering personally into any public scientific debate, he probably was relieved at not having to be present at the readings on July 1. He also continued to worry that he might not be treating Wallace fairly. At the same time, he feared that Wallace's paper, which was to be included in the *Proceedings* of the Linnean Society, would read much better than the abstracts from his 1844 piece and the letter to Gray. Since he had not intended to publish either one of them, he would later confess in his *Autobiography* that both "were badly written." In contrast, Darwin thought Wallace's essay was "admirably expressed and quite clear."[24]

The first part of Darwin's communication to the Linnean society consisted of portions from the 1844 manuscript. As a way of dramatizing the threats faced by any living creature, he included the vivid line "Nature may be compared to a surface on which rest ten thousand sharp wedges touching each other and driven inward by incessant blows." Since more individuals were born every year than could survive in such a harsh environment, "the smallest grain in the balance [meaning the smallest advantage], in the long run, must tell on which death shall fall, and which shall survive. Only a few individuals in each generation could live; hence the struggle for life. . . . Thus is supplied the 'unerring power' of '*Natural Selection*' . . . which selects exclusively for the good of each organic being."[25]

A clearer account of these essential points had been set down in Darwin's letter to Asa Gray on September 5, 1857. In it, he described how humans had for centuries selected certain plants and animals for propagation and, in that way, had improved them. Over the much longer period of geological time, he submitted, nature had also selected certain characteristics to survive. Changing environmental conditions, he added, would tend to speed up the process of natural selection, as when natural disasters wiped out or greatly reduced a species in numbers, thereby exposing remaining individuals to "the mutual action of a different set of inhabitants." Later scientists would point to the disappearance of the dinosaurs as one such monumental change that allowed the full development of mammals (a hypothesis in some dispute at the beginning of the twenty-first century). Finally, Darwin emphasized the advantages of divergence as a survival "strategy," since "the same spot will support more life if occupied by very diverse forms." This divergence also explained why organic beings "always *seem* to branch and sub-branch like a tree from a common trunk; the flourishing twigs destroying the less vigorous—the dead and lost branches rudely representing extinct genera and families."[26]

Wallace's paper "On the Tendency of Varieties to Depart from the Original Type" was in truth more smoothly written and easier to follow than the more piecemeal presentation of Darwin's letter to Gray, together with the extracts from his 1844 sketch. Unknown to the audience at the time, Wallace had not accumulated anything like the mountain of evidence that Darwin had amassed over the years. Another difference was Wallace's rejection of analogies between the breeding of domestic animals and natural selection, since Wallace observed that domestic varieties tended to return to the parental form in successive generations. In contrast, Darwin had made a great point of saying how he thought that domestic breeding and natural selection operated under the same basic principles.[27] Wallace had also not given the specific name of "natural selection" to the engine of evolution, and he differed from Darwin by concentrating on competition between varieties within species—rather than between individuals within a species

Despite Darwin's concerns about how his theory would be greeted, and given the social and intellectual firestorms that would swirl around it in the future, the reaction of the men attending the presentations at the Linnean Society was surprisingly muted. According to Hooker, who was there that day, "There was no semblance of discussion. The interest excited was intense, but the subject too novel and too ominous for the Old School to enter the lists before armouring." Hooker also believed that his—and especially Lyell's approval—"rather overawed those fellows who would have otherwise flown out against the doctrine, and this because we had the vantage ground of being familiar with the authors and their themes."[28] Darwin's "politicking" among these respected scientists had clearly paid off.

Wallace, who was still halfway around the world, was not consulted about the arrangement, but Darwin's worries about what his codiscoverer would think turned out to be groundless when Wallace wrote back that he was delighted about what had transpired. In the years ahead, both men would show great sensitivity and generosity toward each other. Wallace never failed to credit Darwin as the original discoverer of their similar theories, and Darwin always declared Wallace to be a joint discoverer. Still, Darwin knew that he had to bring out a book on natural selection as soon as possible to stake his claim more firmly. As before, Lyell pushed his friend to publish right away. Since his basic ideas had already been put before a group of important scientists, there was no need for the larger academic treatise he had been in the process of writing. Instead, a shorter account that was more accessible to the educated public would do just as well, if not better. Darwin got down to work almost immediately in July 1858 while on a holiday with his family on the Isle of Wight. The result would be his *Origin of Species*, a book that forever changed the social, intellectual, and moral landscape.

While Darwin was taking pen in hand to write what would become his greatest work, Lincoln took to the campaign trail that summer of 1858 as the Republican candidate opposing Stephen Douglas in the race for US Senate. At their state convention in June, the Republicans unanimously resolved that Lincoln was their "first and only choice." Lincoln was not surprised and had spent some time putting together an acceptance speech. Despite much contrary advice from friends and political associates, he decided to use the image of a "house divided" as a major part of the address. He had used these words in his 1856 speech at the organizational meeting of the Republican Party in Illinois but had bowed to a party request not to use the phrase again soon because of its potentially explosive effects. (He had also employed the phrase fifteen years earlier, in 1843, in a message recommending solidarity among fellow Whigs.)[29]

When preparing for the acceptance speech, Lincoln reread Daniel Webster's famous 1850 reply to Robert Hayne in the US Senate, in which Webster insisted that America was one nation, a union of people and not of states, ending with the famous peroration, "Liberty and Union, now and forever, one and inseparable." According to Herndon, Webster's speech "served in part as his model" for Lincoln.[30] And like so many of Webster's stirring addresses, Lincoln's speech took on the tone of a sermon, especially since the "house divided" image came from Matthew 12:25, a passage that Lincoln may have known since childhood days when the Bible was one of the few books in the house available to the voracious young reader. It was also well known to Bible-reading Protestants in Illinois, who made up the great majority of churchgoers in that state. Although the image may have struck Lincoln as particularly apt, he also understood the authority that scripture would carry with the audience. This did not mean that Lincoln had converted and become a practicing Christian, for he surely had not; nor was he acting as a shameful opportunist. He was just operating as a good politician who knew the Bible well and recognized when its familiar words and cadences would resonate with his listeners.

Lincoln gave his "house divided" speech at Springfield on June 16. He began by reminding the audience that they were "now far into the *fifth* year" of agitation over the question of slavery in the territories, and in his opinion, it would not "cease until a *crisis* shall have been reached, and passed." Then came the famous lines: "'A house divided against itself cannot stand.' I believe this government cannot endure, permanently half *slave* and half *free*. I do not expect the Union to be *dissolved*—I do not expect the house to *fall*—but I *do* expect it will cease to be divided. It will become *all* one thing, or *all* the other."[31]

In the very next breath, Lincoln explained himself in such clear and concise terms that no one could mistake what he meant: "Either the *opponents* of slavery, will arrest the further spread of it, and place it where the public mind shall rest in the belief that it is in the course of ultimate extinction; or its *advocates* will push it forward, till it shall become alike lawful in *all* the States, *old* as well as *new*, *North* as well as *South*."[32] Frighteningly, Lincoln believed, the country seemed well on the road to making slavery legal everywhere, given Congress's repeal of the Missouri Compromise and the *Dred Scott* decision. To save the nation from this fate, he intoned, Republicans had to stand firm, whatever the odds.

Douglas answered in a speech that he gave in Chicago on July 9, charging that Lincoln's insistence that the government could not remain half slave and half free would bring about a "war by the North upon the South."[33] In some ways Douglas was correct, since the South was not likely to give up slavery without a fight, and the Republicans, if victorious, would not stand for the further spread of slavery into the territories.

The following day, July 10, Lincoln responded in his own Chicago speech. He freely admitted that he wanted slavery put on a course of "ultimate extinction," but he added that neither he nor anyone else had the right to interfere with slavery where it already existed. During the last part of his speech, he turned to the Declaration of Independence and to the well-known line that "all men are created equal." If it did not apply to "the Negro," it was an easy step to claiming that it did not apply to individuals of another group. Though the country might fall short of this promise in the Declaration, Lincoln declared, "Let it be as nearly reached as we can."[34]

Douglas and Lincoln spoke again during alternating days at Springfield on July 16 and 17, where they went over much the same ground as in their previous verbal sparring. In his presentation, Lincoln refined what he meant by equality regarding the slaves: "Certainly the negro is not our equal in color—perhaps not in many other respects; still, in the right to put into his mouth the bread that his own hands have earned, he is the equal of every other man, white or black."[35]

Many Republicans were embarrassed to see their candidate merely trailing around the state after Douglas and urged Lincoln to challenge the Democrat to a series of formal debates. Lincoln did so in late July, with the result that the two candidates agreed to hold seven debates, one in each of the Illinois congressional districts, with the exception of Chicago and Springfield, where they had already spoken.

In the course of these debates, held between August 21 and October 15, 1858, Lincoln and Douglas covered much of the same material as before. Lincoln assured his audiences that neither he nor the Republican Party had any intention of interfering with slavery where it already existed, that his house divided speech did not invite disunion or civil war, that he was not opposed to the fugitive slave laws, and that he did not believe in full racial equality or in the mixing of the two races. In his most colorful reference to this last point he said, "I do not understand that because I do not want a negro woman for a slave I must necessarily want her for a wife. My understanding is that I can just let her alone. I am now in my fiftieth year, and I certainly never have had a black woman for either a slave or a wife. So it seems to me quite possible for us to get along without making slaves or wives of negroes."[36] Once again he hedged on the question of equality for African Americans, probably out of personal belief and political calculation, a position that would open him to charges of racism in future generations.

Major newspapers throughout the United States published all or part of the Lincoln–Douglas debates. Douglas already had a country-wide reputation, but the debates propelled Lincoln into the national limelight as nothing else could have. He had done well in the debates and had often put Douglas on the defensive, but the Democrats, who retained control of the Illinois legislature, chose Douglas for a third term in the senate.

Lincoln was very disappointed, but not as castdown as Darwin had been when he received the letter from Alfred Wallace just two months before the Lincoln-Douglas debates began. Lincoln knew he had broken new ground with the Republican Party and with many members of the general public in other parts of the country. Although Lincoln and Darwin could not know it, the disappointments of 1858 were setting the stage for their greatest triumphs.

NOTES

1. Francis Darwin, "Reminiscences of My Father's Everyday Life," in *The Life and Letters of Charles Darwin*, edited by Francis Darwin (New York: D. Appleton and Company, 1896), p. 91.

2. Ibid.

3. Ibid., p. 102.

4. David Quammen, *The Reluctant Mr. Darwin* (New York: W. W. Norton, 2006), p. 141.

5. William H. Herndon, *Herndon's Life of Lincoln* (New York: Da Capo Press, 1983), p. 287.

6. Quoted in David Herbert Donald, *Lincoln* (New York: Quadrangle Books, 1995), p. 162.

7. Quoted in ibid., pp. 163–64.

8. Quoted in Allen C. Guelzo, *Abraham Lincoln: Redeemer President* (Grand Rapids, MI: William B. Eerdmans, 1999), p. 111.

9. Jean H. Baker, *Mary Todd Lincoln: A Biography* (New York: W. W. Norton, 1987), pp. 148–53.

10. Herndon, *Herndon's Life of Lincoln*, p. 296.

11. Lincoln, "Speech at Peoria, Illinois" (October 16, 1854), *The Collected Works of Abraham Lincoln*, edited by Roy P. Basler et al. (New Brunswick, NJ: Rutgers University Press, 1953), 2:251.

12. Ibid., p. 255.

13. Ibid., pp. 255–56.

14. Ibid., p. 271.

15. Lincoln to Speed, August 24, 1855, ibid., p. 323.

16. Herndon, *Herndon's Life of Lincoln*, p. 313.

17. Darwin to Lyell, May 3, 1856, *The Correspondence of Charles Darwin* (Cambridge: Cambridge University Press, 1985–[2005]), 6:100.

18. Darwin to Fox, October 3, 1856, *Correspondence of Charles Darwin*, 6:238.

19. Darwin to Hooker, September 25, 1853, *Correspondence of Charles Darwin*, 5:156.

20. Quoted in Randall Keynes, *Annie's Box: Darwin, His Daughter and Human Evolution* (New York: Riverhead Books, 2002), pp. 272–75.

21. This is the conclusion drawn by Michael White and John Gribbon, *Darwin: A Life in Science* (New York: Dutton, 1995), p. 190.

22. Darwin to Lyell, June 18, 1858, *Correspondence of Charles Darwin*, 7:107.

23. Darwin to Lyell, June 25, 1858, *Correspondence of Charles Darwin*, 7:119–20.

24. Nora Barlow, ed., *The Autobiography of Charles Darwin, 1809–1882* (New York: W. W. Norton, 1993), p. 122.

25. Quoted in Edward B. Poulton, *Charles Darwin and the Theory of Natural Selection* (New York: Macmillan and Company, 1902), p. 66.

26. Ibid., pp. 68–70.

27. Ibid., pp. 71–76.

28. Joseph Hooker, quoted in White and Gribbon, *Darwin*, p. 192.

29. Lincoln, *Collected Works of Abraham Lincoln*, 1:315.

30. Herndon, *Herndon's Life of Lincoln*, p. 327.

31. Lincoln, "A House Divided" (speech, June 16, 1858), *Collected Works of Abraham Lincoln*, 2:461.

32. Lincoln, "Speech at Chicago, Illinois" (July 10, 1858), *Collected Works of Abraham Lincoln*, 2:461–62.

33. Ibid., p. 491.

34. Ibid., p. 501.

35. Lincoln, "Speech at Chicago, Illinois," *Collected Works of Abraham Lincoln*, 2:520.

36. Lincoln, "Fourth Debate with Stephen A. Douglas at Charleston, Illinois," *Collected Works of Abraham Lincoln*, 3:146.

Chapter 6

CRISIS AND REVOLUTION

The parallel between political and scientific development should no longer be open to doubt. . . . The historical study of paradigm change reveals very similar characteristics in the evolution of the sciences. Like the choice between competing political institutions, that between competing [scientific] paradigms proves to be a choice between incompatible modes of community life.
—Thomas S. Kuhn, *The Structure of Scientific Revolutions*

*P*olitical and scientific revolutions are similar in telling ways: in both, the old frameworks and ideological underpinnings can no longer accommodate new realities and needs. At first, only a prescient few are aware of these misalignments, and there is much resistance to change until a crisis is reached and some new consensus emerges. Political revolutions are often deadly, resulting in the deaths of thousands, as in France during the 1790s. But scientists who challenge prevailing worldviews have also faced terrible persecution and hideous deaths. In 1600 the Roman Inquisition had Giordano Bruno burned at the stake for embracing Copernicus's sun-centered model of the universe; and a generation later, the Church forced Galileo, with threats of torture, to recant on his knees for elaborating this same theory. Although dissenting scientists did not have to fear torture or death in the nineteenth century, they risked both ridicule and rejection from the scientific community and the public at large.

Darwin's *Beagle* adventure, his wide reading and correspondence, and his continuing experiments all had convinced him that the traditional beliefs in the permanence of species—and their supposed special creation by a benign God—did not fit the mounting facts as he interpreted them. For Lincoln, the contradictions between the promises of the Declaration of Independence and the evils of slavery had become increasingly intolerable.

As the fifty-year-old Abraham Lincoln was beginning his serious bid for the presidency, the fifty-year-old Charles Darwin was working feverishly to complete and publish his seminal work on evolution. For both of them, gathering and marshalling mountains of information to justify their arguments continued to be central methods of presentation and persuasion.

By the beginning of 1859, Abraham Lincoln had plunged into the law again to shore up family finances after long months on the campaign trail. While Darwin's money worries amounted to whether or not he was making wise investments of his large capital funds, Lincoln could only depend on his legal work for significant income. He probably exaggerated his plight, but he did need to get down to preparing and arguing cases with his usual care in hopes of again earning about $3,000 a year from his practice, a very respectable sum for the time, but only a fraction of Darwin's income in the late 1850s. Lincoln's net worth, represented by his house and a few mortgages, notes, and bonds that he owned, came to only $10,000, compared to the hundreds of thousands of dollars worth of property and other assets in mid-nineteenth-century values (millions in the early 2000s) owned by Charles and Emma Darwin.

After all the excitement on the campaign trail, it was hard for Lincoln to resume his legal practice, and his disappointment at losing the recent senate race was evident as he searched for some consolation in the message he had been able to get across during the campaign. To A. G. Henry, a medical doctor and old friend, he wrote, "I believe I have made some marks which will tell for the cause of civil liberty long after I am gone." Still feeling sorry for himself, he added, "I now sink out of view and shall be forgotten."[1] To another correspondent he wrote, "I write merely to let you know that I am neither dead nor dying."[2]

Soon Lincoln was looking for ways to keep his name before the public and he came up with the idea of "entering the lecture field." He worked up a presentation on "Inventions" and delivered it at several towns in central Illinois during the winter of 1859, but according to Herndon, "it was so commonplace, and met with such indifferent success, that he soon dropped it altogether."[3] Anyone reading the lecture a century and a half later would have to agree.

His lecture a failure, Lincoln must have felt a great relief when the Republican leadership in Ohio asked him to campaign during the fall elections for state offices. He gave speeches in Cincinnati (despite having sworn that he would never step foot in the city again), as well as Hamilton, Dayton, and Columbus. His main target was again Douglas, who was campaigning around the Buckeye State for the Democratic ticket and who had just published an article on popular sovereignty for *Harper's Magazine*.[4] In this article Douglas argued that leaving the question of slavery up to the local residents of a territory was exactly what the framers of the Constitution had had in mind. This argument thereby made his own solution entirely consistent with the founders' wishes, as well as a moderate position on the present slavery question. This was a clear attempt to appeal to both Republicans and Democrats during this time of shifting party allegiances, a possibility that terrified Lincoln and many Republican politicians.

Lincoln insisted to Ohio audiences, as he had in the debates with Douglas the year before, that the repeal of the Missouri Compromise and the subsequent *Dred Scott* decision, if taken to their logical conclusions, would open the entire country to slavery and might even allow the revival of the international slave trade. He also blasted Douglas and the Democrats for "debauching public opinion" with their radical and unfounded claim that the Declaration of Independence applied only to white men. In answer to the Southern claim that their slaves were actually better off than workers in the North, who Southerners claimed were the "wage slaves" of ruthless capitalists, Lincoln maintained that free laborers might easily become capitalists themselves: "Men who are industrious, and sober, and honest in the pursuit of their own interests should after a while accumulate capital, and after that should be allowed to enjoy it in peace, . . . and when they have accumulated it to use it to save themselves from actual labor and hire other people to labor for them."[5] Although Lincoln was now a Republican, such sentiments were pure Whig doctrine on both sides of the Atlantic. Twentieth-century Lincoln critics would charge that this concept of the self-made man later played into the hands of wealthy capitalists who used it to block social and economic legislation. (Some capitalists would also twist Darwinian concepts of competition in nature to forestall attempts at reform.)

Lincoln's performances so impressed the Ohio Republicans that they asked to publish the speeches he made for them that fall, along with those from the Lincoln–Douglas debates the preceding year, including Douglas's remarks. Appearing in the spring of 1860, the book became a national best seller.[6] After leaving Ohio, Lincoln went on the stump for Republicans in Indiana, Wisconsin, Iowa, and Kansas, where he also captivated audiences. Heavy newspaper coverage of these appearances, along with the publicity of the earlier Lincoln–Douglas contest, made Lincoln into one of the nation's leading Republicans.

Editors now wanted to know more about this rising man, and in December 1859, in response to a request from the *Chester County Times*, a newspaper published in a county seat just west of Philadelphia, Lincoln himself wrote out a biographical sketch. He began this very brief account of his life by telling what he knew of his ancestry and the moves that his own family had made from Kentucky to Indiana and then to Illinois. He told of the poor frontier schools he had attended, adding, "I have not been to school since. The little advance I now have upon this store of education, I have picked up from time to time under the pressure of necessity."[7] Although Lincoln's recitation of his scanty formal education was honest and straightforward, it helped advertise his rise from humble origins, a theme that had became an integral part of his persona and appeal to voters. After summarizing his working and professional life and political career, Lincoln ended the sketch by describing his personal appearance: "I am, in height, six feet, four inches, nearly; lean in flesh, weighing on average, one hundred and eighty pounds; dark complexion, with coarse black hair, and gray eyes."[8]

Far more important than this biographical sketch was the invitation to give an address in New York City. Lincoln knew immediately that this engagement would give him an unparalleled opportunity to impress an eastern audience and he prepared for this speech more thoroughly than ever before, using sources from his own and Herndon's collections, as well as from the state library in Springfield. As had been his habit in the past, he took notes on small strips of paper and began writing his speech only after all the notes had been taken down and the slips assembled. He then tried out the speech by reading it aloud to a group of trusted political associates, a method that he had often used with success.

The great event took place on February 27, 1860, at New York's Cooper Union before a large audience.[9] Reading the speech nearly one hundred and fifty years later, one is struck with how all but the last few utterances are a dispassionate recitation of historical facts and interpretations to prove that Douglas and the Democrats had misrepresented the founders' firm belief that slavery could and should be banned from the territories. He cleverly began by quoting from a speech that Douglas had made the previous autumn at Columbus: "Our fathers, when they framed the Government under which we now live, understood this question [of slavery in the territories] just as well, and even better, than we do now."[10] Lincoln quoted this line from Douglas no fewer than fifteen times in the course of the speech, often in a gently mocking manner.

Lincoln said that he heartily agreed with this statement by Douglas and then proceeded to demolish him by demonstrating that the majority of the thirty-nine men who signed the US Constitution would now share the Republican Party's policy of keeping slavery out of the territories rather than agreeing with Douglas's idea of popular sovereignty. As proof, Lincoln informed the audience that twenty-three of the thirty-nine framers had also voted, while previously members of Congress, for the Northwest Ordinance of 1787 to ban slavery from the territories acquired from Great Britain after the Revolution. This showed, according to Lincoln, that the founders thought the national legislature—not the residents of the territories—should decide the slavery question. Lincoln purposely made reference to "our fathers" during the Cooper Union speech, knowing full well the biblical resonance of this term, most especially with the opening words of the Lord's Prayer, "Our father, who art in Heaven. . . ."

Piling fact upon fact and conclusion upon conclusion, Lincoln appeared much like a seasoned advocate before a court of appeals. According to Herndon's account, "His speech was devoid of all rhetorical imagery. . . . It was constructed with a view to accuracy of statement, simplicity of language, and unity of thought. In some respects like a lawyer's brief, it was logical, temperate in tone, powerful—irresistibly driving conviction home to men's reasons and their souls"[11] Lincoln's aim was that "sledge-hammer logic," which his listeners had come to admire in the courtroom as well as on the political stump.[12] His inescapable conclusion was that slavery was a blatant hypocrisy, which contradicted the core belief of the Founding Fathers—that all men were created equal.

Conjectural replica of the cabin near Gentryville, Spencer County, Indiana, where Abraham Lincoln spent his childhood from age seven in 1816 to age twenty-one in 1830. *Photo by author.*

"The Mount," Charles Darwin's birthplace and childhood home at Shrewsbury, England. The Darwin home could scarcely have been more different from the crude frontier cabins where Abraham Lincoln was born and grew up. *Reprinted with permission of the Syndics of Cambridge University Library.*

Conjectural replica of the general store at New Salem, Illinois, that Lincoln kept for Denton Offutt, where he enjoyed joking and conversing with his customers and friends. Lincoln's five and a half years at New Salem (1831–1837) represented a time out, or moratorium, from having to decide what he would do in life, and it took place at almost exactly the same time as Darwin's nearly five years on the *Beagle* expedition. By the time Lincoln left New Salem, he had decided on a career in law and politics. *Photo by author.*

Etching of the HMS *Beagle* in the Straits of Magellan, at the southern tip of South America. Darwin's five years (1831–1836) on the *Beagle* expedition gave him the time he needed to decide what he would do in life, and at the completion of the voyage he was well on his way to becoming a naturalist. Print from author's collection. *Original by Conrad Martins, one of the illustrators on the* Beagle.

The Lincoln home in Springfield, Illinois, 1860. Lincoln and his son Willie are standing inside the fence in the corner of the front yard. The house, recently enlarged and remodeled, was entirely fitting for a successful lawyer like Lincoln. *Photograph by John Adams Whipple. Reprinted with permission of the Abraham Lincoln Presidential Library & Museum.*

Down House, from the garden side, at the village of Downe, to which Darwin and his family moved in 1842 and where he spent the rest of his life. Here Darwin wrote *Origin of Species, The Descent of Man,* and all but the earliest of his major publications. *Reprinted with permission of the Syndics of Cambridge University Library.*

Lincoln at age thirty-seven in 1846, the earliest-known photograph of him. *Daguerreotype by N. H. Shepherd. Reprinted with permission of the Abraham Lincoln Presidential Library & Museum.*

Darwin at age thirty-one in 1840. Portrait by George Richmond. *Reprinted with permission of the Syndics of Cambridge University Library.*

The restored exterior of the Lincoln-Herndon law offices in Springfield, Illinois, where Lincoln made a good enough living to afford the accoutrements of an upper-middle-class lifestyle for his family. *Photo by author.*

Darwin's study at Down House. Unlike Lincoln, Darwin and his wife, Emma Wedgwood Darwin, had inherited large estates and did not have to worry about money, freeing Darwin to pursue science as he saw fit. *Reprinted with permission of the Syndics of Cambridge University Library.*

The dead at Gettysburg. The terrible death toll of the Civil War weighed heavily on Lincoln. *Reprinted with permission of the Abraham Lincoln Presidential Library & Museum.*

Darwin regularly read in the English newspapers about the horrors of the American Civil War while sitting comfortably in this drawing room at Down House. *Reprinted with permission of the Syndics of Cambridge University Library.*

Mary Todd Lincoln in her inaugural gown as first lady, 1861. Mary's frequent mood swings and out-bursts of anger and depression often made life difficult for her husband. *Photographed by Mathew Brady. Reprinted with permission of the Abraham Lincoln Presidential Library & Museum.*

Emma Wedgwood, Darwin's wife and first cousin, in 1840, by George Richmond. Unlike Mary Lincoln, the even-tempered and motherly Emma was a constant source of comfort to her husband. *Reprinted with permission of the Down House.*

An obviously tired and care-worn President Lincoln, 1865. *Photo by Alexander Gardner. Reprinted with permission of the Abraham Lincoln Presidential Library & Museum.*

Photograph of Charles Darwin at age sixty-five in 1874, looking like the benign sage that many people envision. *Photo by Darwin's son, Leonard. Reprinted with permission of the Syndics of Cambridge University Library.*

The apotheosis of Lincoln, one of many depictions of the martyred president being welcomed into heaven by George Washington. The fact that Lincoln was never baptized, never joined a church, and never received Communion was not well known at the time of his death, and is little know by the general public nearly a century and a half later. *Reprinted with permission of the Abraham Lincoln Presidential Library & Museum.*

In cartoons, Darwin's head was often superimposed on a monkey's body, as in this cover sketch for a French publication called *La Petite Lune*. The fact that Darwin never claimed humans had descended from monkeys (only that humans and monkeys had evolved from a common ancestry) did not bother the cartoonists or the general public who often dubbed Darwin's ideas as "the monkey theory." *Reprinted with permission of the Syndics of Cambridge University Library.*

Still, Lincoln reminded his audience, the Republicans had no intention of interfering with slavery where it already existed and he vehemently denied that Republicans had had anything to do with the fanatical John Brown's raid at Harper's Ferry the previous October and his failed attempt to incite a slave rebellion. Then, injecting some emotion that had been lacking up to this point, he dismissed the argument that the election of a Republican president would be responsible for any disintegration of the Union. This was perverse logic that attempted to blame a crime on the innocent party: "But you will not abide the election of a Republican President! In that supposed event, you say, you will destroy the Union; and then, you say, the great crime of having destroyed it will be upon us! That is cool. A highwayman holds a pistol to my ear, and mutters through his teeth, 'Stand and deliver, or I shall kill you, and then you will be a murderer!'"[13]

Although Lincoln did not waver from his insistence that slavery was wrong and in conflict with both the Declaration of Independence and mid-nineteenth-century beliefs in equality of opportunity, he added, for the sake of argument, that the Republicans would be more than willing to try to work out a compromise with the South—though not on slavery in the new territories—if only to honor the letter of the Constitution. In this way Lincoln sought to distinguish his position from the abolitionists, who demanded the extinction of slavery everywhere. But he believed the South would not be satisfied with anything short of a declaration by the free states that slavery was good and right: "Their thinking [slavery] right and our thinking it wrong, is the precise fact upon which depends the whole controversy. . . . Can we cast our votes with their view, and against our own? In view of our moral, social, and political responsibilities, can we do this?"[14] He ended with an appeal: "Let us have faith that right makes might, and in that faith, let us, to the end, dare to do our duty as we understand it."[15]

Lincoln's saying that slavery was wrong—but that he would try to block its extension only into the new territories—would lead critics then and later to question his sincerity in opposing slavery. Realistically, Lincoln recognized that the constitutional and practical realities of the day would keep him or anyone else from abolishing slavery in the South without the use of force. Yet Lincoln knew that the spirit of the age was moving in his favor and he would later use the crisis of the Civil War to make that spirit a reality in the United States.

The Cooper Union speech lasted for an hour and a half, far too long for most audiences in the early twenty-first century who are accustomed to the many quick stimulations of electronic media, but it created a sensation back then, once the audience got over the first shock of seeing Lincoln, "the long, ungainly figure, upon which hung clothes that ... were evidently the work of an unskilled tailor; the large feet; the clumsy hands . . . ; the long, gaunt head capped by a shock of hair that seemed not to have been thoroughly brushed out."[16] Several newspapers carried the whole text of the speech, and editorial opinion was overwhelmingly positive. Noah Brooks of the *New York Times* said of Lincoln, "He's the greatest man since St. Paul."[17]

Meanwhile, Charles Darwin had been working just as hard as Lincoln to place his opinions before the world and in somewhat similar ways by amassing overwhelming evidence and organizing it, in the end, through compelling logic. With Alfred Wallace nipping at his heels, Darwin knew he had to act quickly to bring out a book-length account of his theory, though it would be shorter than the "big book" he had been laboring over for the past several years. Like Lincoln, he believed that the old ways—in his case, of viewing nature—no longer fit the facts or the gathering tenor of the age.

The writing process was never easy for Darwin, as he readily admitted and as his son Francis described it years later. He began by spending "much time and labour" in making an outline, Francis explained, which he then enlarged with numerous subheadings. He scribbled a first draft on the backs of old proof sheets or scrap paper, fearing that if he used his best paper it would somehow keep him from creating a rough copy. He revised this first draft on "foolscap" paper, wide-ruled, so that he could make corrections between the lines. He then gave it to the village schoolmaster, who made a "fair copy" that could be sent to the printer. It was only after receiving the printer's proofs that he began to consider style and make further corrections.[18]

Francis wrote that his father "did not write with ease, and was apt to invert his sentences both in writing and speaking, putting the qualifying clause before it was clear what it was to qualify." Darwin was also prone to omitting certain steps in his argument because he was so familiar with the subject that he forgot others were not. Another problem was that his words often failed to replicate his thoughts, and he had the habit of forcing too many ideas into one sentence. He was good-natured about all this, often laughing or grumbling to himself, "If a bad arrangement of a sentence was possible, he should be sure to adopt it."[19] He was always grateful to others for corrections and editorial advice, and without their input, his writing would have been very difficult to read. Yet the final product was very clear, one reason why Darwin's works continue to be read a century and a half later. Still, his process was a far cry from the easy eloquence of Abraham Lincoln in both speech and writing.

Darwin labored away on his "species book" during the rest of the summer of 1858 and into the early autumn. Although he kept referring to it as an "abstract," in comparison to the much larger book he had projected, even this scaled-down version was ballooning. He explained to his friend Hooker in early October: "I am working most steadily at my Abstract; but it grows to an inordinate length; yet fully to make my view clear . . . , I cannot make it shorter."[20] He pressed on into the new year but was soon suffering from vomiting spells and dizziness—which a visit to the water cure establishment at Moor Park alleviated in time for his fiftieth birthday on February 12—only to come down with the same symptoms in March.

By May 1859, Darwin had a manuscript of fourteen chapters and 155,000 words ready to send off to his publisher, John Murray. The writing had proved a real struggle, and he referred to it in letters to scientific friends as his "abominable volume." He had written the manuscript in great haste and was shocked at how awkwardly it read when he received his first proof sheets, promising Murray to "*do my utmost to improve my style.*"[21] The extensive revisions were quite costly, since they meant that each page would have to be reset by hand in this age before typesetting machines. Darwin offered to pay for the extra expenses, but Murray, as a gesture of goodwill toward a loyal author, absorbed the additional charges.

The strain of writing, combined with continuing fears that someone else might put out a book on more or less the same subject, comes through in Darwin's letters to Murray. On April 29, he wrote, "Please to observe, that it is of *real importance* for my health sake to get the work printed as quickly as possible; for I must leave home soon & stay for months at some water-cure establishment."[22] On May 14, he again expressed his concern over the publication schedule: "I am rather alarmed at what you hinted in a previous note about proper period of publication: for I am very anxious to have it published as soon as can be, as to my knowledge two men are already writing more or less on the subject, starting from the foundation of my Paper in Linn. Journal."[23] Just what persons he had in mind as potential rivals (other than Wallace) is uncertain. Two weeks later he was confessing to Murray that many parts of the writing were unclear and that his corrections would take much longer than he anticipated: "I find that my M.S, which I thought was pretty clear is very obscure, & I am sorry to say, both for time & experience sake, that my corrections are rather heavy, & will take me *much* longer time than I anticipated."[24] He had also gotten sick again, but a week of hydrotherapy at Moor Park had done him "a world of good."[25] August found him still worried about the pace of publication, and he asked Murray, "How early in the autumn you will permit the publication of my volume[?]"[26] By September Darwin was so weak that he could barely carry anything, but he pushed on, finishing the proofs on October 1 amid bouts of vomiting, and left the next day for yet another water cure establishment at Ilkley Wells, where he stayed through the appearance of his book on November 22. The spa, which had opened just three years before, had bowling alleys, billiard tables, and a corps of consultants. Darwin and the other invalids stayed in a grand palazzo and were taken by donkeys to springs on a nearby wooded hillside.

The title of Darwin's new book, which had literally sickened him to write, was *On the Origin of Species by Means of Natural Selection, or the Preservation of Favored Races in the Struggle for Life*. Booksellers snapped up the initial printing of 1,250 copies, and Murray immediately brought out a second run of 3,000. Darwin was astounded at the sales, particularly to the educated reading public as opposed to just scientists. The title has never been out of print since it first appeared, and by the early twenty-first century it had gone through over four hundred editions or reprints and had been translated into at least twenty-nine languages.

In his *Autobiography*, Darwin attributed the initial success of *Origin* to two main factors: One was having produced two earlier sketches of his theory (1842 and 1844). These earlier writings, he thought, had allowed him to "select the more striking facts and conclusions."[27] The second factor was his abandonment of a projected multivolume treatise after receiving Wallace's essay: "Had I published on the scale which I began to write in 1856, the book would have been four times as large as the *Origin*, and very few would have had the patience to read it."[28] No doubt the larger work would have been far less readable than the *Origin*, despite Darwin's difficulties in straightening out his prose, since a longer work would have allowed him to give so much more detail and to hedge his arguments to such a degree that readers probably would have had to tease out what the author was trying to say.

Even so, *Origin of Species* was a weighty tome, filled with many examples and careful analyses. At the end of his brief introduction, Darwin boldly stated his general conclusions: "I am fully convinced that species are not immutable; but that those belonging to what are called the same genera are lineal descendants of some other and generally extinct species. . . . Furthermore, I am convinced that Natural Selection has been the main but not the exclusive means of modification."[29] He had become convinced of this because the traditional view of biological origins no longer fit the evidence he had so painstakingly accumulated. For instance, the fossil record failed to show that all life forms, as they existed in the mid-nineteenth century, had always been present on Earth: many creatures that had lived in the past had obviously become extinct, and many plants and animals in the present were not around in past epochs. Yet there were obvious anatomical similarities among all vertebrates that pointed to evolutionary connections among them. The similarities among certain species, such as the Galapagos finches, also pointed to common origins. So did the close structural similarities among primates. The old concepts simply did not fit the facts, which compelled Darwin to embrace and disseminate a powerful new paradigm.

To illustrate and explain natural selection, Darwin's first chapter discussed the breeding of domestic plants and animals, where breeders used variations among individuals to create new varieties. In subsequent chapters, he explained how plants and animals in the wild had gone through natural selection, a process that had taken far longer than with the conscious selection of domestic varieties in order to bring out certain desirable characteristics. Using an insight from Malthus's *Essay on Population*, Darwin explained that both plants and animals overpopulated their living spaces, and that any variation that gave an advantage in the struggle to survive "will tend to the preservation of that individual, and will generally be inherited by its offspring." This was a two-step process: first came some kind of variation, and second, this variation was passed on to succeeding generations if it conferred some survival advantage. Darwin called this principle "by which each slight variation, if useful, is preserved, by the term of Natural Selection, in order to mark its relation to man's power of selection [in domestic breeding]."[30] This process of natural selection, as the prime motor of evolution, had probably taken tens of millions of years to occur, a chronology supported by geologists such as Darwin's friend Charles Lyell, who had spent a lifetime arguing for the earth's ancientness.

Two terms did not appear in *Origin*, which were later used very widely to refer to Darwin's main ideas—*evolution* and *survival of the fittest*. Instead of using the word *evolution*, Darwin spoke of "descent through modification." He did not use the term *evolution* in this first edition, since it had been employed mainly to describe any gradual change over time—whether social, political, or intellectual—and was only gradually being adopted by the scientific community. Not until the sixth edition of *Origin*, published in 1872, did Darwin employ the word *evolution*, now that it had become more widely used to mean the transmutation of plant and animal species.

At the suggestion in a letter from Wallace in 1866, Darwin borrowed the term *survival of the fittest* from Herbert Spencer to describe the struggle for life and the preservation of advantageous characteristics. Wallace argued that adopting the term would make Darwin's main argument less confusing to general readers. The problem, as Wallace saw it, was that the words *natural selection*, especially given Darwin's constant comparisons of it with the selective breeding of plants and animals, caused many readers to assume that there had to be a "selector" in nature, as in the breeding of dogs, pigeons, or orchids. "*The Survival of the Fittest*," Wallace wrote in a closely reasoned argument, "could not possibly be denied or misunderstood. Neither would it be possible to say, that to ensure the '*survival of the fittest*' any *intelligent chooser* was necessary,—whereas, when you say *natural selection* acts so as to choose those that are fittest it *is* misunderstood & apparently always will be."[31] Wallace's argument convinced Darwin, and he began using *survival of the fittest* in the sixth edition of *Origin*, published in 1872.[32] Although the term may have added some clarity to Darwin's presentation, his adopting it from Spencer would have the unfortunate effect of causing many critics over the years to assume, incorrectly, that Darwin agreed with Spencer's concept of social evolution.

At the time he wrote *Origin*—and to the end of his life—Darwin had no idea how inherited characteristics were handed down from one generation to the next, and only decades later would biologists isolate the chromosomes, genes, and ultimately the DNA structure and sequencing that would explain the process. He freely admitted that his ignorance on this subject was a problem and, for the time being, he left it to future scientists to discover the mechanisms of inheritance. He also realized that many scientists would have a hard time accepting the process of natural selection because they could not see the intermediate steps—the so-called missing links from one species to another—though he thought that many of these links would eventually be found in the fossil record. Despite these admissions, critics would pounce on the weaknesses in Darwin's argument and use them to attack or even dismiss his entire theory. In fact, Darwin was not as interested in exploring the history of life on Earth—of tracing it back through various stages to the so-called beginning—as he was in explaining the mechanisms, still at work in the present, that had brought about evolution.

Darwin compared the process of natural selection to a tree with many branches, with present life forms represented by the outermost branches at the top, and their ancestors represented by the larger limbs farther down. The implication was, in Darwin's own words, "that probably all the organic beings which have ever lived on this earth have descended from some one primordial form, into which life was first breathed."[33] He did not attempt to explain how this first life form had come to exist, leaving the door open to the possibility of some divine act, if that was what readers wanted to conclude. However this had happened, his assertion that all life forms were related was truly revolutionary. It undermined the old Judeo-Christian belief that humans were different in kind—and not just in degree—from the rest of creation. A century and a half later, this conclusion would lend tremendous support to an ecological paradigm that holds all life to be interrelated and essential to the preservation of the planet.

At the time *Origin* was published, Darwin allowed that God might have created a natural law of evolution, but he did not agree that the deity had in any way directed evolution toward a specific design or goal—the old teleological argument that had been put forth so convincingly, even to Darwin, by William Paley and so many others down through the ages.[34] Darwin's mild theism at the time he published *Origin* would undergo considerable erosion in the future, and he would end up calling himself an agnostic, a term coined by his friend Thomas Huxley to mean a person who does not deny the existence of God but who believes there can be no proof that God exists. In 1879, three years before his death, he wrote to a correspondent what might be considered a final statement on his religious beliefs: "I have never been an atheist in the sense of denying the existence of God. I think . . . generally . . . that an Agnostic would be the more correct description of my state of mind."[35] But as he explained a year later in a letter to Karl Marx, he had purposely refrained from any public statements about religion: "I have therefore always avoided writing about religion and have confined myself to science."[36] To another correspondent around the same time, he wrote, "Science has nothing to do with Christ."[37] This assertion that science and religion are two separate spheres, which do not and should not intersect, is one that many individuals (religious and irreligious alike) have adopted in the century and a half since *Origin* appeared.

Despite gaps in the evidence and admitted weaknesses in his arguments, Darwin's contribution to the theory of evolution was novel and represented a new scientific worldview. While many others had proposed some sort of evolutionary scheme, Darwin was the first to produce a plausible scientific explanation for it—natural selection—and he was the first to marshal a large body of evidence and experimentation to back it up, ranging from his experiences during the voyage of the *Beagle* a quarter century earlier, to his own experiments with pigeon breeding and seed dissemination. He sincerely believed that he had discovered a law of nature that was simple, clear, and full of wonder, as he concluded in the very last paragraph of *Origin*: "There is grandeur in this view of life, with its several powers, having been originally breathed into a few forms or into one; or that, whilst this planet has gone cycling on according to the fixed law of gravity, from so simple a beginning endless forms most beautiful and most wonderful have been and are being evolved."[38] Tellingly, the prose was almost biblical, and the reference to breathing life "into a few forms" seemed to hint at some higher power at work, perhaps purposeful devices to reassure his public.

Darwin's care in laying the groundwork over the years for a favorable scientific reception of his theory now paid off handsomely, and in this, he was as skilled a politician as Abraham Lincoln. Thomas Huxley, who would become his most outspoken supporter in the British Isles, wrote a very favorable review of the book in the *Times* of London. Most of the geological establishment was also ready to accept the reality of transmutation of species, and Lyell himself, Darwin's long-time supporter and leading light within the discipline, would adopt transmutation in the tenth edition of *Principles of Geology* (1867), despite some continuing religious qualms. In the United States, Harvard botanist Asa Gray arranged to have an American edition of *Origin* published in 1860, in addition to reviewing it positively and speaking widely in its favor, though he, too, had religious reservations similar to Lyell's. Even those scientists who had some difficulty accepting Darwin's assertion that natural selection could account for all aspects of species change largely came around to accepting the fact of evolution. In this regard, as science historian Peter J. Bowler has argued, *Origin of Species* was a powerful catalyst in gaining acceptance for the concept of evolution, even if not all scientists agreed with Darwin's particular version of it.[39]

By the time *Origin* appeared in the United States in May 1860, Lincoln was in the thick of his bid for the Republican nomination for president. Following the Cooper Union speech in February, he had traveled to New Hampshire, ostensibly to visit his son Robert, who had enrolled the previous fall at the Phillips Exeter Academy to prepare himself for the entrance exams to Harvard College, which he had failed miserably on his first try. The father might take pride in rising so far with so little formal schooling, but Mary Lincoln, ever desirous of family prominence, had probably insisted on Harvard for her eldest son.[40] Given his habit of always leaving decisions about the children's welfare up to his wife, Lincoln was not likely to have objected, even if he did not look forward to paying the bills.

When Bob's friends at Exeter saw Lincoln walking up to give his address at the school, they were initially as shocked as the audience had been at Cooper Union. Here came a "tall, lank, awkward" man, "dressed in a loose, ill-fitting black frock coat, with black trousers, ill-fitting and somewhat baggy at the knees," along with the rumpled hair and homely face. Some of the boys even whispered about his appearance and felt sorry for Bob, but as soon as Lincoln began to speak, they forgot about his looks and were impressed by what he had to say.[41]

In truth, Lincoln had gone to New Hampshire as much to make additional political speeches as to see his son. Besides the presentation at Exeter, he gave talks in Concord, Manchester, and Dover. He also spoke in New Haven, Connecticut, where he again turned to the theme of equality of opportunity, a blessing that he had enjoyed: "I am not ashamed to confess that twenty five years ago I was a hired laborer, mauling rails, at work on a flat-boat." Rising from such humble work was an opportunity that everyone should have: "I want every man to have the chance—and I believe a black man is entitled to it—in which he *can* better his condition."[42]

Lincoln returned to Illinois in triumph, well aware that he was now a serious contender for the Republican presidential nomination. When some journalists had advanced his name as a possible contender during the last year or so, he had only scoffed at the idea. In response to one such suggestion, he had roared with laughter: "Just think of such a sucker as me as President." Later he had written a newspaper editor saying, "Seriously, I do not think I am fit for the Presidency."[43] Now, basking in the success of his speeches in New York and New England, he wrote, as something of an understatement to Lyman Trumbull on April 29, "I will be entirely frank. The taste *is* in my mouth a little."[44]

At this point Lincoln was writing to influential members of the party everywhere, asking for support. Yet on paper he was one of the least prepared persons ever to run for president: he had held only one national office, a single term in the US House of Representatives, and he had no executive experience. But all the other leading candidates for the Republican nomination were problematic: William H. Seward, who had served as governor of New York as well as a US senator from that state, struck many as too radical because of his appeal to a "higher law" over the slavery issue and because of his recent predictions of an "irrepressible conflict" between slavery and freedom. Governor Salmon P. Chase of Ohio had plenty of support from the more outspoken antislavery wing of the Republican Party, but he could be politically clumsy and lacked personal charisma. Another contender was Edward Bates of Missouri, a conservative member of the now fading Free Soil Party, who had the backing of *New York Tribune* publisher Horace Greeley, mainly as someone to stop archrival Seward from getting the Republican nomination. Although Lincoln was by no means a dark horse, he had the advantage of not having been in the national political arena and therefore of not having made any important enemies. He also had the virtue of being from what was then considered the west, a qualification that many party operatives thought crucial to success in November.[45]

Luckily for Lincoln, the Republicans had decided to hold their convention in Chicago, which would give him the advantage of favorable statewide publicity. Further aiding him was the state Republican convention's unanimous decision, just one week before the national convention, to name Lincoln as their favorite-son candidate for the nomination. The state convention went wild when John Hanks, Lincoln's cousin, helped by a young assistant, marched onto the floor carrying two weathered split rails, decorated with ribbons, from a fence that Hanks said he and Lincoln had made back in 1830. This was an obvious play on the "common man" theme first used so successfully by Andrew Jackson (Old Hickory) in 1824. In 1840, it was used disingenuously by William Henry Harrison, who, although he was wealthy and had been born in a Virginia plantation house, was said by his supporters to be content with a plain buckeye bench and jug of hard cider. In this political tradition, Lincoln became the "Rail Splitter," even though he had always hated farm work and was now a very successful lawyer. As an astute politician, he played along with the scheme, which nicely complemented his lack of formal education and rise from poverty and obscurity. Even more than Jackson, who had also experienced poverty as a child, Lincoln was on his way to becoming the quintessential model of the American dream, an image that would grow to mythic proportions after his death.

Lincoln did not attend the Republican convention, which took place from May 16 to 18, not because he would have shied away from such a public exhibition, as Charles Darwin always tried to do, but because it would have been unseemly at a time when the party was supposed to seek the man rather than the reverse. Lincoln stayed in Springfield and had to rely for news on terse telegraphic messages sent to the *Illinois State Journal*. When none of the major contenders won a first-ballot nomination, support began to flow to Lincoln, and he won in the third round of votes. Managing the Lincoln forces at Chicago was Judge David Davis, with whom Lincoln had so often ridden the judicial circuit.

Though Lincoln was tempted to break with precedent and go to Chicago in person to accept the nomination, his advisers in Springfield talked him out of it, and he waited until a delegation came to him on May 19, the day after the convention adjourned. He then accepted the nomination in writing on May 23, pledging to respect the Republican platform, which called for federal sponsorship of internal improvements, including a transcontinental railroad, high protective tariffs, and homestead legislation that would give free land to farmers. The party's most important plank, of course, was its implacable opposition to allowing slavery in the territories.

Almost immediately, journalists, party delegations, and curiosity seekers besieged the nominee. In order to feed the demand for more personal information, Lincoln wrote an enlarged autobiographic sketch. This time he referred to himself in the third person so that the sketch was easier for campaign biographers and the press to use. He expanded on his family background, his childhood and youth on the frontier, and a variety of early jobs, along with an account of his elections to public office. He again referred to his lack of formal education: "A[braham] now thinks that the aggregate of all his schooling did not amount to one year. He was never in a college or Academy as a student. . . . What he has in the way of education, he has picked up."[46] Very consciously, he painted the picture of a self-made man, bolstering the image of the rail-splitter and his party's philosophy that freedom and careers open to talent—not slavery and the social oligarchies of the South—were best suited to unleashing the potential of each individual.

Had Lincoln's life not been cut short, he might have written a much fuller account of himself after retiring from the presidency. But being such a private man, who confided very little to anyone, he may have avoided writing any sort of autobiography or memoir; and if he did, it is unlikely that he would have left such a full account of his early life as Darwin's *Autobiography*. Lincoln likely wanted to forget his growing-up times—however much they have been romanticized by others and however helpful they were for political publicity.

The Lincoln home in Springfield was clearly too small and ill-equipped to handle the torrent of visitors, so the candidate welcomed an invitation from Governor John Wood to use his office in the state house until the legislature reconvened in the fall. Once the governor reclaimed the office, Lincoln rented space on the second floor of a downtown office building. Some wealthy Springfield backers contributed money for Lincoln to hire a secretary, John G. Nicolay, a German-American newspaperman who had assisted him and the Republicans with publicity during the 1858 senatorial campaign. When the work soon overwhelmed Nicolay, he took on a young assistant named John Hay, who was then studying law in his uncle's Springfield office. Nicolay and Hay would serve as Lincoln's secretaries throughout his presidency and would later write what for many years was considered the definitive biography of their former chief.

Lincoln's nomination and his outspoken opposition to the spread of slavery led to increasingly strident warnings from Southerners that a Republican victory would trigger secession and disunion. Despite the growing crisis, Lincoln's advisers urged him to say nothing during the campaign and to leave all statements to party leaders, a tactic that he accepted. Nor did he go out and campaign himself, following the customs of the day, which held that it was not appropriate for presidential candidates to make speeches or public appearances on their own behalf.

Saying as little as possible was probably the best tactic, since the breakup of the Democrats all but ensured a Lincoln victory in November. In April, as expected, the Democrats had nominated Stephen Douglas at their convention in Charleston, South Carolina. In June, Southern Democrats, unhappy that Douglas was not proslavery enough, bolted from the party and met in Baltimore, where they nominated John C. Breckinridge, then President James Buchanan's vice president. Potentially dividing the presidential vote even further was the emergence of the Constitutional Union Party, which pledged to uphold only the Constitution and all the laws. It nominated Senator John Bell of Tennessee, whose main support was in the border states, where there was much more uncertainty over disunion. This four-way race boded well for Lincoln, who won in November, sweeping both the North and the west, which gave him a majority—180 out of 303—of the electoral votes. Breckenridge received 72, Bell 39, and Douglas 12. Yet Lincoln carried a little less than 40 percent of the popular vote and was not even on the ballot in most of the Southern states.

During the four months between the election and the inauguration—which at that time was held on March 4—Lincoln continued to say almost nothing about what he would do as president, even when South Carolina, carrying out its threat to secede if Lincoln were elected, voted to leave the Union in December, followed by six more states by the time of the inauguration. Lacking the power to do anything and unclear in his own mind what to do, he simply kept quiet about the matter. At first, he had believed that South Carolina was bluffing and that it would not leave the Union. He also believed that the majority of Southerners opposed secession and that time would allow tempers to cool and the secession crisis to blow over.

Lincoln made no attempts, in either word or deed, to support the efforts of a joint House-Senate committee to work out a compromise that might avoid disunion. Named the Crittenden Compromise, because of the leadership of Kentucky senator John J. Crittenden, the agreement would have extended the Missouri Compromise line of 36 degrees, 30 minutes all the way to the Pacific Ocean. Slavery would not be allowed to exist north of that line during the territorial period. Once statehood had been achieved, the state governments on either side of the line could decide whether or not to allow slavery. If Lincoln had wanted to preserve the Union at any price in late 1860, he could have embraced some sort of compromise that would have avoided war. But he and his party had not achieved victory through a willingness to compromise over slavery in the territories, and Lincoln was not about to stand down from his belief that the evil of slavery should not be extended.

As the nation seemed on the brink of disintegration, Mary Lincoln was thrilled at receiving so much attention and at being elevated to an importance that she had always craved. She determined to arrive in Washington so well dressed that no one would dare look down on her as a social inferior from the west. Encouraged by her husband's presidential salary of $25,000 a year, roughly eight times what he had been making as a lawyer, she went on a shopping spree to New York, where she charged thousands of dollars worth of clothing and other items and then concealed the bills from her husband, a habit that she would continue throughout his presidency.

The Lincolns left Springfield on the morning of February 11, 1861, taking a specially chartered train. From the steps of his private car, the president-elect turned, filled with emotion, to say a final farewell to his friends and neighbors of a quarter century, where his children had been born and one buried, "not knowing when, or whether ever, I may return." Realizing that the challenge awaiting him was greater even "than that which rested upon Washington," he called for the help of that "Divine Being, who ever attended him. . . . To his care commending you, as I hope in your prayers you will commend me, I bid you an affectionate farewell."[47] It is unclear if Lincoln, who continued to shun any kind of organized religion, had been converted to the power of prayer, or if his request for prayer was more a request for the good wishes and positive thoughts of those he was leaving behind, even though it had been phrased in the more familiar rhetoric of Christian petition.

The inaugural train took an indirect route that covered nearly two thousand miles so that Lincoln could address the people as he made his way to Washington, with the aim of shoring up support for the Union. Besides speeches before large audiences in big cities, he often stepped out on the rear platform of the train to speak briefly to curious crowds. The itinerary took him through Indianapolis, Cincinnati, Columbus, Pittsburgh, Cleveland, Buffalo, Albany, New York City, Philadelphia, and Harrisburg. He spoke before the state legislatures of Indiana, Ohio, New York, New Jersey, and Pennsylvania, which were all in session at the time. Over and over, Lincoln continued to insist that the present crisis was an artificial one, created for no legitimate reasons. At Pittsburgh he said, "Take even [the Southerners'] own view of the question involved, and there is nothing to justify the course they are pursuing. I repeat it, then, *there is no crisis*, excepting such a one as may be gotten up at any time by designing politicians." His advice to everyone was "to keep cool. If the great American people only keep their temper, on both sides of the line, the troubles will come to an end, and the question which now distracts the country will be settled."[48]

Standing in front of Independence Hall in Philadelphia, Lincoln took sincere advantage of this powerful symbol of the American republic. "I am filled with deep emotion," he began his impromptu remarks, "at finding myself standing in this place where were collected together the wisdom, the patriotism, the devotion to principle, from which sprang the institutions under which we live." He had often "pondered over the dangers" faced by the men who had assembled to proclaim their country's independence, but now more than ever he was moved by the universal principles proclaimed in Philadelphia, giving "liberty, not alone to the people of this country, but hope to all the world for all future time." Knowledge of assassination plots against him in Baltimore, where his train was scheduled to pass through on the way to the capital, may explain Lincoln's particularly powerful and even haunting conclusion at Independence Hall: "I have said nothing but what I am willing to live by, and, if it be the pleasure of Almighty God, die by."[49]

Finally convinced that the plots to murder him might be real, Lincoln reluctantly agreed to make the last leg of his trip, from Harrisburg to Washington, in the middle of the night and without his usual entourage, which might alert the assassins of his exact whereabouts. To keep anyone from wiring ahead about the changed travel plans, the telegraph wires out of Harrisburg were cut. He arrived safely in Washington early on the morning of February 24. Some newspaper critics derided his surreptitious entry, questioning his courage or doubting that the plot was real. Newspaper cartoonists had fun showing him in various disguises—none of them true—including one of the president-elect wearing a Scottish tam and kilt.

Not quite a month before, representatives from the seven seceded states had met in Montgomery, Alabama, to create the Confederate States of America. With the prospect that even more states might leave the Union and join the Confederacy, Lincoln was careful to reiterate at the very outset of his inaugural address that he had "no purpose, directly or indirectly, to interfere with the institution of slavery in the States where it exists."[50] He also pledged not to interfere with the fugitive slave laws, which gave owners the right to reclaim runaways in the North. The Union, he insisted, was perpetual, since it was "safe to assert that no government proper, ever had a provision in its organic law for its own termination."[51] He would do whatever was necessary to hold and occupy property belonging to the United States in seceded parts, but there would be no violence or bloodshed unless "forced upon the national authority."[52] If there were to be a war, it would be the result of aggression by the seceded states: "In *your* hands, my dissatisfied fellow countrymen, and not in *mine*, is the momentous issue of civil war."[53] In closing, he appealed to patriotic memories of all the sacrifices that had given birth to the American nation just eighty-five years before: "The mystic chords of memory, stretching from every battle-field and patriot grave, to every living heart and hearthstone, all over this broad land, will yet swell the chorus of the Union, when again touched, as surely they will be, by the better angels of our nature."[54] Tellingly, there was no mention of compromise, and if there was to be a war, Lincoln wanted the country to know that the South—not he—would be responsible.

The new president had no opportunity to bask in the afterglow of his inauguration, nor did he have the luxury of taking his time to come up with a strategy for answering Southern threats to military forts in their midst that remained under the control of the national government. One of these was Fort Sumter, located on an island in the harbor of Charleston, South Carolina. On the very next morning after taking the oath of office, Lincoln had to face this challenge when he discovered a report on his desk from Major Robert Anderson, the commander of the garrison at Sumter, saying that he had only six weeks of supplies left. Lincoln could either reinforce Anderson or order him to abandon the fort. Since he had just promised to hold all federal property in the South, surrender was not an option, though giving up the forts may well have kept the peace, if that is what Lincoln wanted most of all. The strain was so great that he "keeled over" at one point and had to be put to bed.

After much agonizing and indecision, Lincoln decided to send supplies on relief ships, with assurances communicated to the authorities in South Carolina that the mission was entirely peaceful. Unwilling to permit even this, artillery batteries in Charleston opened fire on the fort on April 12, 1861, and after thirty-four hours of bombardment, Anderson surrendered. No one was killed, but the attack by South Carolina forced Lincoln to take action against a Confederacy that had fired the first shots and, in his mind, had started the war. Lincoln called for seventy-five thousand volunteers to put down the rebellion, which turned out to be only the first installment in over a million and a half men who would serve the Union cause against the million mobilized by the Confederacy. Four more states, Virginia, North Carolina, Tennessee, and Arkansas, then left the Union; and with Virginia now part of the rebellion, the Confederacy moved its capital to Richmond.

Despite the outbreak of war, Lincoln continued to receive dozens of callers every day. Anyone could come in without an appointment and simply wait around until the president could see him. Often the visitor was there to ask for a government job, but as the war went on there were personal petitions on behalf of deserters or other persons in the ranks who had been convicted of some offense. Lincoln's compassion became famous, as did his continuing storytelling and use of humor to lift his own and others' spirits or to slide around a minor request by distracting the petitioner and not giving a yes or no answer. His secretaries often saw these sessions as a waste of time, but Lincoln believed they were an excellent way of finding out what everyday people thought in this age before public opinion polls. As president, of course, he could not hide away in his office, but, unlike Charles Darwin, who reveled in the seclusion of Down House, he thrived in the company of others, a prime requisite for any successful politician.

Having youngsters in the president's house was a novelty, since most presidential children were gown up, or nearly so, by the time their fathers were elected to that high office. Robert, who turned eighteen in 1861, was away at Harvard except during summer vacations. Willie was ten when Lincoln became president, and Tad was eight. As in his law office back in Springfield, their father let the boys have the run of the place. Caught up in the martial spirit of the day, Willie and Tad gathered up all the neighborhood boys they could find and drilled them on the grounds. They used the roof of the mansion as a make-believe fort, painting small logs to look like cannon and firing them at imagined Confederates on the other side of the Potomac in Virginia. The Lincoln boys also had two pet goats that often tore up the flowerbeds. Tad hitched one of the goats to a chair in the East Room during a reception and had the animal pull him across the polished floor as if on a sled. Lincoln romped with the boys when he had time and enjoyed reading to them.55

Soon after moving in, Mary Lincoln began to refurbish and redecorate the White House. She spent lavishly and when the bills came due, the president discovered that she had vastly overspent the $20,000 that Congress had appropriated. Lincoln was furious and vowed that he would never ask Congress to pay more "for *flub dubs for that damned old house*," but in the end he had no choice, and Congress quietly agreed to cover the cost overruns. Mary also continued her extravagant spending on clothing and obtained money by submitting false bills for items supposedly ordered for the White House but that were never delivered or intended to be delivered, and kept the money for herself.

The improvements to the interior of the president's house were to serve as a backdrop for gracious entertainments over which Mary could preside. To show off the new furnishings, the Lincolns held a grand party for five hundred guests in the East Room on February 5, 1862. There was music by the Marine Band, which introduced a special new piece that evening, "The Mary Lincoln Polka," and a midnight buffet catered by the exclusive Maillard's of New York. Although the guests had a grand time, the Lincolns could not relax and enjoy themselves because Willie was seriously ill upstairs. He died two weeks later, probably of typhoid fever. His brother Tad came down with the same illness but managed to recover.

This loss of a second son was devastating for both parents. For months after Willie's death Lincoln would lock himself in a room and weep. He had frequent happy dreams that Willie was still alive, only to awaken to the awful truth. He also turned to religion for some solace, going so far as to have long conversations with the Reverend Phineas D. Gurley of the New York Avenue Presbyterian Church, where he and Mary rented a pew, and whose sermons the president greatly admired. The minister assured him that Willie was now in heaven, though it is unlikely that he convinced Lincoln, who did not undergo a religious conversion and join the church. Nevertheless, Willie's death and the horrible suffering brought on by the war caused Lincoln to turn more and more to religious ideas to explain the great tragedies of life. Unlike Darwin's situation, the death of a child did not push Lincoln further from religion, but may have drawn him somewhat closer.

Mary Lincoln's grief was much worse than her husband's. She could not bring herself to attend Willie's funeral, went to bed for three weeks, and never again entered the Green Room where Willie's embalmed body had been laid out for viewing. In the months that followed, even the mention of the child's name unleashed rivers of tears, and Lincoln finally had to hire a nurse to take care of her. She draped herself in layers of black clothing and suspended all social activities at the executive mansion.[56]

In other ways, too, Mary Lincoln continued to add to the president's woes. Throughout their marriage, she had been extremely jealous of other women, possibly because of a lifelong fear of abandonment stemming from her mother's death and lack of attention from her father after his remarriage. One of her worst fits of jealousy occurred in March of

1865, when the Lincolns were at City Point, Virginia, paying a visit to General Edward O. C. Ord. His wife, Mary Ord, rode on horseback beside the president while Mary Lincoln was to ride in a coach somewhat behind them. Upon discovering this, the First Lady flew into a rage. When she arrived at Ord's headquarters, she insulted Mary Ord and called her "vile" names in front of a crowd of officers. That night she screamed at Lincoln to remove General Ord from his command. On the boat trip back to Washington, Mary reportedly hit the president in the face and damned and cursed him. General Grant's aide, Adam Badeau, who was at City Point and observed the incident, marveled at how Lincoln had endured this abuse with a resigned but painful stoicism. He "bore it as Christ might have done; with an expression of pain and sadness that cut one to the heart, but with supreme calmness and dignity."57 Mary Lincoln's behavior would have been unthinkable and unfathomable for the calm and sympathetic Emma Darwin, who did everything she could to make life bearable for her husband.

By the early 1860s, Darwin had already launched his great revolution, and Lincoln was on the verge of launching his. Their own personal rebellions were challenging others—often bitter at having old habits of thought and action put into question—to join them, with wide-ranging implications for human equality and human rights and the interconnectedness of all living things.

NOTES

1. Lincoln to Anson G. Henry, November 19, 1858, *The Collected Works of Abraham Lincoln*, edited by Roy P. Basler et al. (New Brunswick, NJ: Rutgers University Press, 1953), 3:339.

2. Lincoln to Alexander Sympson, December 12, 1858, *Collected Works of Abraham Lincoln*, 3:346.

3. William H. Herndon, *Herndon's Life of Lincoln* (New York: Da Capo Press, 1983), p. 362.

4. Douglas's article appeared in the September 1859 issue of *Harper's*.

5. Lincoln, "Speech at Cincinnati, Ohio" (September 17, 1859), *Collected Works of Abraham Lincoln*, 3:459.

6. The book's title was *Political Debates between Hon. Abraham Lincoln and Hon. Stephen A. Douglas, in the Celebrated Campaign of 1858, in Illinois*, and was published in Cincinnati by Follett, Foster and Company in 1860.

7. Lincoln to J. W. Fell, December 20, 1859, *Collected Works of Abraham Lincoln*, 3:511.

8. Ibid., p. 512.

9. The best and fullest account of this speech and its importance in making Lincoln president is Harold Holzer, *Lincoln at Cooper Union: The Speech That Made Abraham Lincoln President* (New York: Simon and Schuster, 2004).

10. Quoted in Lincoln, "Address at Cooper Institute" (February 27, 1860), *Collected Works of Abraham Lincoln*, 3:522.

11. Herndon, *Herndon's Life of Lincoln*, p. 368.

12. Holzer, *Lincoln at Cooper Union*, p. 112.

13. Lincoln, "Address at Cooper Institute" (February 27, 1860), *Collected Works of Abraham Lincoln*, 3:546–47.

14. Ibid., pp. 549–50.

15. Ibid., p. 550. In the original, this quotation was in capital letters.

16. George Haven Putnam, quoted in David Herbert Donald, *Lincoln* (New York: Quadrangle Books, 1995), p. 238.

17. Quoted in ibid., p. 239.

18. Francis Darwin, "Reminiscences of My Father's Everyday Life," in *The Life and Letters of Charles Darwin*, edited by Francis Darwin (New York: D. Appleton and Company, 1896), pp. 129–30.

19. Ibid., p. 131.

20. Darwin to Hooker, October 6, 1858, *The Correspondence of Charles Darwin* (Cambridge: Cambridge University Press, 1985–[2005]), 7:165.

21. Darwin to John Murray, May 14, 1859, *Correspondence of Charles Darwin*, 7:298.

22. Darwin to Murray, April 29, 1859, *Correspondence of Charles Darwin*, 7:286.

23. Darwin to Murray, May 14, 1859, *Correspondence of Charles Darwin*, 7:298.

24. Darwin to Murray, May 31, 1859, *Correspondence of Charles Darwin*, 7:301.

25. Ibid.

26. Darwin to Murray, August 31, 1859, *Correspondence of Charles Darwin*, 7:327.

27. Nora Barlow, ed., *The Autobiography of Charles Darwin, 1809–1882* (New York: W. W. Norton, 1993), p. 123.

28. Ibid., p. 124.

29. Charles Darwin, *On the Origin of Species* (London: John Murray, 1859), p. 6. This quote is from a facsimile of the first edition, with an introduction by Ernest Mayr (Cambridge, MA: Harvard University Press, 1964).

30. Ibid., p. 61.

31. Wallace to Darwin, July 2, 1866, *Correspondence of Charles Darwin*, 14:228.

32. The 1872 publication, in which Darwin used Spencer's phrase *survival of the fittest* was *The Variations of Animals and Plants Under Domestication*.

33. Darwin, *On the Origin of Species*, p. 484.

34. On this matter, see Darwin's *Autobiography*, pp. 85–96.

35. Quoted in Arthur Keith, *Darwin Revalued* (London: Watts and Company, 1955), p. 233.

36. Quoted in ibid., p. 234.

37. Quoted in ibid., p. 242.

38. Darwin, *On the Origin of Species*, p. 490.

39. Peter J. Bowler, *Charles Darwin: The Man and His Influence* (Oxford, UK: Basil Blackwell, 1990), p. 128.

40. Jean H. Baker, *Mary Todd Lincoln: A Biography* (New York: W. W. Norton, 1987), pp. 123–24.

41. Donald, *Lincoln*, p. 240.

42. Lincoln, "From a Speech at New Haven, Conn." (March 6, 1860), *Collected Works of Abraham Lincoln*, 4:24.

43. Lincoln, quoted in Donald, *Lincoln*, p. 235.

44. Lincoln to Lyman Trumbull, April 29, 1860, *Collected Works of Abraham Lincoln*, 4:45.

45. Donald, *Lincoln*, p. 236.

46. Lincoln, "Autobiographical Sketch Written for Use in Preparing a Campaign Biography," *Collected Works of Abraham Lincoln*, 4:62.

47. Lincoln, "Farewell Address at Springfield, Illinois" (February 11, 1861), *Collected Works of Abraham Lincoln*, 4:190.

48. Lincoln, "From an Address at Pittsburgh" (February 15, 1861), *Collected Works of Abraham Lincoln*, 4:211.

49. Lincoln, "Speech at Independence Hall, Philadelphia" (February 21, 1861), *Collected Works of Abraham Lincoln*, 4:240–41.

50. Lincoln, "First Inaugural Address" (March 4, 1861), *Collected Works of Abraham Lincoln*, 4:250.

51. Ibid., p. 252.

52. Ibid., p. 266.

53. Ibid., p. 271.

54. Ibid.

55. Donald, *Lincoln*, pp. 307–308.

56. Baker, *Mary Lincoln*, pp. 208–11.

57. Quoted in Michael Burlingame, *The Inner World of Abraham Lincoln* (Urbana: University of Illinois Press, 1994), p. 289.

Chapter 7

TRIUMPH AND TORMENT

O, my offence is rank it smells to heaven;
It hath the primal eldest curse upon't, . . .
My stronger guilt defeats my strong intent;
And, like a man to double business bound, . . .
My fault is past. But, O, what form of prayer
Can serve my turn? 'Forgive me my foul murder'?
That cannot be; since I am still possess'd
Of those effects for which I did the murder, . . .
Try what repentance can: what can it not?
Yet what can it when one can not repent?
O wretched state! O bosom black as death!
O limed soul, that, struggling to be free, . . .
　　　　　　　　—William Shakespeare, *Hamlet*, act 3, scene 3

D uring the Civil War, Abraham Lincoln wrote to a well-
　　 known Shakespearean actor that the line from *Hamlet*
beginning with the words "O, my offence is rank" was among his
favorites. Again and again he turned to Shakespeare's accounts of

kings—Hamlet, Lear, Macbeth, and others—whose vaulting ambitions left them with bloodstained hands. Lincoln's thirst for fame had propelled him into the White House, had resulted in the secession of the Southern states, and had provoked a war that many around the world, including Charles Darwin, believed was unnecessary.

Darwin, too, had reveled in Shakespeare's tragedies, but now they "nauseated" him.[1] He gave no explanation for this change of heart, but his insights into nature may have been tragic enough, for he had come to believe that suffering, death, and endless cruelty were at the very center of the evolutionary process. Earlier he had confessed to feeling like a murderer for proposing a theory that undermined age-old beliefs about God and humankind and the relationship between human beings and the rest of living nature. Meanwhile, Lincoln seemed to be drowning in death and destruction as the Civil War raged on and on. Both Lincoln and Darwin suffered mightily for their acts, even though many believed, and would continue to believe, that their thoughts and deeds opened a truer and nobler chapter for all humankind.

The Civil War that absorbed nearly all Lincoln's waking hours and disturbed his sleep has been examined, pored over, written about, discussed, depicted, commemorated, and argued about endlessly. More important than the war itself is how Lincoln came to understand the war and how he used it to launch a second American revolution, and in the process to force a larger reexamination of humanity—despite the terrible price in blood and treasure.

The personal means that allowed Lincoln to persevere and ultimately to triumph were his great intelligence, his refusal to adopt doctrinaire positions, a willingness to change his mind and tactics in the face of altered facts, and his growing ability to marshal the English language. His lifelong suffering from depression also may have steeled him for the emotional agony of the war and caused him to redouble his desire to accomplish some great work for humankind that would justify his decision, taken so many years ago, that he would continue to live. Then there was his dogged tenacity in the face of opposition. Lincoln's reading of Shakespeare's tragedies and his falling back on a providential view of God were also powerful coping strategies. Intelligence, pragmatism, determination, and recurrent bouts of deep depression were characteristics that he shared with Darwin. Lincoln remained the better writer and the more public figure, as befits a politician. Darwin did not share Lincoln's growing sense of Providence and had lost his taste for Shakespeare. But during the first half of the 1860s these two men, born on the same day, sustained their far-reaching revolutions.

Lincoln's practicality was nowhere more evident than in how he went about freeing the slaves, a process filled with such inconsistencies and contradictions that he would lay himself open to tremendous criticism at the time—and ever after. Virtually from the outset of the war, the abolitionists in his party pressured Lincoln to free the slaves, but he refused, even to the point of initially ordering field commanders to return runaways who had crossed into Union lines seeking freedom. He did this fearing that any attempts to free slaves could tip the balance toward secession in the border states—those slaves states, namely Delaware, Maryland, Kentucky, and Missouri, which had not seceded. Keeping Maryland in the Union was especially crucial since it lay just north of Washington. With Virginia just across the Potomac River to the south of the capital, Maryland's secession would make Washington into an island surrounded and besieged by the Confederacy.

Lincoln continued to insist that his first priority was to save the Union, and in truth he could not free the slaves unless he preserved the Union. On the other hand, he also came to realize that freeing the slaves might help to save the Union by giving the North an advantage in international public opinion. Freeing the slaves would also weaken the South's war-making power by depriving it of a huge segment of its workforce and by allowing newly emancipated slaves to join the United States Army and fight for their own freedom.

Lincoln spelled out these complexities in a letter to *New York Tribune* editor Horace Greeley, who had been urging immediate emancipation: "If I could save the Union without freeing *any* slave I would do it; and if I could save it by freeing *all* the slaves, I would do it; and if I could save it by freeing some and leaving others alone, I would also do that." To make sure that Greeley understood that he nonetheless continued to oppose slavery everywhere, he added, "I intend no modification of my oft-expressed *personal* wish that all men every where could be free."[2] Knowing and intending that the letter would be published in the *Tribune* and reprinted by numerous other newspapers, Lincoln was attempting to allay fears in the border states as well as in the North where many citizens were either opposed to or ambivalent about freeing the slaves. In this letter he was careful to portray himself as a moderate and reasonable man, a far cry from the more outspoken abolitionists.

Lincoln also held a seemingly inconsistent though pragmatic view of secession itself. Continuing to insist that secession was illegal, he refused to admit that the Confederate States were now a separate country, arguing that it was rebels within the seceded states and not the states themselves that had defied federal authority. He ordered captured Southern troops to be treated as if they were prisoners of war from another sovereign country and not as criminals or traitors who should be tried and convicted for their misdeeds. He also refused to admit that his blockade of Southern ports, defined in international law as an act of war against another sovereign nation, was a tacit recognition of Confederate independence.

By the summer of 1862, Lincoln decided that the border states were enough under Union control for him to free the slaves. Meanwhile, abolitionists, various newspapers, and a growing number of Republicans had been putting increased pressure on him to act as soon as possible. On July 17, Congress passed the Second Confiscation Act, which authorized the military to confiscate slaves as contraband of war, since owners were using their labor in support of the rebellion. Having made up his mind to emancipate the slaves, Lincoln nevertheless bowed to advice from his cabinet to wait until there was a significant Union victory on the battlefield, especially in view of a recent string of military disasters. Otherwise the world might view emancipation as an act of desperation. Later, he told his cabinet that he had made a covenant with the Almighty: If God gave him a victory, it would be a sign to move forward with emancipation. He would be "an instrument in God's hands of accomplishing a great work," as he had told a delegation of Quakers in June.[3]

The Battle of Antietam, fought on September 17, 1862, provided just such a sign. Robert E. Lee had invaded Maryland, hoping to rally support for the Confederacy and to demonstrate to Britain and the other powers in Europe that the South had a fighting chance of winning independence, thereby opening the way for diplomatic recognition and material assistance. Although Lee's army was not destroyed, it was forced from the field and had to retreat back into Virginia.

Lincoln's Emancipation Proclamation was another case of astute contradiction. He had always claimed that the slaves were in fact persons. Yet for the sake of legality in freeing them, he cited his powers as commander in chief, in concert with Congress's Confiscation Act of July 17, 1862, as all the authority he needed to seize the slaves as rebel property. In fact, the proclamation freed only the slaves in those states still in rebellion against the United States and it did not touch the institution of slavery in the border states, which had not seceded. In fact, if any one of the rebellious states had come back into the Union between September 22 and December 31, Lincoln could not have emancipated the slaves in those areas. Such realities were part of the reason why he would later support the Thirteenth Amendment to the Constitution, which would leave no doubt that slavery was wholly illegal in the United States and in any of its territories.

Compared to the eloquence of so many other messages that Lincoln composed during the war—and he did write them himself—the documents of emancipation were surprisingly dull and legalistic. This was done on purpose, since Lincoln the lawyer wanted to argue the legality of his order in every way possible and to avoid any impression that he had acted out of emotion. When taken together with other Lincoln writings, the two emancipation documents show him to be a master of language, capable of using whatever tone and manner of expression he chose.

As a war leader, Lincoln's intelligence and pragmatism also served him well. With his own military experience confined to his uneventful service in the militia during the Black Hawk War thirty years before, he was well aware of his ignorance about how to fight a large-scale conflict. To compensate for this, he borrowed a number of books on strategy from the Library of Congress, including Henry W. Halleck's *Elements of Military Art and Science*. As he had done in learning the law, he would teach himself what he needed to know. He also frequently went into the field to talk to his top generals, hired and fired commanders, and on one occasion seriously considered taking field command himself, but changed his mind. He finally discovered the tenacious qualities of Ulysses S. Grant, who became the architect as well as the executioner of final victory. Lincoln also personally approved William Tecumseh Sherman's strategy for taking Atlanta, Georgia, which fell on September 2, 1864, and which probably saved him from defeat for reelection that November—and the nation from the distinct possibility of a negotiated settlement with the South that could have left slavery intact.

Lincoln realized from the outset that support from War Democrats was essential to victory and placed Democrats such as General George McClellan in positions of high command. Later, when he had to dismiss his Republican secretary of war, Simon Cameron, he replaced him with Democrat Edwin M. Stanton, who turned out to be an excellent choice.

He likewise turned to former Democrat Andrew Johnson to serve as vice president during his second term.

Understandably, the strain of war took a terrible physical and emotional toll on Lincoln. After hearing news of the Union rout at the first battle of Bull Run in July 1861, he exclaimed, "If hell is [not] any worse than this, it has no terror for me." Describing his feelings over the failure of the Peninsular campaign a year later, he said, "I was nearly inconsolable as I could be and live," and after the Union's humiliating defeat at Fredericksburg in December 1862, he moaned, "If there is a worse place than hell[,] I am in it."4 During the early summer of 1863, he had terrible nightmares and often could not sleep. He was too busy to eat proper meals and simply grabbed a bite here or there, causing him to lose weight on an already spare frame. With dark bags under his eyes and a face lined with worry, Lincoln aged rapidly in office. News of great victories at Gettysburg, Pennsylvania, and Vicksburg, Mississippi, in early July brought temporary relief, but battlefield reverses over the next year continued to wear the president down, often leaving him very depressed. Even Union victories made him shudder in horror at the staggering numbers killed and wounded—on both sides.

As Lincoln agonized over the killing, Charles Darwin's Britain was profoundly shaken by the American Civil War.5 There were many reasons for this: The two countries remained each others' most important trading partners, and the question of Britain's continued economic and political relations with the American South were particularly delicate, given the large exports of Southern cotton to the British textile industry. There were also the apparent lessons of the American Revolution, which British liberals, at a time when their country's imperialism was at a low ebb, took to mean that the natural course of the English-speaking peoples was independence; and when conditions pointed to separation, the break should be as amicable as possible. The South's low tariff policies, in contrast to the high tariffs supported by Lincoln's Republican policies, were more in harmony with Britain's free-trade stance. Furthermore, informed opinion makers in Britain, and especially the powerful *Times* of London, did not believe that the North could force the South back into the Union and that attempts to do so would amount to a hopelessly bloody war. Both supporters and critics of democracy in Britain viewed the American Civil War as a severe test for self-government. The shapers of British foreign policy realized full well that Southern independence would weaken the United States as a potential world power and thus compromise a rising competitor. Finally, a common language and a common history could not help but stir interest in the mother country over the dramatic events unfolding in the former American colony.[6]

Darwin read about the war in the newspapers with a mixture of fascination and horror. He also had definite views about what he thought Lincoln and the North should do. He communicated his shifting ideas in a series of letters to Asa Gray, the Harvard botanist who had shared his knowledge of American plants with Darwin and was his staunchest supporter in the United States. Gray was also well connected socially and politically in Boston.[7]

In June 1861, not long after the war had broken out but before there had been any large-scale fighting, Darwin, who had opposed slavery all his life, wanted Lincoln to make the conflict a crusade against this despicable practice, even if it meant the loss of many lives: "I am one, even wish to God, though at the loss of millions of lives, that the North would proclaim a crusade against Slavery. In the long run, a million horrid deaths would be amply repaid in the cause of humanity.—What wonderful time we live in."[8] But by late July, after the North's humiliating defeat at the first Battle of Bull Run, Darwin began to have doubts about the price that would have to be paid for reunion and whether or not there could ever be reconciliation between the North and the South even if Lincoln prevailed. The war, Darwin wrote, was now "a great misfortune in the progress of the world," but he thought it still might be worth the cost if slavery could be annihilated in the process.[9] Unfortunately, he added, "Your president does not even mention the word [emancipation] in his Address [to Congress in July]." A war against slavery would be just, Darwin and many others in Britain believed, but not if it was a war merely to save the Union. Two months later, in September, Darwin was still trying to find a silver lining in the war: "If abolition does follow with your victory, the whole world will look brighter in my eyes & and in many eyes."[10]

By the end of 1861, the Trent Affair threatened war between the United States and Great Britain. This crisis erupted on November 8, 1861, when Captain Charles Wilkes of the USS *San Jacinto* forcibly stopped and boarded the British mail packet *Trent* in international waters. Onboard were two Confederate agents being sent to England and France in hopes of opening up diplomatic relations. Wilkes took the men with a superior show of force and arrested them. The British government, the British press, and the British public were outraged at this violation of international law and of their national sovereignty. For several weeks it looked as if there might be war between the two countries, until Lincoln assured the government in London that Wilkes had acted without instruction and agreed to release the two siezed men. One war, he realized, was more than enough.

Darwin shuddered at the thought of armed conflict with the United States: "What a thing it is," he wrote to Gray,

> that when you receive this we may be at war, & we two be bound, as good patriots, to hate each other, though I shall find this hating you very hard work.—How curious it is to see two countries, just like two angry & silly men, taking so opposite a view of the same transaction! . . . I fear there is no shadow of doubt we shall fight, if the two Southern rogues are not given up. And what a wretched thing it will

be if we fight on the side of slavery. . . . Again how curious it is that you
seem to think you can conquer the south; and I never met a soul, even
those who would most wish it, who thinks it possible,—that is to conquer and retain it.[11]

As Darwin and many others knew well, revolutions and civil wars were
often protracted, and even when they appeared to be over, they were
likely to flare up again as endless guerilla actions—one reason why he
was so pessimistic about the possibility of forcing the South back into
the Union.

Darwin was careful to be polite in his responses to Gray, but to his
friend Joseph Hooker, who was also receiving letters from Gray and was
very irritated by them, he was more than blunt, especially about the
high-handed way he thought the United States was behaving at the
beginning of the Trent Affair. In this context, Darwin wrote to Hooker
in mid-January 1862, "Asa Gray is evidently sore about England: he does
not say much; nor do I: but I have hitherto been able two [sic] write with
some sympathy; now I must be silent; for I look at the [American]
people as a nation of unmitigated blackguards."[12]

Put out by Darwin's comment about the seeming impossibility of
the North's conquering and retaining the South, Gray wrote back that
he and most Northerners had no doubts about their eventual success.[13]
What Gray did not know was that Darwin was passing his letters on to
Hooker, who in turn made comments about them to Darwin. In one of
his comments written in early 1862, Hooker blamed Gray's and the
North's blindness over the war on the failings of democracy: "Our aristocracy may have been (& has been) a great draw back to civilization—
but on the other hand it has had its advantages—has kept in check the
uneducated and unreflecting—& has forced those who have intellect
enough to rise to their own level. . . . There is a deal in *breeding* & I do
not think that any but high bred gentlemen are safe guides in Emergen-
cies such as these [in America]."[14] This was a telling comment, since

Lincoln and many others on both sides of the Atlantic saw both secession and the war as the greatest test for democracy since the founding of
the nation, while many Englishmen who had doubts about democracy
saw the American Civil War as proof that democracy—or at least excessive democracy—was bound to fail.

Darwin responded to Hooker that Alexis de Tocqueville, in his
classic *Democracy in America*, had warned against the excesses of popular
government, in this case the "tyranny of the majority," which was
blocking Southern independence: "By Jove you must write your book on
Aristocracy—I read De Tocqueville some years ago with great
interest."[15] Darwin put the democracy problem a little more gently to
Gray, emphasizing that the war in American would set back the case for
democracy in England for many years: "This war of yours, however it
may end, is a fearful evil to the whole world; & its evil effect will, I must
think, be felt for years.—I can see already it has produced wide spread
feeling in favour of aristocracy & monarchism; no one in England will
speak for years in favor of the people governing themselves."[16]

Gray was not amused at these remarks and shot back that what was
happening in the United States had nothing to do with the fate of democracy in England: "I never thought anything of American institutions for
England. Aristocracy is a natural & needed appendage to Monarchy. You
work out your own type—and you will liberalize fast enough,—and leave
us to do ours. We'll make it do,—with some jangling."[17]

By early 1862 Darwin was ready to confess to Gray that he had
changed his mind about Lincoln's continuing the war and concluded
that the best option for the president was to let the South go: "It is well
to make a clean breast of it at once; & I have begun to think whether it
would not be well for the peace of the world, if you were to split up into
two or three nations. . . . Well I can't help my change of opinion—It is all
owing to that confounded Longitude.—Bad man, as you will think me,
I shall always think of you with affection,—Here's an insult! I shall
always think of you as an Englishman."[18]

Most especially, Darwin believed that once the North had taken Kentucky and Tennessee and secured other parts of the border areas, Lincoln should have "agreed to a divorce," especially since there was no desire for reunion in the rest of the South.[19] Many in Britain, as well as the *Times* of London, shared this opinion. So did the Peace Democrats in the United States. And for years before the Civil War broke out, William Lloyd Garrison, one of America's most radical and outspoken abolitionists, had called for the free states to secede from a Union that had been forged through an evil compromise with slavery. Once the South did secede, Garrison, joined by Horace Greeley of the *New York Tribune* and a number of other influential Republicans, declared that the Southerners should be allowed to go and rot in their own immoral and backward way of life.[20] Given that context, Darwin's advice about a divorce was not so outlandish; it was an opinion that Lincoln had heard frequently enough in his own country and that he could not have ignored, even if he did not agree with it.

Gray responded to such opinions from Darwin by writing that if the North had kept on giving in to the South, he himself would probably have left in disgust and gone to England: "I thank God, it has been otherwise, and that I have a country to be proud of, and which I will gladly suffer for, if need be."[21]

Darwin assured Gray that he was following the war news with nearly as much interest as Americans did.[22] In fact, Darwin's view of the war—not unlike that of many Americans—was greatly influenced by how the conflict was going. In April 1862, he congratulated Gray on a series of Northern victories in the western theaters, but he added that the English still did not believe that there could ever be a single "Union again."[23] When the tide of battle turned against the North once more in the summer of 1862, Gray admitted to Darwin that defeating the South was going to be more difficult than he thought, but he added that the North would only have to fight harder: "For my part, I would fight till 4/5 of our property and half our men were destroyed before I would give up!—and I think that is the general opinion."[24]

Darwin was pleased about Lincoln's Emancipation Proclamation, which went into effect on January 1, 1863, but he was afraid that it would not have too much effect on British public opinion about the war: "Well, your President has issued his fiat against Slavery—God grant it may have some effect.—I fear it is true that very many English do not now really care about Slavery; I hear some old sensible people saying here the same thing; & they accounted for it . . . by the present generation never having seen or heard much about Slavery."[25]

As time went on, Gray believed that emancipation had created a strong and irrevocable determination in the North to smash slavery for good. He wrote Darwin in early 1864, "The sentiment of our country, you must see—at least I assure you—has settled—as I knew it would if the rebellion was obstinate enough—into a determination to do away with Slavery. Homely, honest, ungainly Lincoln is the *representative man of the* country."[26]

Understandably, Lincoln was more horrified about the bloodletting than Darwin. As the war continued and the death toll mounted to heartrending proportions, Lincoln struggled to find both meaning and explanation for the terrible and seemingly endless suffering and destruction. He went to Gettysburg, Pennsylvania, on November 18, 1863, to help dedicate a national cemetery to those who had fallen the summer before in a costly but critical turning point of the war. He began by connecting the battle with the great sacrifices of the American Revolution and to the bold new experiment that the revolution had begun for the United States—and ultimately for the whole world: "Four score and seven years ago our fathers brought forth on this continent, a new nation, conceived in Liberty, and dedicated to the proposition that all men are created equal." The present war was a great test to show "whether that nation, or any nation so conceived and so dedicated, can long endure." The duty of the living was to make sure that those who had fallen had not died in vain—that "this nation, under God, shall have a new birth of freedom and—that government of the people, by the people, for the people, shall not perish from the earth."[27] Although the Gettysburg Address has become trite through memorization by millions of schoolchildren, along with the many paraphrases and saccharine references, it remains one of the most beautifully constructed and moving passages ever written in the English language.

Six weeks earlier, in a proclamation making the last Thursday in November a day of general thanksgiving, Lincoln had tried to answer the question being asked by so many as to why God would allow such endless, hideous suffering. He found great comfort in reading the Bible, though he continued to shun membership in any church, with creeds and doctrines that he could not accept. More and more, he seemed to fall back on the Calvinistic beliefs of his parents' Baptist faith, combined with his old deistic belief in the "Doctrine of Necessity." Such was the context for his haunting "Second Inaugural Address" on March 4, 1865:

> Neither party expected for the war, the magnitude, or the duration, which it has already attained.... Both read the same Bible, and pray to the same God; and each invokes His aid against the other.... The Almighty has His own purposes. "Woe unto the world because of offenses! for it must needs be that offenses come; but woe to that man by whom the offense cometh!" If we shall suppose that American Slavery is one of those offenses which, in the providence of God, must needs come, but which, having continued through His appointed time, He now wills to remove, and that He gives to both North and South this terrible war, as the woe due to those by whom the offense came, shall we discern therein any departure from those divine attributes which the believers in a Living God always ascribe to Him? Fondly do we hope—fervently do we pray—that this mighty scourge of war may speedily pass away. Yet, if God wills that it continue, until all the wealth piled up by the bonds-man's two hundred and fifty years

of unrequited toil shall be sunk, and until every drop of blood drawn with the lash, shall be paid by another drawn with the sword, as was said three thousand years ago, so it still must be said "The judgments of the Lord, are true and righteous altogether."[28]

Lincoln knew that a quotation from scripture (in this case Matthew 18:7) about divine retribution would resonate powerfully with a Bible-reading public.

However soaring the rhetoric, Lincoln was a sick and exhausted man as he began his second term. His eyes were swollen and encircled with black rings, and he looked like he had lost thirty pounds on an already thin body. This and the deep creases down his face made him look far older than his fifty-six years. He went to bed for several days after the inauguration and, more than a week later, he held a cabinet meeting in his bedroom.

During these dark times, the Bible was not the president's only source of solace, as he read Shakespeare's tragedies over and over, most of them about kings or heads of state—rulers whose overreaching ambitions had led to tragedy. Lincoln had learned to love Shakespeare thirty years before while living at New Salem and he kept a copy of Shakespeare's plays on top of his desk in the White House. Blessed with a good memory, he could recite hundreds of lines from Shakespeare and enjoyed doing so for friends and associates. While president, he went to several dozen Shakespearean plays and was especially drawn to *King Lear*, *Hamlet*, and *Macbeth*. The first presentation of *Hamlet* that he saw in Washington starred Edwin Booth, the brother of John Wilkes Booth, who would later assassinate him.

Of all Shakespeare's tragedies, Lincoln had a special affinity for *Macbeth*, and when riding the judicial circuit back in Illinois, he had carried around a worn copy of the play. During his presidency, he wrote a letter to Shakespearean actor James Hackett: "I think nothing equals Macbeth."[29] Lincoln was probably drawn to *Macbeth* because of his own drive for power. Ironically, he had warned about such dangerous ambitions in his 1838 Lyceum lecture. In both his first and second inaugural addresses, Lincoln insisted that the South had started the war. Yet he knew there had been alternatives—some compromise with the South or allowing the Southerners to secede in peace—but he had gone with war, a war that turned out to be more terrible than he or anyone else could have imagined.

While aboard the *River Queen* during his way back from visiting army headquarters at City Point, Virginia, in April 1865, Lincoln was particularly fascinated by Macbeth's envy of Duncan, whom Macbeth had murdered, but who is in his grave and can suffer no more. Senators Charles Sumner and James Harlan were on the boat with the president that day and remembered vividly how he had read to them from the play for several hours.

Like any tragic hero, Macbeth is a prisoner of fate, as foretold in the witches' prophesy at the beginning of the drama. In thrall to hidden forces over which he has no control, Macbeth is doomed to act as he does. This view of leadership could only strengthen Lincoln's wish to believe that the course of the war—and the fate of the nation—were not his to command. He could salve his conscience by allowing at least one part of himself to believe that God—or fate—were in control. Yet he could not be sure and he was desperate to end the killing. During their meeting with Lincoln on the *River Queen*, General Grant and General Sherman predicted at least one more great and bloody battle before the war came to an end. "My God," Lincoln pleaded, "my God! Can't you spare more effusions of blood? We have had so much of it."[30]

By the end of March, Lincoln was cheered by the news that Richmond seemed about to fall and that Grant was finally closing in on Lee. On April 3, federal troops entered Richmond, the Confederate capital, and Lincoln himself visited the city the following day, walking through the streets with his son Tad, attended by only a few guards. Most of the white residents stayed behind closed doors, but newly emancipated slaves came into the streets to catch a glimpse of "Father Abraham." One account, which has been questioned by some historians, has a group of black workmen recognizing the president and falling to their knees to kiss his feet. Embarrassed by this display, Lincoln told them, "Don't kneel to me. That is not right. You must kneel to God only, and thank Him for the liberty you will hereafter enjoy."[31]

When the news of Richmond's fall reached England, Darwin had to admit to his friend Asa Gray that he had been wrong about the North's ability to crush the South and went on to contradict what he had been saying about the war not being worth the cost:

> The grand news of Richmond has stirred me up to write. I congratulate you, & I can do this honestly, as my reason has always urged and & ordered me to be a hearty good wisher for the north, though I could not do so enthusiastically, as I felt we were so hated by you . . . —Well I suppose we shall all be proved utterly wrong who thought that you could not entirely subdue the South. One thing I have always thought that the destruction of Slavery would be well worth a dozen years war.[32]

On April 9, Lee surrendered to Grant at Appomattox Court House, Virginia, effectively ending the conflict, though not all Confederate troops had yet surrendered and there remained concerns about the possibility of ongoing guerilla war. By April 14, Good Friday, Lincoln was more relaxed and happier than he had been at any time since becoming president. That afternoon, he and Mary went for a carriage ride in the country outside Washington and envisioned a pleasant retirement. They would travel to Europe and perhaps to the Holy Land in Palestine and out west to the Rockies and on to California. "Dear husband, you almost startle me with your cheerfulness," Mary laughed, prompting Lincoln to respond, "I have never felt better in my life."[33]

That evening a relieved and exultant president and Mrs. Lincoln attended Ford's Theater in the company of a young couple, Major Henry R. Rathbone and his wife, Clara. The play was an English comedy, *Our*

American Cousin. During the second scene of the third act, Shakespearean actor John Wilkes Booth, a Southerner filled with bitterness
over the recent defeat, crept up behind Lincoln in his private box and
shot him in the head at point-blank range with a small derringer pistol.
Booth jumped down onto the stage but caught his spur on some flags
decorating the box and broke his leg as he hit the boards. Waving a
dagger in the air, Booth shouted, according to some in attendance, "*Sic
Semper Tyrannis*" ("Thus Always to Tyrants," the state motto of Virginia) or, according to others, "The South is avenged." Well acquainted
with Shakespeare's *Julius Caesar*, Booth, in fact, likened himself to
Brutus, who had struck down the Roman tyrant. On April 21, 1865,
Booth, who had not yet been found, wrote in his journal, "[W]ith every
man's hand against me, I am here in despair. And why; For doing what
Brutus was honored for . . . And yet I for striking down a greater tyrant
than they ever knew am looked upon as a common cutthroat." Shakespearean tragedy was with Lincoln to the very end.

Soldiers carried the unconscious president to a boardinghouse
across Tenth Street and placed him on a bed in a "small, narrow" room
at the back of the first floor. The bed was too short for the president, and
they had to lay him across it diagonally. Mary Lincoln became frantic at
one point, leapt up from her chair with a piercing shriek and fell fainting
to the floor. After surviving for nine hours, Lincoln breathed his last at
7:22 on the morning of April 15. Secretary of War Stanton, who had
taken charge that night, said in sad salute, "Now he belongs to the ages."

Lincoln was cut down in his greatest moment of triumph with his
work incomplete, as he had envisioned it in his second inaugural address a
little over a month before: "[To] strive on to finish the work we are in; to
bind up the nation's wounds; to care for him who shall have borne the
battle, and for his widow, and his orphan—to do all which may achieve and
cherish a just, and a lasting peace, among ourselves, and with all nations."[34]

Had Darwin died just several days after publishing *Origin of Species* in November 1859, he would have left his own labors equally unfinished. As it was, he lived for another twenty-three years and had the chance to experiment, gather, elaborate, and defend his work. Although his trials in the aftermath of publishing the *Origin of Species* had been very different from Lincoln's, and may appear insignificant by comparison, he continued to suffer over the revolution he had launched and continued to nurture.

Darwin saw grandeur in his theory, but there was much about *Origin* that threatened contemporary thinking about nature, religion, and the human order in the universe. In many ways, what he was proposing completed the revolution begun by Copernicus, Bruno, Galileo, and others who had insisted that the earth was not in the center of the cosmos. Now Darwin was questioning the primordial belief that humans were wholly different in kind from the rest of creation

Among the threats represented by Darwin was the long period of time necessary for evolution to take place, which contradicted the Genesis account of creation in just six days. Furthermore, many religious people of the day continued to agree with seventeenth-century Archbishop James Ussher that the earth was only six thousand years old, having been created precisely on Sunday, October 23, 4004 BCE.[35] Ussher arrived at this date by correlating Middle Eastern and Mediterranean histories with persons, genealogies, and events in the Bible. In 1701, his chronology was incorporated into an authorized version of the English Bible and came to be accepted as holy writ by many Bible readers, who believed that dates printed on the pages had been part of the Bible from the beginning. To question this chronology was therefore to question the truth of Scripture itself.

Darwin's assertion of natural selection, as opposed to supernatural, or divine creation, also rankled many of the devout. His insistence that random variations, which were selected by nature for their survival value alone, undercut the old "argument from design" of God's existence and benign creative power, regardless of what Darwin would later say about remaining a theist at the time he wrote *Origin*. Evolution was one thing, and many liberal believers could swallow it by saying that God had simply used this law to perfect his creation. But the stark materialism of natural selection, with its assumption that there was no overarching goal or purpose in nature, and with the implication that humans were merely a cosmic accident, was downright frightening.

Darwin did not discuss human evolution in the book, though he did write in the conclusion that "light will be thrown on the origin of man and his history," and anyone who wished to do so could easily extrapolate his arguments to humans.[36] Worse still, if all living things had evolved from a single source, then humans were only different in degree from the rest of living creation and *not in kind*, with a unique conscience and immortal soul made in the image of God, as Christians, Jews, and others had long been taught. If this were true, there seemed nothing to keep humans from acting like beasts. And without the promise of eternal life, there would be no divine sanctions to keep people from misbehaving more than they already did, and nothing to give them hope of a better life beyond the grave.

Darwin's old Cambridge professor, Adam Sedgwick, was one who shared these fears with Darwin after reading *Origin of Species* when it came out in November 1859: "I have read your book with more pain than pleasure.... There is a moral or metaphysical part of nature as well as a physical. A man who denies this is deep in the mire of folly.... You have ignored this link.... Were it possible (which thank God it is not) to break it, humanity in my mind, would suffer a damage that might brutalize it—& sink the human race into a lower grade of degradation than any into which it has fallen since its written records tell us of its history."[37] Darwin responded two days later by saying that he had expected Sedgwick's disapproval, but he did not answer any of his objections. For decades, Sedgwick's fears about Darwin's materialism and the effect that it would have on morality would lay at the heart of so many attempts to dismiss natural selection, or at least to infuse the process with some sort of divine guidance or intent.

Finally there was nothing to keep radical thinkers and godless revolutionaries from using Darwin's theory to undermine the social hierarchy of church and state in the British Isles. If God did not exist, there was no reason to have an established Church of England or any justification, based on religious concepts of hierarchy, for monarchy and aristocracy. In fact, fears that his theory might be used to destabilize society had been one of the reasons that Darwin hesitated to publish for so long.

Darwin had also held back from going public because he feared rejection and ridicule from the scientific establishment, a fear that caused him to gather as much evidence as possible and to conduct as many experiments as he could. These were realistic concerns, since some scientists turned out to be his most formidable critics. One of these was Britain's highly respected anatomist, Richard Owen, who had examined, categorized, and placed into a wider context the fossilized bones that Darwin had sent back from the *Beagle* a quarter century before. Now Owen feared that belief in evolution would brutalize humankind. He long argued that God had engaged in continuous acts of creation over time that could explain the changes in the fossil record. Even Darwin's long-time friend and mentor, Charles Lyell, balked at applying natural selection to human beings and for essentially the same reason as Owen—that it would debase humanity—even though Darwin had stopped short in *Origin* of specifically applying his theory to humans.

As always, Darwin shrank from taking on his critics personally and he willingly allowed Huxley to take up the cudgel for him. Huxley went after Owen in the *Times* at the end of December and in the liberal *Westminster Review* the following April, where he claimed that "man might be a transmuted ape." But Huxley's most memorable salvos came in an exchange with Bishop Samuel Wilberforce, son of the famous British abolitionist, William Wilberforce. The verbal fireworks took place at a meeting of the British Association for the Advancement of Science, held at Oxford in June 1860 before a crowd of seven hundred faculty, students, and members of the educated public. Darwin had thought of attending, but a sick stomach gave him an excuse to stay home.

The organizers of the meeting had set aside a session for the life sciences, with a focus on evolution. The main speaker on June 30 was John W. Draper, originally from Liverpool and now a professor at New York University. His topic was "The Intellectual Development of Europe, Considered with Reference to the Views of Mr. Darwin." Besides Wilberforce, the others expected to comment on Draper's presentation were Richard Owen, Thomas Huxley, and Joseph Hooker. Wilberforce was a conservative Anglican as well as the Bishop of Oxford who accepted the Genesis story of creation. His nickname was "Soapy Sam" because of his slippery rhetorical ability to turn any debate in his own favor and because he had a habit of wringing his hands while speaking, as if rinsing off soapsuds.

Wilberforce could be counted on to criticize Darwin—as could Owen. Huxley and Hooker, of course, would stand up for their friend. Owen had spent the previous night at the Wilberforce residence and probably had armed the bishop with several arguments against Darwin's theory; he was expected to chair the climatic Saturday morning session. In fact, for unexplained reasons, Owen did not attend the session. Taking his place in the chair was Darwin's old Cambridge professor, the Reverend Robert Stevens Henslow.

At the end of Draper's two-hour presentation, Wilberforce thought he would inject a note of humor. Turning to Huxley, he reportedly asked him whether it was on his grandfather's or grandmother's side of the family that he had descended from an ape. Huxley quickly flung the bishop's words back at him, to the delight of the audience: "If then, said I, the question is put to me would I rather have a miserable ape for a grandfather or a man highly endowed by nature and possessed of great means & influence & yet who employs these facilities & that influence for the mere purpose of introducing ridicule into a grave scientific discussion I unhesitatingly affirm my preference for the ape."[38]

In fact, Huxley and Wilberforce had not been part of a "grave scientific discussion" that day but participants in a popular program for the majority of the audience, who were not scientists and who came for the intellectual enjoyment and self-improvement that were the hallmarks of these British Association meetings. More than anything else, the exchange between Huxley and Wilberforce dramatized the deepening fault lines between science and religion, and as the years passed, the Oxford contest was blown up in public opinion as an epic struggle between two giants battling for their respective intellectual worlds. At the time, however, there seemed no real winner, and each combatant believed he had bested the other.

A little over two years before, at a meeting of the Harvard Science Club in April 1858, and a full year and a half before the publication of *Origin of Species*, Darwin's American friend Asa Gray had thrown down the gauntlet, not against a clergyman, but against the great Louis Agassiz, his colleague on the Harvard College faculty. Agassiz was a confirmed catastrophist, who referred to glaciers as "God's great plows." (In fact, Agassiz is credited with discovering the impact of glaciers on the earth's surface.) He insisted that each species had been specially created and was an implacable foe of evolution, as Gray well knew. To irritate Agassiz, Gray decided to use the college's science club to present Darwin's theory of natural selection to an American audience for the first time, based on the 1857 outline that Darwin had sent to him. In the winter of 1860–61, Gray and Agassiz, two titans of American science, debated each other before a series of packed audiences in Boston, arguing whether species were divine constructs or if they were the result of purely natural forces and had evolved over time.[39]

The Agassiz–Gray debates were widely reported in the American press, but Abraham Lincoln may well have been too preoccupied by his recent election as president to pay any attention to them, or to take note of the May 1860 American publication of *Origin of Species*, which was published the same month he received the Republican nomination. Even if Lincoln never lifted the cover of *Origin*, he had long been fascinated with the subject of evolution according to Herndon, who reported that a friend in Springfield had given his partner a copy of *Vestiges of Creation*, first published in the United States in 1845. According to Herndon, Chambers's book "interested [Lincoln] so much that he read it through. The volume was published in Edinburgh, and undertook to demonstrate the doctrine of development or evolution. The treatise interested him greatly, and he was deeply impressed with the notion of the so-called 'universal law'—evolution; he did not extend greatly his researches, but by continued thinking in a single channel seemed to grow into a warm advocate of the new doctrine."[40] Herndon had also purchased various works by Darwin. There can be little doubt that Lincoln would have been fascinated by the *Origin of Species*.

As a universal law, evolution would have reinforced Lincoln's belief in the Doctrine of Necessity and his continuing acceptance of a creator God, though not of the divinity of Christ or any set of creeds. Lincoln's earlier law partner, John T. Stuart, said of him, "He was an avowed and open infidel . . . and sometimes bordered on atheism. . . . Lincoln always denied that Jesus was the Christ of God—denied that Jesus was the son of God as understood and maintained by the Christian Church." Judge David Davis, with whom Lincoln traveled on the judicial circuit, told Herndon that Lincoln "had no faith, in the Christian sense of the term—had faith in laws, principles, causes and effects." Another associate related that Lincoln "believed in a Creator of all things. . . . A reason he gave for his belief was that in view of the order and harmony of all nature which we behold, it would have been more miraculous to have come about by chance than to have been created and arranged by some great thinking power."[41] William Paley could not have said it better.

Although Darwin started out in life as a believer, his faith had become weaker over the years, and by the end of his life it had largely disappeared.[42] Darwin took specific issue with American supporter Asa Gray's belief in some sort of intelligent design. Gray accepted the reality of evolution, as shown in his writings and his many arguments with Louis Agassiz. However, unlike Darwin, Gray believed that the whole process of evolution should be seen as the unfolding of a divine plan. In response to Gray's query about what would make his friend believe in design, Darwin answered politely but sarcastically, "If I saw an angel come down to teach us good, & I was convinced from others seeing him, that I was not mad, I shd. believe in design."[43]

A few months later, Darwin offered Gray a more scientific answer, arguing that the existence of rudimentary organs in humans, which served no purpose, would seem to rule out some sort of divine intension: "With respect to Design, I feel more inclined to show a white flag than to fire my usual long-range shot. . . . If anything is designed, certainly man must be; one's inner consciousness' (though a false guide) tells one so; yet I cannot admit that man's rudimentary mammae; bladder drained as if he went on four legs; & pug nose were designed. If I was to say that I believe this, I should say it in the same incredible manner as the orthodox believe the Trinity in Unity."[44] Darwin was also disgusted over the many attempts by others to reconcile his theory with the Genesis account of creation. To a correspondent he exclaimed, "I am weary of all these various attempts to reconcile, what I believe to be irreconcilable."[45]

Although Darwin seemed very self-assured in his comments about science and religion, he fell into another bout of debilitating sickness. By the end of 1863, he was so ill that Emma had to maintain his correspondence with Hooker. Excusing Charles from not writing, she explained to him, "One day is a little better and one a little worse but I cannot say that he makes progress at present. He stays in his bed room and gets frequently in and out of bed and occasionally goes down stairs for a very short time, but he can only stand very short visits even of the boys. When not very uncomfortable his spirits are wonderfully good, but I am afraid he may remain just as he is very long before there is a struggle in his constitution and that the sickness is conquered."[46]

Despite feeling wretched much of the time, Darwin was able to take up his experiments again and often found some peace of mind through them. His work with orchids convinced him that their flowers had developed intricate forms to ensure cross-pollination. In his *On the Various Contrivances by which British and Foreign Orchids are Fertilized by Insects*, published in May 1862, he demonstrated how the structure of orchids had eliminated self-fertilization and come to depend on insects to carry pollen from plant to plant, thereby producing numerous variations that were conducive to natural selection.

In January 1868, Darwin published another book he had been working on for years: *The Variations of Animals and Plants under Domestication*. It was an elaboration of the comparisons he had made in *Origin* between the conscious selections of breeders and the process of natural selection. In this work, he also came up with a "provisional hypothesis or speculation" to explain the process of biological inheritance, which he called pangenesis. According to this idea, every cell in the body contributed tiny particles called "gemmules" that circulated throughout the system and congregated in the reproductive organs, and in this way passed parental characteristics down to the next generation. Darwin was wrong about this and he did not live to see a scientific explanation of heredity, but his term *pangenesis*, later foreshortened, became the origin of the word *gene*.

Meanwhile Darwin was collecting everything he could find on human evolution, a subject about which he had hinted though not explored in *Origin*, but which others had readily taken up. In 1862 Huxley came out with a book titled *Zoological Evidences as to Man's Place in Nature*, and the following year Lyell published his *Antiquity of Man*. Although Lyell agreed with the mounting evidence from the fossil record that humankind was far older than anyone had imagined until recently, he still could not bring himself to accept the proposition that modern humans were merely the transmuted descendants of some "primitive brute." Darwin was very disappointed with Lyell's reservations and fell into one of his violent vomiting spells as he read *Antiquity*. He also suffered from terrible headaches and was so weak that he could not walk even a hundred yards. Lyell's continued insistence on some sort of divine intervention in the creation of humankind could only have reminded Darwin of how far he had gone in challenging orthodox views.

Also weighing in on the subject of human evolution was Alfred Wallace, who had finally returned to England from Malaya. In May 1864, Wallace delivered a paper before the Anthropological Society, a racist, proslavery organization that Darwin and his supporters detested. Wallace himself did not subscribe to their views and seemed to have simply used the group as a platform for his own ideas about human evolution, which were increasingly socialist in nature. The title of his paper was "The Origin of Human Races from the Theory of Natural Selection."

Finally, in 1871, Darwin published his own findings about human evolution, titling his book *The Descent of Man and Selection in Relation to Sex*. He began by saying that he had collected notes on human origins over the years with no intention to publish anything on the subject, since he thought that this would "only add to the prejudices against my views." But because of the increasing number of younger naturalists around the world who now admitted that "species are the modified descendants of other species," he believed that the time had come for him to speak out.[47]

Darwin noted that anatomists had long realized that humans were generally constructed along the same lines as other mammals: "All the bones in his skeleton can be compared with corresponding bones in a monkey, bat, or seal. So it is with his muscles, nerves, blood-vessels and internal viscera."[48] He added that the reproductive process in all mammals is "strikingly the same," and that embryos at a very early stage of development are almost identical among all vertebrates. Rudimentary parts of the human body, such as the tailbone, likewise suggested connections with other mammals.

As in the *Origin*, Darwin pointed in *Descent* to the variations among humans and the fact that, as Malthus observed, they were capable of doubling their populations under favorable conditions in as little as twenty-five years. Under these circumstances nature had acted to select individuals with advantageous traits that allowed them to survive longer than others and to reproduce, passing these traits along to their offspring. The two most important human traits developed by this process were the "intellectual powers, through which [humankind] has formed for himself weapons, tools, &c, . . . and, secondly, by his social qualities which lead him to give and receive aid from his fellow man."[49]

Cooperation was an important ingredient in human evolution, as it was in many other animal species. In Darwin's words, "With those animals which live permanently in a body, the social instincts are ever present and persistent. Such animals are always ready to utter the danger-signal, to defend the community, and to give aid to their fellows in accordance with their habits. . . . So it is with ourselves. A man who possessed no trace of such feelings would be an unnatural monster."[50] Those who later heaped blame on Darwin for emphasizing ruthless competition above all other human traits should have paid more attention to his writings on cooperation.

Although Darwin admitted that human intellectual powers were superior to all the other mammals, they were superior only in degree—and not in kind. "As man possesses the same senses as the lower animals," he wrote, "his fundamental intuitions must be the same. Man also has some few instincts in common [with the lower animals], as that of self-preservation, sexual love, the love of the mother for her new-born offspring, the desire possessed by the latter to suck, and so forth."[51]

Animals and humans also shared many similar emotions, according to Darwin: "The lower animals, like man, manifestly feel pleasure and pain, happiness and misery. Happiness is never better exhibited than by young animals, such as puppies, kittens, lambs, &c., when playing together, like our own children." He added that fear produced similar reactions in humans and in animals, "causing the muscles to tremble, the heart to palpitate, the sphincters to be relaxed, and the hair to stand on end."[52] Jealousy, too, was a shared emotion: "Every one has seen how jealous a dog is of his master's affection, if lavished on any other creature; and I have observed the same fact with monkeys."[53]

Darwin also believed that animals "possess some power of reasoning. Animals may constantly be seen to pause, to deliberate, and resolve."[54] This reasoning ability allowed chimpanzees in the natural state to use a stone to crack open fruits, and in captivity it allowed trainers to teach monkeys how to use a stick as a lever to open a box.

Darwin went on to give numerous examples of social cooperation among animals. Insects formed large colonies and worked together to build hives and collect food; many of the higher animals warned each other of danger; and many species hunted together in packs. Animals also formed herds for mutual self-protection. These realities, as well as similarities in thought patterns and emotions, led Darwin to conclude that "the difference in mind between man and the higher animals, great as it is, certainly is one of degree and not of kind."[55] Of course, this statement flew in the face of age-old Judeo-Christian belief, though Darwin was in no danger of being punished as a heretic in mid-nineteenth-century Britain.

Darwin devoted a large amount of space in *Descent* to what he called sexual selection, explaining how sexual reproduction allowed the traits of two individuals to combine for maximum variation, an observation that he now made for humans as well as for other animals. Briefly put, any advantages in mating or in nurturing the young would be passed on to subsequent generations. In Darwin's words, "for those individuals which generated or nourished their offspring best, would have . . . the greatest number to inherit their superiority; whilst those which generated or nourished their offspring badly, would leave but few to inherit their weak powers."[56] The often fierce competition among males for mates also helped to ensure that the strongest would be able to pass on their fitter characteristics: "So it appears that the strongest and most vigorous males . . . have prevailed under nature, and have led to the improvement of the natural breed or species."[57]

What Darwin wrote about the so-called races of man is of special interest because of how some "social Darwinists" would later use evolutionary theories to argue for the natural inferiority of some races and the dominance of others. In reality, Darwin dismissed the claim, made by some in his time, that the different races were separate human species by observing that individuals of different races could and did reproduce across so-called racial lines, something that members of separate species generally could not do. Furthermore, if all humans had "descended from a single primitive stock," as Darwin believed they did, it would not make sense to claim separate species status for each race.[58] Most telling for Darwin was the fact that individuals of different races resembled each other in physical characteristics more than not.

Because Darwin had long concluded that living animals were closely related to the extinct species of a region, he surmised that the first humans had come from Africa: "It is therefore probable that Africa was formerly inhabited by extinct apes closely allied to the gorilla and chimpanzee: and as these two species are now man's nearest allies, it is somewhat more probable that our early progenitors lived on the African continent than elsewhere."[59] Decades later, both the fossil and DNA evidence would prove him right in his belief that human life had begun in Africa.

Darwin also rejected the idea of separate human species because of the "mental similarity" and the "close similarity between the men of all races in tastes, dispositions and habits."[60] This did not mean that more "civilized" peoples did not enjoy advantages over more "primitive" groups, such as when Europeans came in contact with the aborigines of Australia, but this appeared to Darwin to have more to do with broad environmental conditions than with any innate biological differences. For example, when Europeans came into contact with the native peoples of the Americas or with the aborigines of Australia, who had been isolated from the rest of the world, they unintentionally spread diseases that decimated local populations with no immunities to them. Still, Darwin had no doubt, like virtually all his contemporaries, that white Europeans were superior to others. Abraham Lincoln felt the same, and he also shared Darwin's abhorrence of slavery and racial cruelty. Such conclusions, however qualified by Darwin, would offer aid and comfort to those who believed that racial inferiority was genuine and a natural product of evolution.

Toward the end of *Descent*, Darwin observed that his conclusions about human evolution would be "highly distasteful" to many people who would not want "to acknowledge that the blood of some more humble creature flows in [their] veins." Having heard stories about the noble actions of so-called lower animals, Darwin had no such qualms: "for my own part I would as soon be descended from that heroic little monkey, who braved his dreaded enemy in order to save the life of his keeper, or from that old baboon, who descending from the mountains, carried away in triumph his young comrade from a crowd of astonished dogs—as from a savage [human being] who delights to torture his enemies."[61]

Nowhere, of course, did Darwin assert that humans had come from monkeys. What he said was that monkeys and humans had descended from a common ancestor. The general public would frequently fail to make this distinction, and in the popular imagination Darwin's concept of human evolution simply became the "monkey theory." Cartoonists had great fun with the image, often depicting Darwin himself as half man/half monkey.

Surprisingly, the reactions to *Descent* were milder than what Darwin anticipated. Most of the reviewers agreed to some form of evolution, but a number of them insisted that humans had somehow been separately endowed with a conscience and that a higher power had lifted them above the brutes. It helped that there had already been plenty of controversy over the implications of natural selection for humans ever since the publication of *Origin* a dozen years earlier, even though Darwin himself had only hinted at the subject in the earlier book. In a sense, the subject of human evolution was old news.

Predictably, Alfred Wallace joined the critics who insisted that the human moral dimension must have had some external source and was not a mere product of the struggle for existence. In his review of *Descent*, Wallace wrote, however politely: "[Man's] absolute erectness of posture, the completeness of his nudity, the harmonious perfection of his hands, the almost infinite capacities of his brain, constitute a series of correlated advances too great to be accounted for by the struggle for existence of an isolated group of apes in a limited area."[62]

Far less polite and far more irritating for Darwin was the review by St. George Mivart, a brilliant and once warm supporter of Darwin and *Origin* when the book first appeared. As a convert to Roman Catholicism, Mivart came to have serious misgivings about human evolution, and in his review of *Descent*, he castigated Darwin on a number of issues. He argued that complex organs like the eye could not have evolved through a vast series of intermediate stages, each one of which had to be an improvement on the one before, an objection that has been repeated by anti-Darwinists ever since. He also castigated Darwin for undermining the religious beliefs of even well-educated people. Far worse, Darwin's theories would unsettle "our half-educated masses." Without belief in a supernatural soul, people would feel free to do whatever they liked, resulting in moral anarchy.[63]

Darwin felt betrayed by Mivart's criticisms and he fought back on many fronts, as did supporters like Huxley. Darwin himself responded by adding a whole new chapter to his sixth edition of *Origin*, where he toned down some aspects of natural selection by embracing certain

Lamarckian ideas, especially the mechanisms of use and disuse. In the end, Mivart was the real loser. Excommunicated by Darwin, Huxley, and their crowd from the circle of "respectable scientists," he was also excommunicated by the Catholic Church for trying to reconcile evolution with Roman theology.

Mivart's objections might be dismissed as unscientific, but such a charge could not be laid at the feet of William Thompson (later raised to the peerage as Lord Kelvin), who invented the science of thermodynamics. Unaware of radioactivity, Thompson calculated that the earth would have cooled down and solidified enough to support life only one hundred million years ago, not the hundreds of millions of years that Darwin believed was necessary to bring about evolution through natural selection. It turned out that Thompson was wrong, but his great stature as a physicist gave ammunition to Darwin's critics, and made it difficult for him to counter what Thompson was saying. Darwin's response, once again, was to endorse Lamarckian use and disuse proposals that would have the effect of speeding up the evolutionary process.

In reality, Thompson was not just an objective scientist with no axes to grind. He was a devout Scottish Presbyterian who opposed evolution and the support it received from uniformitarian geologists like Lyell. For years Thompson had been objecting to such theories and he now turned his criticisms against Darwin, though he was careful to couch them in scientific terms.

Even as *Descent* was going through the press, Darwin was hard at work on a book called *Expression of Emotions in Man and Animals*, published in 1872. This was the culmination of observations and studies that he had begun as far back as 1839 when taking notes on the behavior of his first son, William, whose expressions as an infant, his father believed, could not have been learned and must be inherited instincts. This led Darwin to conclude "that the most complex and fine shades of expression must all have had a gradual and natural origin."[64] The new book greatly expanded the observations about expressions Darwin had made in *Descent*. Again, its main purpose was to demonstrate the many links between animals and humans and, as such, to advance his argument for human evolution. In researching *Expression*, Darwin relied heavily on photographs, and his publication was one of the first to include photographic images. The book was an immediate success, selling over nine thousand copies in the first four months, the greatest initial sale of any Darwin title.

Darwin considered *Expression* to be the last of a trilogy on evolution, the other two being *Origin of Species* and *Descent of Man*. Now he felt free to indulge his curiosity in several areas, which resulted in a spate of books during the last ten years of his life: *Insectivorous Plants* (1875), *Effects of Cross and Self Fertilization in the Vegetable Kingdom* (1876), a new and enlarged edition of *Fertilization of Orchids* (1877), the *Different Forms of Flowers on Plants of the Same Species* (1877), *Power of Movement in Plants* (1880), and *The Formation of Vegetable Mould through the Action of Worms* (1881). He researched these books through his vast network of correspondents, along with help from family members and friends who shared information and sent him specimens. He also carried out experiments in his own greenhouse and outdoor planting beds. Besides satisfying his curiosity, the work continued to contribute structure for his days and a partial defense against related physical and nervous disorders. With his evolution tracts behind him, he could occupy himself with uncontroversial studies that still fulfilled his need to be busy. Work, he often said, made him feel like himself—to feel alive. As with Lincoln, Darwin's work had become a prime reason for living.

However therapeutic these researches were for Darwin personally, they did give him some further proof of evolution. The fact that the leaves of plants moved during the day to seek the light or that insect-eating plants actually "reached out" to catch or enfold their prey allowed him to claim that the so-called higher and lower forms of life shared many characteristics—and, again, that humans were only different in degree rather than in kind from the rest of the living world. "It has always pleased me," he wrote, "to exalt plants in the scale of organized beings."[65] The experiments on cross- and self-fertilization reinforced his conclusions about sexual selection as one of the most important factors in the process of evolution, finding again and again that crossing resulted in more vigorous plants. These conclusions also contributed to a growing worry about first-cousin marriages, since several of his children had suffered from illnesses very much like his own

By the 1870s, Darwin was a famous man. In photographs of the time, he looks like a benign sage, with gentle, deep-set eyes, a flowing white beard, and furrowed brow. He received letters from all over the world. Some of them contained helpful ideas and information and others harebrained and sometimes humorous observations and suggestions from amateur readers who thought they might somehow contribute to the great man's work. Darwin tried to answer as many letters as he could, but he finally became so inundated that he agreed to have his son Francis serve as a secretary, as well as a research assistant.

In 1873 Karl Marx, who had long lived in England, sent Darwin a copy of his *Das Kapital*, with the inscription "Mr. Charles Darwin on the part of his sincere admirer Karl Marx." Marx believed that Darwin's theory of natural selection reinforced his own materialistic views of society and social change. His revolutionary ideas would have as much impact during the next century as Darwin's, but Marx's gift remained in the study at Down House, its pages uncut and unread, partly because Darwin always had to struggle to read German and also because what Marx had to say was of little interest to him. Still, he was flattered by the gift and wrote back, "Though our studies have been so different, I believe that we both earnestly desire the extension of knowledge & that this in the long run is sure to add to the happiness of mankind."[66] Although Darwin praised Marx in this letter, he cannot be blamed for failing to foresee the evil that would be done in Marx's name, as some of his later detractors would charge.

There was also a mounting stream of visitors to Down House, some unannounced and quite unwelcome. Many were simply turned away at the door. When Darwin felt he had to receive certain callers, he would typically spend a few minutes with them and then make excuses about having to return to his work, attend to some household or family matter, or rest because he was feeling unwell. This was very different from Lincoln's device of telling stories to avoid serious conversation with unwanted visitors, but Darwin's method was just as effective.

A most welcome visitor to Down House was the Liberal prime minister William Gladstone, who came in March 1877. Both Charles and Emma were devoted to the Liberal Party (which had succeeded the Whigs) and were deeply honored by the visit, which made them feel a personal connection to their country's politics at the highest level. The fact that Gladstone was a devout Christian who had never wavered from church teachings signaled that Darwin was now respected for his pathbreaking scientific work and not necessarily for the most controversial implications of his theories.

Darwin clearly deserved a knighthood for his accomplishments, and the government had proposed such an honor back in 1859. That was the same year *Origin* came out, and Queen Victoria's ecclesiastical advisers, including Bishop Wilberforce, had opposed it, saying that the gesture would be taken as approval of Darwin's unorthodox views. Eleven years later, in 1870, as Darwin was working hard to complete the *Descent of Man*, he was both delighted and surprised to be offered an honorary degree of Doctor of Laws (LLD) from ultra-orthodox Oxford University, where the famous debate between Huxley and Bishop Wilberforce had taken place a decade earlier. Huxley had also been nominated for a degree, but the faculty had angrily turned it down. Although Darwin's nomination was approved, there had been considerable opposition among some members. After learning the details from Huxley, Darwin declined the degree, with the excuse that he was too ill to travel to Oxford to receive it.

His own alma mater, Cambridge, which was more dedicated to science than Oxford and less insistent on religious orthodoxy, granted Darwin an honorary degree of Doctor of Laws (LLD) with virtually no dissent from the faculty. His son George, who was then a student at the university, wrote to him directly about the overwhelmingly positive vote. He received the degree at a special ceremony on November 17, 1877, held in the university's grand, neoclassical Senate House. When Darwin appeared in his crimson robes and mortarboard, some students dangled from the ceiling a stuffed monkey wearing an identical academic costume, much to Darwin's amusement, as the audience roared its approval. He enjoyed the whole event, including the receptions in his honor, the tours of new campus buildings, and the luncheon that his son George hosted for him at Trinity College.

Emma had worried that Charles could not withstand the strain of the degree festivities, but he came through very well. In truth, his health seemed better than before, probably because he was now out from under the pressure of worrying about how his work on evolution would be received and could enjoy his continuing and far less controversial research. Still, whenever he appeared to be working too hard, Emma whisked him off on some vacation. Beginning in 1872, she arranged for them to be in London for the month of January, where they could visit Charles's brother Eras. The first year they rented a house, but beginning in 1873 they stayed with their married daughter Henrietta and her husband, who had moved to the city. These forays to London allowed Darwin to visit old friends such as Lyell, Huxley, and Hooker.

Back at Down House, their lives were enlivened by a first grandchild, a boy named Bernard, born to son Francis and his wife, Amy, in September 1876. As too often happened in those days, Amy contracted a fever and died several days after giving birth. A grief-stricken Francis and the baby moved in with his parents, who secured a nanny and made every arrangement for their son and grandson to feel comfortable and welcome. Despite the tragedy, Charles and Emma were both delighted to have a baby in the house again and doted on little Bernard. It was then that Charles enlisted Francis as his assistant, partly to help him over his grief and also because he really needed him.

The birth of his grandchild and the aging of his own children set Darwin to thinking about leaving a record of his life for all of them to have when he was gone. In this frame of mind he started writing in May 1876 what became his *Autobiography*. As time went by, he would add paragraphs as various memories came to mind, completing the work during the summer of 1881. He enjoyed the process immensely, in part because he did not have to look up sources and carefully check his facts. Since he did not intend that his autobiography would ever be published, he felt free to be as personal as he wanted about his life and those associated with it. He was particularly frank about his lack of religious faith and compared belief to a sort of primitive instinct, not unlike a monkey's "instinctive fear and hatred of a snake."[67]

Although writing about himself, conducting enjoyable experiments, and receiving meaningful honors allowed Darwin to find a sense of peace and freedom from the worst of the debilitating sickness that had plagued him in the past, he began to receive warnings of a genuine life-threatening illness. One day at home in August 1873, he had what Emma called "a fit," and for twelve hours, he temporarily lost his memory and could not move. These were all symptoms of a mild stroke, but he soon recovered. Another warning came in June 1881, while vacationing in the Lake District, when climbing up some low hills caused him to see spots before his eyes and he almost fainted. The doctor's diagnosis was angina pectoris, or congestive heart disease. In December of the same year he had another heart attack while attempting to pay a call on a friend in London. Back home, he suffered attacks in February and March. He died on April 19, 1882, after suffering terrible pain for three and a half days, passing away in his own bed attended by his beloved family. Almost exactly seventeen years before, his fellow birthday revolutionary had met a violent end and had died without regaining consciousness. Unlike Lincoln, Darwin had had a chance to come to terms with his own life amid the comfortable surroundings of a place he had loved for so many years. It can never be known if Lincoln could have achieved the same degree of peace and contentment, despite the happiness he had felt on that afternoon before his death.

Both Abraham Lincoln and Charles Darwin had unleashed revolutions as broad and as deep as anyone in history. Lincoln had used his ideas and words to bring about a new birth of freedom, but he had not shrunk from using overpowering violence to realize his second American revolution. Darwin's revolution had provoked a war of words, but the implications of what he was saying had the power to threaten some of the oldest and most cherished beliefs about religion, the nature of humanity, and the connections among all life forms. Neither man could escape knowing about the trials that others experienced because of their actions. After suffering from what he described as the torments of the damned, Lincoln himself became a casualty of war, while Darwin was sickened by publishing ideas that he knew would horrify others. The revolutions that they spawned would not end with their deaths but would continue to ferment for generations to come and with implications that could not yet be foreseen.

NOTES

1. Darwin wrote, "Even as a school-boy I took intense delight in Shakespeare, especially in the historical plays. . . . I have tried lately to read Shakespeare, and found it so intolerantly dull that it nauseated me." Nora Barlow, ed., *The Autobiography of Charles Darwin, 1809–1882* (New York: W. W. Norton, 1993), p. 13.

2. Lincoln to Horace Greeley, August 22, 1862, *The Collected Works of Abraham Lincoln*, edited by Roy P. Basler et al. (New Brunswick, NJ: Rutgers University Press, 1953), 5:388–89.

3. Quoted in David Herbert Donald, *Lincoln* (New York: Quadrangle Books, 1995), p. 354.

4. These quotes are from Michael Burlingame, *The Inner World of Abraham Lincoln* (Urbana: University of Illinois Press, 1994), pp. 104–105.

5. R. J. M. Blackett, *Divided Hearts: Britain and the American Civil War* (Baton Rouge: Louisiana State University Press, 2001), p. 7.

6. On this subject, see Alfred Grant, *The American Civil War and the British Press* (Jefferson, NC: McFarland and Company, 2000); Sheldon Vanauken, *The Glittering Illusion: English Sympathy for the Southern Confederacy* (Worthing, UK: Churchman Publishing, 1988) and Blackett, *Divided Hearts.*

7. For more context on the Darwin–Gray exchange of opinions during the Civil War, see A. Hunter Dupree, *Asa Gray: American Botanist, Friend of Darwin* (Baltimore, MD: Johns Hopkins University Press, 1988), pp. 307–31.

8. Darwin to Gray, June 5, 1861, *The Correspondence of Charles Darwin* (Cambridge: Cambridge University Press, 1985–[2005]), 9:163.

9. Darwin to Gray, July 21, 1861, *Correspondence of Charles Darwin*, 9:214.

10. Darwin to Gray, September 17, 1861, *Correspondence of Charles Darwin*, 9:266.

11. Darwin to Gray, December 11, 1861, *Correspondence of Charles Darwin*, 9:368.

12. Darwin to Hooker, January 16, 1862, *Correspondence of Charles Darwin*, 10:25.

13. Gray to Darwin, December 31, 1861, *Correspondence of Charles Darwin*, 9:383–84.

14. Hooker to Darwin, January 19, 1862, *Correspondence of Charles Darwin*, 10:29.

15. Darwin to Hooker, December 24, 1862, *Correspondence of Charles Darwin*, 10:625.

16. Darwin to Gray, October 16, 1862, *Correspondence of Charles Darwin*, 10:471.

17. Gray to Darwin, November 10, 1862, *Correspondence of Charles Darwin*, 10:512.

18. Darwin to Gray, January 22, 1862, *Correspondence of Charles Darwin*, 10:41.

19. Darwin to Gray, October 16, 1862, *Correspondence of Charles Darwin*, 10:471.

20. See Henry Mayer, *All on Fire: William Lloyd Garrison and the Abolition of Slavery* (New York: St. Martin's Press, 1998), pp. 452, 524–25.

21. Gray to Darwin, February 18, 1862, *Correspondence of Charles Darwin*, 10:86–87.

22. Darwin to Gray, June 10, 1862, *Correspondence of Charles Darwin*, 10:241.

23. Darwin to Gray, April 21, 1862, *Correspondence of Charles Darwin*, 10:163.

24. Gray to Darwin, September 22, 1862, *Correspondence of Charles Darwin*, 10:429.

25. Darwin to Gray, January 19, 1863, *Correspondence of Charles Darwin*, 11:56.

26. Gray to Darwin, February 16, 1864, *Correspondence of Charles Darwin*, 12:48.

27. Lincoln, "Address at the Dedication of the Cemetery at Gettysburg," final text (November 19, 1863), *Collected Works of Abraham Lincoln*, 7:23.

28. Lincoln, "Second Inaugural Address" (March 4, 1865), *Collected Works of Abraham Lincoln*, 8:332–33.

29. Lincoln to James H. Hackett, August 17, 1863, *Collected Works of Abraham Lincoln*, 6:392.

30. Quoted in Jay Winik, *April 1865: The Month That Saved America* (New York: HarperCollins, 2001), p. 67.

31. Quoted in Donald, *Lincoln*, p. 576.

32. Darwin to Gray, April 19, 1865, *Correspondence of Charles Darwin*, 13:125.

33. Quoted in Winik, *April 1865*, p. 220.

34. Lincoln, "Second Inaugural Address," *Collected Works of Abraham Lincoln*, 8:333.

35. On Ussher's chronology and the whole matter of geological time, see Jack Repcheck, *The Man Who Found Time: James Hutton and the Discovery of the Earth's Antiquity* (Cambridge, MA: Perseus Publishing, 2003), especially pp. 42–43.

36. Darwin, *Origin of Species: A Facsimile of the First Edition* (Cambridge, MA: Harvard University Press, 1964), p. 488.

37. Adam Sedgwick to Darwin, November 24, *Correspondence of Charles Darwin*, 7:397.

38. Thomas Huxley, quoted in Adrian Desmond and James Moore, *Darwin: The Life of a Tormented Evolutionist* (New York: Warner Books, 1991), p. 497.

39. Dupree, *Asa Gray*, pp. 252–53, 285–88.

40. William H. Herndon, *Herndon's Life of Lincoln* (New York: Da Capo Press, 1983), p. 354.

41. Ibid., p. 356.

42. Barlow, *Autobiography of Charles Darwin*, pp. 92–93.

43. Darwin to Gray, September 17, 1861, *Correspondence of Charles Darwin*, 9:267.

44. Darwin to Gray, December 11, 1861, *Correspondence of Charles Darwin*, 9:369.

45. Darwin to Bartholomew Sullivan, May 24, 1861, *Correspondence of Charles Darwin*, 9:138.

46. Emma Darwin to Hooker, December 26, 1863, Ms Box 115: 214:4359 in the Darwin Papers at the Cambridge University Library.

47. Charles Darwin, *The Descent of Man and Selection in Relation to Sex* (New York: Modern Library, n.d.), p. 389.

48. Ibid., pp. 395–96.

49. Ibid., p. 444.

50. Ibid., p. 483.

51. Ibid., p. 446.

52. Ibid., p. 448.

53. Ibid., p. 450.

54. Ibid., p. 453.

55. Ibid., p. 494.

56. Ibid., pp. 568–69.

57. Ibid., p. 570.

58. Ibid., p. 537.

59. Ibid., p. 520.

60. Ibid., 539.

61. Ibid., p. 919.

62. Alfred Russell Wallace, review of *The Descent of Man*, in *Academy* (December 1, 1871): 183.

63. Quoted in Desmond and Moore, *Darwin*, p. 583.

64. Barlow, *Autobiography of Charles Darwin*, pp. 131–32.

65. Ibid., p. 135.

66. Quoted in Janet Browne, *Charles Darwin: The Power of Place* (Princeton, NJ: Princeton University Press, 2002), p. 403.

67. Barlow, *Autobiography of Charles Darwin*, p. 93.

Chapter 8

AFTERLIVES

[Do] not to forget [that] there is a skeleton in every house.
— William Herndon

Mr. Darwin has taught many readers how to think of God working in nature during long periods of time, not how to think of nature as excluding God.
— H. P. Liddon, canon residentiary
at St. Paul's Cathedral, London

*D*arwin's agnosticism and Lincoln's unorthodox views were no obstacles to the churches and religious establishments that rushed to embrace them in death. While many believers would never accept Darwin's ideas, other religious men and women grappled with the implications of natural selection and believed they could reconcile his science with their faith. Lincoln's religious beliefs, which were less well known and then largely forgotten except among certain scholars, would have virtually no effect on his posthumous reputation.

Both Lincoln and Darwin would suffer criticism outside religious circles. Members of the scientific community continued to question Darwin's theories, though mainly in the two or three generations after his death, before the genetic breakthroughs of the early twentieth century. Not unexpectedly, Lincoln would be excoriated in the South. More surprisingly, some Northern historians would play down his commitment to human equality and accuse him of undue sympathies with the Southern way of life. Meanwhile many Americans would have a hard time seeing their martyred sixteenth president as a real flesh-and-blood human being. In contrast, Darwin's private life was more accessible to the public. He kept copious records, lived long enough to write an autobiography, and died of natural causes. Still, he remained a figure of mythic proportions for many.

Darwin expected to be buried at Downe, in the family vault in the St. Mary's churchyard, but his friend Thomas Huxley and first cousin, Francis Galton (also the father of modern eugenics), immediately initiated a campaign for a far grander interment. Galton went to William Spottiswoode, president of the Royal Society, and asked him to telegraph the Darwins to see if they would allow Charles to be buried in Westminster Abbey with England's other scientific and literary heroes. A friend of the family in high ecclesiastic circles then petitioned the dean of Westminster to permit the burial. John Lubbock, Darwin's anthropologist neighbor at Downe, a supporter of his evolutionary theory and a member of the House of Commons, collected twenty-eight signatures among fellow members of Parliament urging that Darwin be laid to rest in the abbey. The *Standard*, a leading conservative newspaper of the day, likewise called for such a burial, boldly stating that "one who has brought such honor to the English name, and whose death is lamented throughout the civilized world, . . . should not be laid in a comparatively obscure grave. His proper place is amongst those other worthies whose reputations are landmarks in the people's history."[1] Many other newspapers followed suit, emphasizing a patriotic theme and often comparing Darwin to Sir Isaac Newton. The press generally discounted any conflicts between evolution and religion by insisting that Christians could accept the main facts of evolution just as they accepted the basic facts of the other sciences.

Typical of the sermons that attempted to show that Darwin had been a believer was one preached on April 23, just three days after Darwin's death, by H. P. Liddon, canon residentiary at St. Paul's Cathedral. Darwin's own books, Liddon insisted, showed him to be "a believer in Almighty God," since he had stated twice in *The Descent of Man* that belief in God was "ennobling." "No one," he insisted, "would thus speak unless he believed in God himself."[2] Liddon then added, as many clergy would remark over the years, that natural selection "is not of itself opposed to faith in God's relation to the material universe as its Maker and ever-Present Upholder and Ruler."[3] The good canon, of course, had not read Darwin's still private and unpublished *Autobiography*, in which he boldly proclaimed his agnosticism, his statements of unbelief in letters to close friends, or his objection to attempts to reconcile his theories with religion.

Darwin's funeral took place on April 26, a week after his death, attended by hundreds of eminent guests. Serving as pallbearers were political and governmental dignitaries: Lord Derby, the dukes of Argyll and Devonshire, and American ambassador James Russell Lowell, along with leading lights from the scientific community, including Spottiswoode, Lubbock, Huxley, Hooker, and Alfred Wallace. Fittingly, Darwin's grave, in the floor with an inscribed stone slab covering it, was in the side aisle below Newton's raised and elaborately carved tomb.

Seventeen years before, clergymen in America had rushed to embrace the fallen Lincoln. The president's assassination on Good Friday was a godsend to preachers likening him to Christ, who, they proclaimed, had also died to make men free. Two days later, in what was long known as

"Black Easter" because of the black mood and black mourning crepe that draped worshipers and churches alike, homilists attempted to reconcile the great tragedy. In Boston, the Reverend Edward Everett Hale took the parallel with Christ back a little further to Lincoln's return from Virginia on Palm Sunday, April 9, not long after newly freed slaves had reportedly hailed him as a messiah as he walked through the streets of Richmond with his son Tad. Like Jesus, Lincoln had died a martyr's death less than a week after his greatest triumphs.

According to historian Merrill D. Peterson, the Black Easter sermons fell into two main categories.[4] The first argued that God had allowed the president to be killed because he had finished his work to save the Union and free the slaves. So that Lincoln's well-known reputation for mercy and forgiveness would not lead him to undermine his own accomplishments, God had removed him from the scene so that sterner men could take his place and preside over reconstruction. The second and more lasting explanation held that Lincoln died as atonement for his nation's sins, just as Jesus' death had been a payment for the sins of all who believed in him. This explanation echoed Lincoln's own words from the second inaugural address—that the Civil War was a divine punishment for two hundred and fifty years of slavery. Lincoln as well as Darwin loomed so large in the public consciousness that religious authorities could not afford to ignore them, despite their unorthodox or even subversive beliefs.

Lincoln's funeral was a long, drawn out affair that began on April 18. The day before, the president's body lay in the East Room of the White House, dressed in the same black suit he had worn at his first inaugural, where twenty-five thousand mourners passed by his bier. Mary Lincoln, prostrate with grief, remained upstairs all that day and during the funeral the next day. Beginning at 2:00 p.m. on the nineteenth, it took the procession two hours to move up Pennsylvania Avenue to the Capitol, where Lincoln lay in the rotunda beneath the great dome that he had insisted on finishing during the war as a symbol that the Union would endure. Throughout the Northern states, most businesses closed for the afternoon as churches filled to capacity for more prayers and sermons.

Early in the morning of April 21, the body was placed on board a special train that would retrace, in reverse, the nearly two thousand-mile journey that Lincoln had made to Washington a little over four years earlier. Everywhere it stopped, there were long processions from railroad stations to sites where the body would be viewed—in the state capitol buildings at Harrisburg, Columbus, and Indianapolis, and at Independence Hall in Philadelphia. Finally, on May 4, Lincoln was laid to rest in Springfield's Oak Ridge Cemetery, almost three weeks after the assassination.

This "long funeral" had been possible only because of intravenous embalming, one of the latest miracles of science that had been practiced in the United States for only a few years. The public's amazement at how Lincoln's body had been preserved for so long a period gave a tremendous boost to the practice of embalming, which became widespread in the United States over the next several decades.

Mary Lincoln, who had so often found her husband wanting in social graces and personal attention, remained in deep mourning and never fully recovered from the assassination. She wore black crepe for the rest of her life and wrote all her letters on mourning paper with wide black borders. Her grief only deepened when son Tad died of pleurisy at age eighteen in 1871. Mary exiled herself to Europe, living first in Germany and then in France. Wild shopping sprees and erratic behavior led son Robert to commit his mother to a mental institution for a brief period in 1875 until she managed to get herself released. She died nearly blind and with multiple illnesses at her sister's house in Springfield on July 15, 1882, just under two months after the death of Charles Darwin.

Emma Darwin's widowhood could not have been more different from Mary Lincoln's. She did not attend Charles's funeral at Westminster, partly because she was exhausted and partly out of Victorian etiquette. She did not grieve excessively, for their marriage and years together had been happy, despite religious differences and the loss of three children, and she did not have to endure the shock of a husband's sudden and violent death. Emma was also more balanced mentally and emotionally than Mary Lincoln and better able to bear her sorrows, along with the normal ups and downs of daily life. She eventually moved to a house in Cambridge to be near her sons George, Francis, and Horace, who were all at the university in various capacities, though she returned to Down House every summer. She died there, at age eighty-eight, in 1896—fourteen years after her husband and Mary Lincoln and thirty-one years after the assassination of President Lincoln.

Emma was content to let others tend her husband's legacy, but Mary Lincoln was not. She was furious when in 1872 William Herndon gave one of his many lectures in Springfield and claimed that Mary herself had told him in an 1866 interview that Lincoln had "never joined a Church . . . and was never a technical Christian."[5] Not only was this an attack on the widely held popular belief that Lincoln had indeed been a true Christian believer, but it also struck at the heart of Mary's faith in spiritualism and, through its mediums, her belief that she could communicate with Abraham from beyond the grave. If her husband had not accepted Jesus as his personal savior, then he could not have gone to the afterlife and she could not communicate with him. She lashed out by denying that she had ever said anything remotely like this to Herndon.[6]

Robert Lincoln, who became the custodian of his father's papers, guarded this treasure jealously, eventually giving the collection to the Library of Congress, with the stipulation that it could not be opened to the public until twenty-one years after his own death. Since Robert died in 1926, the papers remained sealed until 1947, eighty-two years after the assassination.⁷ By then, several generations of biographers had done much to shape the Lincoln story.⁸

The earliest biography, *The Life of Abraham Lincoln* by Josiah G. Holland, appeared in 1866, the year following his subject's untimely death. Holland was the first to undertake serious research on Lincoln; his work included interviews of people who had known the slain president. Although well written, the book was essentially a hagiography that glorified the fallen leader. Holland, a devout Christian and Sunday school teacher, had asked Herndon about Lincoln's religious beliefs, and when Herndon replied, "The less said about that the better," Holland reportedly remarked, "Oh, never mind. I will fix that!"⁹ Holland's solution was a dubious quotation from Newton Bateman, the Illinois superintendent of education, to the effect that Lincoln had once confessed to him a belief in the divinity of Christ. If this were true, it was the one and only time that Lincoln ever made such a confession, and it contradicts every other known testimony about Lincoln's faith. Yet it was something that the public very much wanted to believe and it remains a widespread though erroneous view.

Pious assertions about Lincoln drove Herndon to continue his own researches, which he had begun shortly after Lincoln's death by interviewing or writing to everyone who had known the man in his earlier life. In 1889 Herndon finally brought out his long-promised *Life of Lincoln*, which covered the period before Lincoln's presidency. Although an assiduous collector of Lincolniana, Herndon had lacked the discipline to write the book himself and he engaged Jesse W. Weik, a former federal pension agent and fellow Lincoln aficionado, to smooth out and stitch together the mass of information that he had written or collected over the years. In the introduction Herndon said that his main object was "that the whole truth concerning [Lincoln] should be known ... [and] the reader will see and feel the presence of the living man." Otherwise, if "the story is colored or the facts in any degree suppressed, the reader will be ... misled."¹⁰

And there was much that had been suppressed, according to Herndon, including the allegedly lazy and shiftless Tom Lincoln, Abraham's deep melancholy, the stormy marriage to Mary Todd, and, of course, Lincoln's religious infidelity.[11] Although Herndon was subsequently proven wrong in a few of his facts, virtually every biographer and historian who has written about Lincoln's early years has had to depend on the information gathered by Herndon from Lincoln neighbors, friends, and acquaintances. Not surprisingly, most of the reading public did not like what Herndon had to say, and although the reviews were generally favorable, the book was not a financial success. It sold about five thousand copies compared to the eighty thousand of Holland's laudatory book published a generation earlier. Mary Lincoln surely would have despised Herndon's book, but mercifully for her, she was already at peace beside her husband in Oak Ridge Cemetery.

The ten-volume *Abraham Lincoln: A History* by Lincoln's private secretaries, John Hay and John Nicolay, published in 1890, returned to the theme of general glorification. Both authors had idolized Lincoln from the first, and this attitude only increased after his death. Nicolay wrote that Lincoln "is our ideal hero." For Hay, Lincoln was "the greatest character since Christ."[12] Both authors wanted future generations to worship the fallen president as much as the two of them did and, in particular, they wished to counter the supposed heresies spun by Herndon. As Hay wrote to Nicolay, "God-fearing men make up the reading public. They want a model for all the good little boys to follow, and Billy Herndon's model won't do."[13]

Hay and Nicolay were the only biographers to gain access to the Lincoln Papers before they were opened to the public in the late 1940s. Robert Lincoln, their custodian, demanded the right to read and make corrections to their manuscript as the price for his permission to use the papers. Because the authors trusted only documented evidence and disdained the interviews done by the likes of Herndon, they contributed little to an understanding of Lincoln's early life. They had only praise for the Lincoln presidency, though they were the first to write about the terrible pessimism and deep depression that overcame him as he faced reelection in 1864. The multivolume work sold respectably at the time and it was reviewed favorably in the press and in academic journals, but it has been little read in recent generations.

A decade after the Hay and Nicolay biography, the United States entered a multifaceted period of reform that historians have since labeled the Progressive Era. Theodore Roosevelt, an outspoken progressive reformer who restored a strong presidency after years of congressional domination, saw Lincoln as an exemplary chief executive. Roosevelt even had a personal connection to the sixteenth president through John Hay, whom he made his secretary of state. Hay liked to tell his new chief stories about how Lincoln, unable to sleep, would roam the halls of the White House and come into his room and sit on the bed to talk or have Hay read Shakespeare to him. On the night before Roosevelt's inauguration in March 1905, Hay gave him a ring containing a snippet of Lincoln's hair, which he wore the next day and treasured for the rest of his life.[14] Roosevelt, who kept a large portrait of Lincoln behind his desk, once told a reporter, "When I am confronted with a great problem, I look up at that picture, and I do as I believe Lincoln would have done . . . were he in my place."[15]

Lincoln was also an inspiration during the Progressive Era for the many private efforts to solve a multitude of modern problems. From the time she was a child, Jane Addams admired Lincoln and was determined to do something important to help her country. She went on to head Hull House in Chicago, the nation's most famous settlement house, and to become an informal adviser to presidents, including Theodore Roosevelt.

Another reformer inspired by Lincoln was the muckraker Ida Tarbell, best known for her scathing exposé of the Standard Oil Trust. In 1900 she published a two-volume biography of Lincoln, as laudatory of Lincoln as she would be critical of Standard Oil founder John D. Rockefeller. As a good progressive who tended to see increased democracy as vital to good government and reform, Tarbell explained in her preface to the Lincoln book how she had cast her net widely, putting out calls from her desk at *McClure's Magazine* to "all persons possessing or knowing of Lincoln material." She received hundreds of replies and traveled thousands of miles to collect information, making her work "one in which the whole country co-operated."[16] From both new and old sources she shaped a model character for all Americans. "The man has stood the test," she wrote. "He comes out of each examination and re-examination still sound, wise, honest, humorous, merciful. . . . It is good to see what a man can make of heart and brain if he will set himself for life to the task—what can be done in spite of the multiplied handicaps."[17] For Tarbell, Lincoln was proof of equality of opportunity—a centerpiece of the American dream.

A quarter century later, Tarbell published *Boy Scouts' Life of Lincoln* (1921), which held him up as a model for boys, much as Mason Weems had done with *Life of Washington*, a copy of which Lincoln had borrowed and devoured as a youth. Typical of a book aimed at boys, Tarbell concentrated on Lincoln's early life, the lessons and skills that prepared him for greatness. He had learned early that labor was "a necessary and dignified part of man's life. . . . The idler was a nuisance to himself and his fellows." Lincoln had also realized the importance of education, especially self education—"that no man is so placed that he does not have the opportunity to feed, train and rule it." Keeping his impulses "clean and noble" had been equally important to Lincoln, and from his earliest years, he had never allowed himself to "despise any man."[18] The greatest idea he took from his early life was the universal desire for freedom, that compelling impulse at the center of his hatred for slavery. In case her message was not absolutely clear, Tarbell ended by saying, "The history of this or no other land offers to the American Boy a more worthy and beautiful model on which to base and rear his own than Abraham Lincoln."[19]

American biographers were not alone in their praise of Lincoln. In

1879, English biographer Charles G. Leland concluded, "Whatever may be said of Lincoln, he was always simply and truly *a good man*. He was a good father to his children, and a good President to the people whom he loved as if they had been his children. America and the rest of the world have had many great rulers, but never one who, like Lincoln, was so much one of the people, or who was so sympathetic in their sorrows and trials."[20] A dozen years later another English writer, William M. Thayer, assured his readers that Lincoln was a devoutly religious man by quoting one of Lincoln's neighbors in Springfield: "I have known him long and well, and I can say in truth, I think (take him altogether) he is the best man I ever saw. Although he has never made a public profession of religion, I nevertheless believe that he has the fear of God before his eyes, and that he goes daily to a throne of grace, and asks wisdom, light, and knowledge, to enable him faithfully to discharge his duties."[21]

The need to see Lincoln in a religious light appeared inexhaustible. In 1920, John Wesley, who was then chancellor of the Lincoln Memorial Library, published *Abraham Lincoln: Man of God*. Ignoring the fact that Lincoln was not baptized, had never belonged to a church, and did not believe in the divinity of Christ, Wesley wrote, "He worked out a theology in general conformity with the accepted standards of Christianity. In the darkest hour of his White House days when personal bereavement was added to national anxiety, he literally lived on his knees."[22] Wesley admitted that Lincoln had once read Paine and various French philosophes who openly scorned Christianity, but he dismissed this fact by asserting that he had read them with the same avidity as he read Weems's *Life of Washington* or the "Revised Statutes of Indiana": "A man of Lincoln's intellectual comprehensiveness could read books of the most powerful skeptics without fear that his faith would be disturbed by disbelief."[23]

The progressives, most of them white and upper-middle class, generally showed little concern about the continuing plight of black Americans a half century after the Emancipation Proclamation. However, to those who had actually lived in slavery and to the vast majority of their descendants, Lincoln remained a great hero. Lincoln had freed African Americans, who could also associate with his humble origins and his struggles to improve himself. Children and students in the black community heard endless stories about Lincoln's Bible reading, his patience, and his scrupulous honesty.

The last attempts to protect black voting rights in the former Confederacy had been abandoned in 1890, and the United States Supreme Court had upheld racial segregation in its landmark decision *Plessy v. Ferguson* (1896). Tellingly, the Lincoln Centennial in 1909 focused on Lincoln as savior of the Union, man of the people, and champion of democracy, with little said about Lincoln the Great Emancipator.

A continuing legacy of the 1909 centennial is the Lincoln penny, issued that year to commemorate his birth. Heated controversies over its appearance shed light on the differing views of Lincoln at the time: Some argued that Lincoln deserved to be on a higher division of coinage, given his great importance to the nation, but supporters of the idea argued that Lincoln had seen himself as the common person's president and that putting his face on the humble one-cent piece was entirely fitting. Others objected to this first-ever instance of placing the image of an American president on a coin, claiming that it seemed too reminiscent of European monarchies, where the ruling sovereign appeared on all the coinage. Up to this point, with the exception of the Indian head penny that directly preceded the Lincoln cent, American coins had generally carried abstract images of "Lady Liberty," as on the liberty head dollar, half dollar, quarter, dime, and nickel. Some Southerners, still unreconciled to the results of the Civil War, found the image of Lincoln on the penny to be especially offensive.

The renewed awareness of Lincoln raised by the centennial was partly behind the decision in 1913 to designate the country's first coast-to-coast motor road (from New York to San Francisco) as the Lincoln Highway. Backers of the project thought the name would give it great patriotic appeal and be a fitting memorial "in memory of Abraham Lincoln."[24] It was an especially suitable honor for Lincoln, who believed his entire life in transportation improvements.

Hundreds and eventually thousands of places and enterprises of all sorts would carry the Lincoln name. This process was well under way even before 1909. In 1867, the new state of Nebraska named its capital Lincoln; it was among the first of many new towns, counties, villages, and subdivisions to adopt the name.

Just a year before the two centennials, in August 1908, a deadly race riot erupted in Lincoln's own Springfield, Illinois. Two black men were lynched, four more were killed, fifty were wounded, houses and stores were sacked and burned, and almost two thousand blacks fled from the city. In the preceding two months there had been twenty-five lynchings in various other communities, mostly in the South. The response was the Lincoln Conference on the Negro Question, which met in New York in May of the following year. From this conference came the National Association for the Advancement of Colored People (NAACP), founded in the Lincoln centennial year of 1909. Its principal mission was to complete "the work . . . the Great Emancipator began."[25]

While the NAACP and the black community in general were appealing to the memory of Lincoln as emancipator, a number of writers, including some respected historians, were painting a very different picture of him. Perhaps the most outrageous distortion of Lincoln came from the pen of Thomas Dixon, best known for his novel *The Clansman* (1905), which served as the basis for D. W. Griffith's controversial film *Birth of a Nation* (1915). In both the book and the movie, the Ku Klux Klan is depicted as saving the South from the "Black Beast." President Woodrow Wilson had the film shown in the White House— the first movie ever screened there—and enthusiastically approved of it: "It is like writing history with lightening," he said. "My only regret is that it is all so terribly true."[26] In *Clansmen* as well as in *Birth of a Nation*, Lincoln is depicted as a strong advocate of racial discrimination and segregation, with great emphasis placed on his support for sending blacks back to Africa. The Radical Republicans, who wanted to punish as well as to transform the South, are the real Northern villains in both the book and the film, not Lincoln.

During the early twentieth century, other writers began to revise popular views of Lincoln. At the time, there were growing desires for greater reconciliation between North and South, and one way to encourage this was to soften the view of Lincoln toward both slavery and the South.

Doubtless pleasing to the South was William P. Pickett's *The Negro Problem: Abraham Lincoln's Solution* (1909), whose publication coincided with the Lincoln centennial. Pickett, who was a Brooklyn attorney and law professor, proposed that Lincoln's earlier support for the idea of sending black Americans back to Africa should be renewed. Pickett begins by insisting that "Negroes" belonged to an "alien and inferior race" that could never be assimilated. If Lincoln had not been shot, Pickett was convinced, he would have returned to this solution of the race problem: "Emancipation first, and colonization afterward. Fortunately, he lived to see the first effected; in some form the second is yet to come. Each passing year emphasizes the tremendous error of the reversal of Lincoln's long-cherished and profoundly contemplated plan for the solution of the problem by means of a policy of colonization. . . . Nobly did Lincoln do his part. The present duty is ours."[27]

Although not an outspoken racist, Albert J. Beveridge, a former US senator from Indiana, took a very benign view of slavery before the Civil War in his *Abraham Lincoln* (1928). He argued that the self-interest of slave owners caused most of them to treat their slaves humanely—often better than laborers in Northern factories (an assertion that Southerners had made to defend slavery in the years leading up to the war).[28] Beveridge argued that a presidential victory in 1860 for Stephen Douglas, who was trying to work out a compromise over slavery, might well have avoided the Civil War. Instead, Lincoln and the Republicans pushed the South into secession. Beveridge died before writing about Lincoln's presidential years, but Southerners were understandably happy with what he had written up to that point, and the book was reviewed positively in the Southern press.

Also pleasing to the South was the work of professional historians belonging to what is called the revisionist school, many of them influenced by the horrors and seeming futility of World War I. One of its founders was James G. Randall, who in his four-volume *Lincoln the President* (1945–1955), contended that there was no real difference between Lincoln and Stephen Douglas on the subject of slavery.[29] Having been born in the slave state of Kentucky, according to Randall, Lincoln had supposedly understood and sympathized with the South. Randall even managed to depreciate the Emancipation Proclamation, contending that it had been forced on Lincoln by military necessity and that it kept him from realizing his preferred method of gradual, compensated emancipation tied to colonizing the freed slaves back to Africa.

Randall also had no use for Herndon, finding his biography full of gossip, half-truths, and downright falsehoods. He had particular contempt for the Ann Rutledge story and for Herndon's dismal description of the Lincoln marriage, especially his characterization of Mary Todd Lincoln. In 1953, Randall's wife, Ruth Painter Randall, published *Mary Lincoln: Biography of a Marriage*, in which she defended the First Lady to the hilt and in the process poured even more scorn on Herndon, a necessary action if she was going to be successful in rehabilitating Mrs. Lincoln.

For the revisionists, the real culprits were the extremist abolitionists, who made compromise between North and South impossible (a position that Darwin might well have accepted, given his views of the war). For them the Civil War was no more inevitable than World War I and was caused by what Randall called "A Blundering Generation." After the Civil War, it had been the Radical Republicans who torpedoed any possibility of sectional reconciliation by insisting on punishing the former Confederacy and remaking Dixie in the image of the North. If only Lincoln had lived, the revisionists never tired of preaching, his magnanimity and essentially moderate Republicanism would have saved the country from the worst excesses of reconstruction, and the wounds of sectional strife would have healed far faster. The most outspoken historian of this viewpoint was T. Harry Williams in his *Lincoln and the Radicals* (1941). His view would have baffled Northerners who had lived through the war and just after and was no doubt one that would have been rejected by Lincoln himself.

In posthumous images, Lincoln was often paired with Washington, as in an 1865 engraving by John Sartain titled "Abraham Lincoln the Martyr Victorious." In it Washington, surrounded by clouds and hosts of angels, welcomes Lincoln into heaven. Other images memorialized Lincoln as the Great Emancipator. For instance, the Freedman's Monument sculpted by Thomas Ball and erected in Washington, DC, in 1876 shows Lincoln with the Emancipation Proclamation in his right hand and with his left arm outstretched over a kneeling slave, whose wrist shackles have just been broken. Lincoln's face is kindly yet careworn. Attracting nearly universal acclaim was the 1886 statue of Lincoln at Fort Wayne, Indiana, by Augustus Saint-Gaudens, the foremost sculptor of the day. Lincoln, in plain rumpled clothing, stands before a very formal Roman-style chair of state, the two images emphasizing the contrast between the humble man and his heroic deeds.

In 1917, the aim of sculptor George G. Barnard was to capture the plain and homely Lincoln as he might have appeared before becoming president. His statue was erected in Cincinnati, Ohio, with a replica mounted in London, England. Many critics thought the image much too crude, including Robert Lincoln, who called it "a monstrous figure ... grotesque as a likeness of President Lincoln ... [and] defamatory as an effigy."[30]

Best known of all is Daniel Chester French's statute (1922) in the Lincoln Memorial in Washington, DC. There the colossal seated Lincoln looks every bit like Father Abraham—or even God himself. All in all, the artists were far more respectful of the Lincoln image than the revisionist historians who questioned his dedication to racial equality and wanted to see him as something of a Southern sympathizer and a victim of the Radical Republicans.

Imagery of Charles Darwin was well established by the time of his death. Cartoonists had tremendous fun superimposing Darwin's head on a monkey's body, a depiction greatly assisted by their subject's long, shaggy beard, bushy eyebrows, and high forehead due to baldness. *Punch's Almanac* for 1882 published a cartoon of a sagelike Darwin clad in a Roman toga encircled by evolving creatures, beginning with worms and proceeding though more and more advanced monkeys who morph into cavemen and finally into modern humans. Below is the caption "Man Is But A Worm," a reference to Darwin's recently published book on worms.[31] The 1885 statue in the Natural History Museum at South Kensington depicts Darwin as a sage, with the contemplative but benign-looking man seated, with legs crossed, in a Roman-style chair.[32] In the cases of both Darwin and Lincoln, neoclassical imagery was a way that artists could convey the stature of their subjects.

In contrast to Lincoln, Darwin was not connected by the public with a life-and-death struggle involving hundreds of thousands of lives and the survival of a nation. Perhaps as a result, his name has not been attached to as many places as Lincoln's. Mount Darwin in Rhodesia; Darwin, Australia; Charles Darwin University (also in Australia); and Darwin College at Cambridge University are the most noteworthy places bearing his name.

Darwin's posthumous reputation did not depend quite as much on biographers as Lincoln's, since he had had the opportunity in his later years to compose an autobiography. Although written expressly for his family, his son Francis included portions of it in 1887 in his *Life and Letters of Charles Darwin*. Because only five years had passed since his father's death, and because many of the people Darwin had mentioned or written about were still alive, Emma and daughter, Etty, persuaded him to withhold certain parts of the *Autobiography*. They also convinced Francis to omit Darwin's starkest statements of disbelief in Christianity or in any other religion.³³ Subsequent editions of the *Autobiography* restored various omitted portions until the entire, uncut work was available by the late 1950s.

Francis Darwin's 1887 *Life and Letters* in no way qualifies as a comprehensive biography, since he tells his story through the expurgated *Autobiography*, followed by his own "Reminiscences of My Father's Everyday Life." Nevertheless, these reminiscences accurately portray the older Charles Darwin's common routine at Down House, including his work habits and processes of writing, but they mainly add to the persona of the gentle sage that his father had already sketched out in the *Autobiography*. Filling the remainder of this two-volume work are selected Darwin letters, grouped together in categories that correspond to his major researches and writings. Francis briefly introduces these sections of letters and sometimes supplies a connecting narrative, but he does not attempt to place his subject into any larger context, draw conclusions, or hazard any speculations or judgments about why his father thought, spoke, or acted as he did. He left out letters or portions of letters that were personal in nature and also withheld correspondence about what might be considered his father's blind alleys of research and speculation that had not stood up to scrupulous examination. Darwin scholar Jon Hodge has called this largely laudatory approach by a dutiful son the "Franciscan view" of Charles Darwin.³⁴ It would be decades before anyone would write anything approaching a definitive biography, perhaps because the *Life and Works* seemed to say it all. Another obstacle to anyone's writing a complete biography was lack of access to Darwin's papers, which remained in the custody of the family until they were given to Cambridge University in 1942. Nor did any of Darwin's associates imitate William Herndon by interviewing nearly everyone who had known the man. Rather than being a subject of numerous biographies in the several decades after his life, Darwin became inextricably tied to his theory, and it was the theory that attracted the most attention.

By the time Darwin died in 1882, the theory of biological evolution was widely accepted in scientific circles. The early biographer Grant Allen stated this situation very well in 1888. Comparing Darwin's contribution to that of Alfred Wallace, Allen insisted that it was the mountain of facts put forth by Darwin, and not Wallace's speculative essay, that had won the day for evolution as a generally accepted idea: "The prodigious mass of Darwin's facts, the cautious working of Darwin's intellect, the immense weight of Darwin's reputation, the crushing force of Darwin's masterly inductive method, bore down before them all opposition in the inner circle of biologists, and secured the triumph of the evolutionary system even in the very strongholds of ignorance and obscurantism."[35] The impetus that Darwin gave to evolution, Allen believed, "gained us at least fifty years of progress; it set us at a bound from Copernicus to Newton; so far as ordinary minds were concerned, indeed, it transcended at a single leap the whole interval from Ptolemy to Herschel."[36]

Yet twenty years later, the precise meaning of just what Darwin had accomplished remained unclear at his centennial in 1909. To commemorate the hundredth anniversary of Darwin's birth and the fiftieth anniversary of *Origin of Species*, Cambridge University Press published a large volume of essays called *Darwinism and Modern Science*.[37] As the volume's introduction clearly stated, there was no general agreement at the time about the validity of Darwin's main explanation for evolution through natural selection: "The divergence of views among biologists in regard to the origin of species and as to the most promising directions in which to seek for truth is illustrated by the different opinions of contributors." Particularly in question was "whether Darwin's views on the *modus operandi* of evolutionary forces receive further confirmation in the future, or whether they are materially modified."[38]

Cambridge also honored its famous student with a three-day

Darwin commemoration in June 1909. On the twenty-second, there was a reception for delegates from various colleges and universities around the world and other invited guests at the Fitzwilliam Museum. The following day, the delegates presented their addresses at the Senate House, where Darwin had received his honorary degree four decades earlier, followed by a garden party at Christ's College and the opportunity to visit Darwin's old rooms at the college. That evening there was a banquet at the Fitzwilliam. On the twenty-fourth, honorary degrees were conferred at the Senate House, followed in the afternoon by a party hosted by the Darwin family in the Fellows Garden. There was also an exhibit of portraits, books, and other objects relating to Darwin.[39]

Although Darwin received credit at the centennial for making evolution widely accepted within the scientific community, his most original contribution to the study of evolution—the mechanism of natural selection—had been under attack and was in retreat. Historian Peter J. Bowler explains this seeming paradox by saying that Darwin was a powerful catalyst who hastened the acceptance of evolution as a concept but left many scientists unconvinced about its mechanism.[40] There were two reasons why so many contemporary scientists had difficulty with natural selection: one was ignorance about the process of biological inheritance and the other was Lord Kelvin's very respectable, and at the time, very persuasive attack on Darwin's assertions about the ancientness of the earth.

Darwin's doubters continued to include many conservative Christians who rejected evolution on religious grounds, not only because of conflicts with a literal interpretation of the Bible and various doctrinal positions but also because of the analogies being made between the operations of human society and biological evolution, known collectively as social Darwinism. In many ways the term *social Darwinism* was an inaccurate and unfair label, since all sorts of evolutionary ideas—many if not most of them unrelated to Darwin's work—were lumped together under the term.

If anything, the cluster of ideas, comparisons, and opinions loosely grouped together under the concept of social Darwinism owed more to Lamarck's beliefs in acquired characteristics, and especially to the works of the English sociologist Herbert Spencer, than to Darwin himself. Although Spencer later adapted a number of insights from Darwin, his original concept of evolution had been rooted in physics and astronomy. Spencer saw evolution as the inexorable, cosmic movement from chaotic, undifferentiated homogeneity to ordered, differentiated heterogeneity. This was a shorthand way of saying that all the matter in the universe had begun as a swirling mass of simple, uniform particles that had coalesced into larger and more varied forms that performed complex functions. Primordial particles had developed into stars, planets, rocks, trees, rabbits, and human beings. In the same sense, primitive societies were like the early universe: over time, intricate divisions of labor emerged, as did highly developed institutions, bringing with them increasing social order. The key to this process among living beings was competition and "survival of the fittest," as Spencer liked to call it.[41] Spencer also was a strong supporter of Lamarck's belief in acquired characteristics that could be passed down from one generation to the next.

Darwin's adoption of the term *survival of the fittest* in his later writings was unfortunate, since it allowed others to connect his work too closely with Spencer's. Further complicating the picture were the differences between "conservative social Darwinism" and "reform social Darwinism," a distinction that Eric Goldman explored in his book *Rendezvous with Destiny* (1965).[42] According to Goldman, late nineteenth- and early twentieth-century capitalists and their supporters in public office used the conservative version to reinforce laissez-faire economics and to block any kind of governmental intervention in business. There would be winners and losers in the process, with fitness invariably defined by economic success. The worst thing that government could do, conservative social Darwinists argued, was to aid the unfit and allow them to pass on their unfit characteristics to their offspring. The American spokesman most associated with this point of view was sociologist William Graham Sumner (1840–1910) of Yale University.

In foreign affairs, conservative social Darwinists argued that, in the competition among nations, the fittest would win out and dominate the less fit, thereby justifying the conquest of colonies and an imperialistic policy. Such arguments could also be applied within a country to argue that certain races or ethnic groups were fitter than others, justifying racial discrimination. In the United States, these ideas were used to assert the inferiority of black citizens and of the "new immigrants" from southern and eastern Europe. Accordingly, only those whose ancestors came from the Protestant British Isles and from other parts of northern and western Europe could be seen as belonging to a superior and more desirable group. In the sense that Darwin did believe in a hierarchy of civilizations, and in the context of his explaining how contact between more advanced and more primitive peoples led to the diminishment or even disappearance of the latter, he was vulnerable to being classed with conservative social evolutionists. Yet his hatred of slavery and sympathy for the plight of aboriginal people, combined with a strong humanitarian disposition, would have kept Darwin from embracing the harsh views of Spencer toward social inequality.

Although there is no evidence that Darwin ever condemned these views in writing, he did criticize Spencer's reasoning: "His deductive manner of every subject is wholly opposed to my frame of mind. His conclusions never convince me."[43] Darwin would also have objected to Spencer's belief that evolution was essentially the realization of an archetype (an ideal model after which similar forms are patterned), the origins of which he could not explain. To Darwin the notion of an ideal type species was utter nonsense, since a species' "success" could be measured only by its ability to reproduce and pass on advantageous traits.[44]

Reform social Darwinists also used social evolutionary arguments to advance their cause, claiming that governments should hasten progress by ameliorating the social conditions that led to poverty or to exploitation by powerful economic interests. Antitrust legislation, safety regulations in factories, limitations of working hours, outlawing child labor, progressive income and inheritance taxes, votes for women, secret ballots, and popular referenda were all devices to bring about such changes. Liberals also insisted that governments could do much to help citizens cope with their environments through better schools, public libraries, health regulations, parks, and playgrounds. Some historians such as Robert C. Bannister have argued that reformers were much more likely to use evolutionary insights and analogies than their conservative foes, but that they also found it convenient to accuse their enemies of brutal Darwinian competition.

All of this would have surprised Darwin, who never really understood how his scientific work could apply to politics or society in the way that the social Darwinists wanted it to relate. When a Manchester newspaper held that *Origin of Species*, if true, meant that might made right, Darwin thought the charge ludicrous. A decade later, when he heard that German sociologists and economists were occupied in applying the implications of his theories to social questions, he wrote to one of them that it had never occurred to him that his ideas had any relevance to current social issues.[45]

As the progressive era of reform was coming to an end in the United States, biblical literalists, who believed that the book of Genesis could never be squared with the book of Darwin, became more vocal about their objections to evolution. A coalition of such groups formed the World Fundamentalist Association in 1918, claiming that a belief in cut-throat survival of the fittest and a naturalist amorality had helped to bring about World War I, along with other evils.

Many of these fundamentalists focused their attention on the teaching of evolution in the schools. There were several reasons for this: One was the coming together of a neo-Darwinist synthesis, which caused increasing numbers of scientists to accept natural selection over Lamarckianism. In contrast, many Christians found Lamarck's theories more palatable than Darwin's natural selection because they allowed a role for volition (or deliberate choice in the case of humans) in the evolutionary process. Thus, for Christians who wanted to emphasize the role of free will and conscious moral progress in the world, Lamarck was far more appealing than Darwin. A second and more important factor, thanks to compulsory education laws, was the tremendous increase in the numbers of students attending high school and college who were now exposed to the teaching of evolution. There was a tenfold increase between 1890 and 1920 in those attending American high schools, an increase of just two hundred thousand to almost two million during this period. Finally, modernist religious ideas had made increasing headway among the clergy of the "mainline" Protestant denominations, which rejected literal interpretations of scripture and saw the Bible as a product of the society and culture of the times it was written. This resulted in a greater divergence of opinions among Christians on the subject of evolution, with the more liberal denominations having little problem with it and the conservatives hardening their opposition.

The most publicized American crusade against Darwin and the theory of evolution—including social Darwinism—centered on the antievolution campaign of William Jennings Bryan and the climatic Scopes "Monkey Trial" held during the summer of 1925 in Dayton, Tennessee.[46] Ironically, Bryan (1860–1925) had been regarded as one of the most reform-minded and progressive of American politicians, but had been defeated three times as the Democratic candidate for president of the United States. But to Bryan, reform and human betterment were impossible if divorced from the truths of Christianity. If men and women were only different in degree from the rest of creation, as Darwin had asserted, rather than different in kind and uniquely endowed with a conscience and an immortal soul, there was nothing to keep them from behaving like wild animals.

In addition, Bryan believed that conservative social Darwinist arguments had been used to defeat progressive legislation and to pit worker and capitalist against each other. "Survival of the fittest," he wrote, created a "life-and-death struggle from which sympathy and the spirit of brotherhood are eliminated."[47] The pacifist Bryan also believed that evolution supported a materialistic view of reality and that it had helped to prepare the ground for the terrible slaughter of World War I. As evidence, he often cited a book called *Headquarters Nights* (1918), in which author Vernon Kellogg, a highly respected zoologist from Stanford University, recounted conversations he had had with German military leaders. As Kellogg put it, "Natural selection based on violent and fatal competitive struggle is the gospel of the German intellectuals" and was their justification for the war.[48]

Bryan, like many other religious adults in the country, worried that Christian faith was declining among the most educated young people in the country and frequently cited a landmark 1914 survey by James H. Leuba, a professor of psychology at Bryn Mawr College. Leuba reported that belief in immortality decreased greatly from the freshman to the senior year, though he did not cite exposure to evolutionary teachings as a specific cause. But the book prompted Bryan to ask, "What shall it profit a man if he shall gain all the learning of the schools and lose his father in God?"[49]

Bryan incorrectly interchanged the terms *Darwinism* and *evolution*, since there continued to be different versions of evolution, not all of them Darwinian. He also gleefully pointed to various criticisms of natural selection, some of them, ironically, by scientists who accepted evolution as true but who were not convinced that natural selection was a valid explanation—or in some cases the only explanation for the evolutionary process. Bryan nevertheless combined these criticisms with his other concerns about evolution into a speech called "The Menace of Darwinism," which he began delivering in 1921.

Meanwhile, Bryan used his many political contacts to urge the states to pass laws that would permit public school teachers to present Darwinism as only an "unproven hypothesis"—and not as a scientific fact. As a progressive reformer with great faith in democracy, he held that the majority of people in a state had a perfect right to pass legislation to protect the welfare of their children, even if it meant limiting some individual rights. For Bryan, majority rule was much more important than the individual liberty of a faculty member to teach evolution in a public school.

On March 21, 1925, the Tennessee legislature went even further than what Bryan had proposed and completely prohibited the teaching of evolution, defining any violation as a misdemeanor (rather than a crime), punishable by a fine ranging from $100 to $500. Two weeks later, the recently formed American Civil Liberties Union (ACLU) denounced the Tennessee law as a violation of the First Amendment guarantee of free speech and offered to defend any teacher in court who defied it.

Several civic leaders in Dayton, Tennessee, with the connivance of the local school superintendent, came up with the scheme of putting their town on the map in the hopes of rejuvenating its flagging economy. Their idea was to hold a sensational trial in Dayton that would attract national publicity. John Scopes was a popular member of the local high school faculty and was eager to cooperate with them, allowing himself to be charged with teaching Darwin, as presented in the textbook *Civic Biology* by George W. Hunter, which had been officially adopted statewide.

In actuality, Scopes's main assignment in Dayton had been to teach general science, but at the end of the school year he had substituted for the regular biology teacher, who was also the high school principal. In his memoirs, *Center of the Storm* (1967), Scopes explained that he was not even sure he had taught evolution, since his main assignment, as a substitute, had been to prepare the students for their final examination in biology, which would be based on the Hunter text. He could not even remember at the time of the trial whether or not he had gone over evolution with the students in preparation for the test. "If the boys had got their review of evolution from me" he wrote, "I was unaware of it. I didn't remember teaching it."[50] But unlike the regular biology teacher, who was married and had a family to support, Scopes was single and did not need to stay in town.

The plans for a trial in Dayton succeeded spectacularly. Clarence Darrow, the most famous criminal defense lawyer in the country at the time and an avowed agnostic, volunteered to head the defense team; and when Bryan learned of this while speaking before the annual meeting of the World's Christian Fundamentalist Association in Memphis, he eagerly volunteered to represent that organization in the case by offering his services, free of charge, to the prosecution. Ironically, Scopes had lived for several years and gone to high school in Bryan's native hometown of Salem, Illinois, where Bryan had given the commencement address at Scopes's graduation from Salem High School. He had no ill feeling toward Scopes and even offered to pay the teacher's fine if he was found guilty.

A circus atmosphere surrounded the trial, which was held from July 10 to July 21. Bible sellers, preachers of all stripes, souvenir peddlers, and food hawkers descended on the town, as did correspondents from newspapers all over the country, including the acerbic H. L. Mencken of the *Baltimore Sun*, who delighted in ridiculing Bryan and everyone in the South as ignorant hayseeds. Newsreel cameras received permission to set up shop in the courtroom, and radio station WGN out of Chicago gave the first live coverage of a trial in the United States. Predictably, the press dubbed the whole proceeding as the "Monkey Trial," a term first attributed to Mencken, even though neither Darwin nor any other respectable evolutionist claimed that humans had descended directly from monkeys. Newspaper cartoonists also had great fun placing the heads of Darwin and main actors in the trial on monkey bodies, as songwriters poured out musical ditties about humans and their simian relatives.

When the judge refused to allow the defense to put a number of expert witnesses on the stand—who were both scientists and believers in God—to testify for the truth of evolution, Darrow asked to call a witness on the Bible. When the judge assented, Darrow called Bryan, who, despite objections from the rest of the prosecution team and the judge's own doubts, insisted on cooperating in this highly unusual and inappropriate examination by the defense of a prosecuting attorney. Because of the oppressive heat and concerns about the floor of the courtroom collapsing under the weight of so many spectators, the judge moved the trial outside, where Darrow proceeded to flay Bryan with one question after another to show the intellectual shallowness of his opponent: Did Bryan really believe that Jonah had survived in the belly of a whale (or big fish) for three days? Since Adam and Eve had only two sons, Cain and Abel—and Cain killed Abel—where had Abel found a wife to carry on the human race? Or had God created some women somewhere in another county that the book of Genesis failed to mention? Bryan had no answers.

Did Bryan believe that God had stopped the sun in the sky so that Joshua could win the Battle of Jericho, meaning, of course, that God had actually stopped the earth from turning on its axis? When pressed, Bryan admitted that he accepted the heliocentric view of the solar system and in the process revealed that he was not an absolute biblical literalist. He also admitted to not believing that the Genesis story of creation required one to believe that God had made everything in just six twenty-four-hour days, but he said he thought it could be interpreted to mean six periods of time that could each be many thousands of years, so long as it comported with Archbishop Ussher's chronology beginning in 4004 BCE. The point Darrow hoped to make was that if Bryan admitted that the Bible could be interpreted in some instances, it could be interpreted to the point of allowing Christians to accept evolution.

Put on the defensive, Bryan was forced to say that he believed in miracles, to profess his ignorance of or indifference to a whole host of issues, and to contradict his statements about the Bible being wholly and literally true. The judge finally intervened, stopped the questioning, and ordered the testimony expunged from the record. Bryan died of a stroke four days later, and many of his supporters blamed his death on Darrow's hostile questioning, but Bryan was a known diabetic and had pushed himself to the limit over the past few years. The heat and stress of the Scopes trial may have tipped the balance, but Bryan would likely have died anyway within a relatively short period of time.

The jury found Scopes guilty as charged and fined him $100 (the minimum prescribed by law), to the delight of the defense team, who all along planned to challenge the constitutionality of the Tennessee antievolutionary law, hopefully all the way to the US Supreme Court. But when the Tennessee Supreme Court ruled on the appeal on January 19, 1927, it upheld the constitutionality of the law at the same time that it overturned Scopes's conviction on a legal technicality. This technicality turned on the fact that, at the end of the original trial in Dayton, the judge had determined Scopes's fine instead of the jury, as directed by the state legislation, thereby allowing the state supreme court to reverse Scopes's conviction and, as a consequence, to remove any basis for appeals to the federal bench. Tennessee's antievolution law remained on the books for another forty years, until the US Supreme Court declared such statutes to be unconstitutional. Neither Bryan nor Darrow had changed many minds, and the nation would remain divided on the subject of evolution for generations to come. Yet scientists and religious modernists alike came away from the trial believing that they had exposed the ignorance and backwardness of the anti-Darwinist cause once and for all. Time would show that they were very wrong.

While debates over the implications of Darwin's works raged in the mid-1920s, the stage was being set for a more human and benign view of Abraham Lincoln. Very different from the revisionists, who emphasized Lincoln's sympathies with the South, was poet Carl Sandburg, who set out to rescue Lincoln's humanity from the professional historians. He achieved this brilliantly in his two-volume *Abraham Lincoln: The*

Prairie Years, published in 1926. For Sandburg, Lincoln was the common man "writ large." Not a trained historian, Sandburg accepted any and all stories about the young Lincoln that might humanize him and allow readers to relate to him emotionally. In many cases, the *Prairie Years* reads more like a historical novel than a biography, the author making up colorful dialogue that might have passed between Lincoln and others, or what he imagined young Abe must have thought in a particular situation. Sandburg, who accepted the Ann Rutledge romance without question, said of it, "He was twenty-six, she was twenty-two; the earth was their footstool; the sky was a sheaf of blue dreams; the rise of the blood-gold rim of a full moon in the evening was almost too much to live, see, and remember."[51] Historians castigated the work for its disregard for the facts, but many reviewers admired Sandburg's lyrical prose, and it sold forty-eight copies in the first year. *The Prairie Years* became the inspiration for many films and dramatizations.

During the first half of the twentieth century, some three or four generations after Charles Darwin and Abraham Lincoln had made their greatest contributions, their legacies were still in question. Had Lincoln fought an unnecessary war? Was he really a racist and Southern sympathizer? Had he been duped by the Radical Republicans? Or was he the Great Emancipator, the savior of the Union, and a prime exemplar of America as a land of opportunity? Although Darwin's name had been inextricably linked to any and every kind of evolutionary theory, including social evolution, it was still unclear if his main contribution to the field of biology—natural selection—would stand up to continuing scientific scrutiny or be cast aside by better and more plausible explanations. Would the clash between religion and Darwin's theory subside or grow more intense, and would racists and imperialists alike continue to use the ever-expandable category of social Darwinism to advance their agendas? A century and more after they were born, the legacies of these rebel giants were as controversial as ever.

NOTES

1. Quoted in Adrian Desmond and James Moore, *Darwin: The Life of a Tormented Evolutionist* (New York: Warner Books, 1991), p. 668.

2. Liddon. "The Recovery of St. Thomas," pp. 2, 4. Liddon explains that the sermon was preached three days after Darwin's death, in which he had made only an allusion to Darwin with little premeditation. The quotations here and just below are from a "Prefatory Note" that he added to the sermon in its published form.

3. Ibid., p. 4.

4. Merrill D. Peterson, *Lincoln in American Memory* (New York: Oxford University Press, 1994), pp. 7–8.

5. See William H. Herndon, *Herndon's Life of Lincoln* (New York: Da Capo Press, 1983), pp. 359–60.

6. Jean H. Baker, *Mary Todd Lincoln: A Biography* (New York: W. W. Norton, 1987), p. 312.

7. For an account of Robert Todd Lincoln and the Lincoln Papers, see Peterson, *Lincoln in American Memory*, pp. 258–360.

8. For excellent synopses and analyses of books about Lincoln, see Michael Burkhimer, *100 Essential Lincoln Books* (Nashville, TN: Cumberland House, 2003).

9. Quoted in ibid., p. 7.

10. Herndon, *Herndon's Life of Lincoln*, p. v.

11. Ibid., p. vi.

12. Quoted in Peterson, *Lincoln in American Memory*, p. 118.

13. Ibid.

14. Vice President Theodore Roosevelt had succeeded to the presidency in September 1901, as the result of President William McKinley's assassination. Roosevelt ran for president in 1904 and won and was inaugurated in his own right as president in March 1905.

15. Quoted in Peterson, *Lincoln in American Memory*, p. 164.

16. Ida Tarbell, *The Life of Abraham Lincoln* (New York: Macmillan Company, 1928), p. xiii.

17. Ibid., pp. xvii–xviii.

18. Ibid., pp. 245–46.

19. Ibid., p. 247.

20. Charles G. Leland, *Abraham Lincoln* (London: Marcus Ward & Co., 1879), p. 244.

21. William M. Thayer, *The Pioneer Boy and How He Became President* (London: Hodder and Stoughton, 1892), p. viii.

22. John Wesley, *Abraham Lincoln: Man of God* (New York: G.P. Putnam's Sons, 1920), p. x.

23. Ibid.

24. Quoted in Brian A. Butko, *The Lincoln Highway: Pennsylvania Traveler's Guide* (Mechanicsburg, PA: Stackpole Books, 1996), p. xix.

25. Quoted in Peterson, *Lincoln in American Memory*, p. 168.

26. Quoted in ibid., p. 170.

27. William P. Pickett, *The Negro Problem: Abraham Lincoln's Solution* (New York: G. P. Putnam's Sons, 1909), p, 330.

28. Albert J. Beveridge, *Abraham Lincoln, 1809–1858*, 2 vols. (Boston: Houghton Mifflin, 1928).

29. Randall died before completing the fourth volume and it was finished by Richard Current, then a young Lincoln scholar.

30. Quoted in Peterson, *Lincoln in American Memory*, p. 210.

31. See Randall Keynes, *Annie's Box: Darwin, His Daughter and Human Evolution* (New York: Riverhead Books, 2002), pp. 340, 349.

32. See Desmond and Moore, *Darwin*, plate 90.

33. Nora Barlow, in her introduction to the 1958 edition of the *Autobiography* (p. 12) tells of receiving a letter from Leonard Darwin (1850–1943), the last surviving child of Charles and Emma Darwin, who told her about the family disagreement over publishing the *Autobiography* without omissions.

34. M. J. S. Hodge, "Darwin as a Lifelong Generation Theorist," in *The Darwinian Heritage*, edited by D. Kohn (Princeton, NJ: Princeton University Press, 1985) pp. 207–44.

35. Grant Allen, *Charles Darwin* (London: Longmans, Green, and Co., 1888), p. 194.

36. Ibid.

37. A. C. Seward, ed., *Darwin and Modern Science: Essays in Commemoration of the Centenary of the Birth of Charles Darwin and of the Fiftieth Anniversary of the Publication of the Origin of Species.* (Cambridge: Cambridge University Press, 1910).

38. Ibid., p. vii.

39. Scrapbook of the University of Cambridge Darwin Commemoration, June 22–24, 1909. This handsomely mounted volume may be found in the rare book room of the Cambridge University Library.

40. Peter J. Bowler, "Darwin," *Cambridge Scientific Minds*, 103–104.

41. For somewhat differing views of Spencer's connections to social Darwinism, see Robert C. Bannister, *Social Darwinism: Science and Myth in Anglo-American Social Thought* (Philadelphia: Temple University Press, 1979), pp. 34–78 and Richard Hofstadter, *Social Darwinism in American Thought* (Boston: Beacon Press, 1955), pp. 31–51.

42. Eric F. Goldman, *Rendezvous with Destiny* (New York: Alfred A. Knopf, 1965), especially pp. 90–155.

43. Quoted in Janet Browne, *Charles Darwin: The Power of Place* (Princeton, NJ: Princeton University Press, 2002), p. 185.

44. Greta Jones, *Social Darwinism and English Thought: The Interaction between Biological and Social Theory* (Sussex: Harvester Press, 1980), pp. 6–7.

45. Gertrude Himmelfarb, *Darwin and the Darwinian Revolution* (New York; Doubleday, 1959), pp. 390–91.

46. On the Scopes trial, see Edward J. Larson, *Summer for the Gods: The Scopes Trial and America's Continuing Debate Over Science and Religion* (Cambridge, MA: Harvard University Press, 1998) and, as told from a creationist point of view, Marvin Olasky and John Perry, *Monkey Business: The True Story of the Scopes Trial* (Nashville, TN: Broadman and Holman Publishers, 2005). Of great value is John Scopes's memoir of the trial, with James Presley, *Center of the Storm: Memoirs of John T. Scopes* (New York: Holt, Rinehart and Winston, 1967).

47. Quoted in Robert W. Cherny, *A Righteous Cause: The Life of William Jennings Bryan* (Boston: Little, Brown, 1985), p. 173.

48. Quoted in Larson, *Summer for the Gods*, p. 40.

49. Quoted in Cherny, *Righteous Cause*, p. 172.

50. Scopes and Presley, *Center of the Storm*, p. 134.

51. Quoted in Burkhimer, *100 Essential Lincoln Books*, p. 49.

Chapter 9

LEGACIES

The issues that Lincoln grappled with will never become obsolete: The meaning of freedom; the limits of government power and individual liberty in time of crisis; the dimensions of democracy, the nature of nationalism; the problems of leadership in war and peace; the tragedies and triumphs of a revolutionary civil war.

—James McPherson,
Abraham Lincoln and the Second American Revolution

New knowledge has led to the recognition of the theory of evolution as more than a hypothesis.

—Pope John Paul II, speech to the
Pontifical Academy of Science

*D*ebates over Lincoln and Darwin flowed into new and unexpected channels, and sometimes came full circle, as earlier praises and condemnations reappeared and then faded away. The key to proving or disproving Darwin in the twentieth century, at least among scientists, depended on a better understanding of heredity, and by the middle of the century, breakthroughs in this area vindicated Darwin's theory of natural selection for most scientists. Religious opposition to Darwin remained and even intensified in some quarters of the faith community, especially in the United States. Meanwhile, Lincoln's reputation fluctuated with political trends and with larger cultural shifts. Conversations over what these two towering figures said, did, and represented remained intense on the approach of their two-hundredth-birthday anniversaries in 2009.

A most important though unappreciated breakthrough for Darwin occurred, ironically, in 1858, the year before *Origin* was published, when German scientist Rudolf Virchow (1821–1902) showed that every living cell comes from a preexisting cell, through the process of cell division.[1] Virchow also discovered that each cell was made up of a "bag of watery jelly" known as the protoplasm, in the center of which was a concentration of material he called the nucleus. When cell division took place, the nucleus divided itself into two identical portions, which moved to opposite sides of the cell. Then the cell split into two new cells, each with its own nucleus and surrounding protoplasm. Ironically when Virchow became a member of the German Reichstag, he voted against the teaching of Darwin's theory in the public schools, declaring that there were not yet enough facts to prove natural selection.[2]

In the 1880s another German scientist, August Weismann (1834–1914), realized that the nucleus contained the hereditary material then labeled the "germ plasm." Another German researcher, Walther Flemming (1843–1905), identified threadlike structures in the nucleus that were later called chromosomes. Weismann went on to find that when chromosomes divided to produce the special reproductive cells of sperm and egg, they were "halved," and that only when the sex cells fused through fertilization was the full chromosomal complement restored and the potential for creating a new individual realized. Weismann also demonstrated through the examination of the embryos of small marine creatures that the reproductive organs developed very early, that they did not contribute to the formation or growth of the rest of the body, and that cells in the rest of the body did not contribute to the sexual organs. Consequently, there was no possibility that acquired characteristics, such as a giraffe stretching its neck, could affect sperm or egg cells and thus be transmitted to any offspring.

Weismann concluded that Lamarck was wrong about acquired characteristics and that Darwin was right about natural selection. Yet the Lamarckians would not give up so easily, even when Weismann cut off the tails of sixteen hundred mice through twenty-two generations bred in his laboratory, with the result that there was no shortening of tails in successive generations of mice. For the time being, the "Darwinists" remained in the minority.

Unknown to Weismann and the other researchers were the experiments of an Augustinian monk named Gregor Mendel (1822–1884) who lived in Brünn, Bohemia, now part of the Czech Republic. Over a period of seven years, from 1856 to 1863, Mendel examined the way characteristics are inherited by experimenting with ten thousand pea plants of six varieties, including tall versus short plants, wrinkled versus smooth peas, and green versus yellow peas. When, for example, he cross-pollinated yellow and green peas, he discovered that all of the hybrid peas came out yellow. But when he crossed these peas, the "grandchildren" came out one-fourth green and three-fourths yellow. More peas had turned out yellow because "yellowness" was a dominant trait and "greenness" was a recessive trait. However, when two green factors were paired in the process of reproduction, the resultant peas were green. Many later experiments with a variety of characteristics in many different species, animals as well as plants, resulted in these same three to one ratios.

Most importantly, Mendel realized that a blending of characteristics had not taken place in his pea experiments and that both green and yellow characteristics had been passed intact to the next generation. These discoveries could only mean one more blow against Lamarckianism, since external circumstances of use and disuse had nothing to do with the transmission of characteristics. However, Mendel published his results in a relatively obscure scientific journal, the *Transactions of the Brünn Natural History Society* in 1866, at a time just before the discovery of chromosomes and of how reproductive cells were created. Knowledge of these factors might have caused some scientists to become more aware of Mendel's work and its relevance to their own research. Under the circumstances, there was no obvious audience for Mendel's conclusions. Mendel did visit London in 1862 to see the second Great Exhibition (held eleven years after the first), but there is no evidence that he had heard of Darwin at that point or, as Darwin's meticulous diary shows, that the two of them met. Later, Mendel did purchase a German translation of *Origin*, but he did not communicate to Darwin any reactions that he might have had to it.

Beginning in the 1890s, several scientists began conducting experiments very similar to Mendel's, though they remained ignorant of the earlier work by the now dead Augustinian monk. One of them was Dutch botanist Hugo De Vries (1848–1935), who proposed that species characteristics were due to a single hereditary factor that could be passed from one generation to the next. (In 1899, while checking out the scientific literature before publishing his own work, he came across Mendel's article.) With a bow to Darwin's mistaken theory of pangenesis, he called these factors "pangens"—or in English, "pangenes" (later shortened to "genes").

In England, zoologist William Bateson (1861–1926) came to similar conclusions and agreed with De Vries in thinking that some variations in inheritance could be quite large. They called these "saltations," derived from a Latin word meaning "to jump." In the end, Bateson and De Vries believed that there were two kinds of evolution, a gradual type in which species became more tightly fitted into an ecological niche and another, where sudden jumps produced new species. Later researchers would conclude that Bateson and De Vries were wrong to propose these two types, but that they were on the right track about evolution as a whole. De Vries invented the term *mutation* to describe his idea of jumps, and Bateson coined the word *genetics* for the study of heredity.

Mendelian-type experiments with fruit flies by American Thomas Morgan between 1907 and 1917—and then by others—showed that small changes, accumulating over many generations (two-week generations in the case of fruit flies), could account for large changes over long periods of time that did not require dramatic saltations. Morgan also showed that the genes were "individual units" strung like beads along the chromosomes. In 1930, English scientist R. A. Fisher calculated that if a mutation gave an organism just a one percent advantage over others, the new characteristic would spread throughout the entire population in only one hundred generations. Among humans, according to science historians Michael White and John Gribbin, the evolution from *Homo erectus*, with a brain size of 900 cubic centimeters to Neanderthal man, with a brain size of 1,400 cubic centimeters, could have occurred in about 13,500 years.[3] This seems like a long time in human terms, but in geological time it is nothing, which may explain why the intermediate fossil remains of many evolutionary changes—the so-called missing links—are often never found, though this has not kept religious opponents of evolution from using them as "proofs" against evolution and particularly against natural selection.

In 1942, Julian Huxley, the grandson of Darwin's great friend and defender Thomas Huxley, called these collective conclusions the "evolutionary syntheses."[4] Leonard Darwin, Charles and Emma's last surviving child, who died the following year at age ninety-three, lived to see this vindication of his father's work.

The final piece in what has come to be called neo-Darwinism was the announcement in 1953, by James Watson and Francis Crick, of the double helix structure of DNA. This was a four-letter genetic code that determines how cells work and how they combine to form tissues, organs, species, and individual features. Mutations take place when the code in reproductive cells becomes scrambled or when a chunk of DNA is accidentally dislodged and spliced in at a different location. Purposeful genetic engineering takes place when DNA is manipulated in the laboratory to make plants more disease or drought-resistant, or to improve crop yields. In animals, including humans, genetic engineering holds the potential for preventing or even reversing certain hereditary diseases.

The recent sequencing of DNA in various species also sheds light on how closely some species are related. For example, the difference between the DNA in humans and chimpanzees varies by only 2 to 4 percent, demonstrating that the two species diverged from a common ancestor, just as Darwin had predicted based on the close structural similarities between humans and African apes. Given the time required for such a genetic divergence, it has been estimated that a common ancestor existed between four and five million years ago. This estimate, along with the fact that the most ancient human remains have been found on the African continent, reaffirms Darwin's conviction that the first humans arose in Africa.

DNA evidence has allowed criminal investigators to connect suspects more accurately to a crime scene or to clear those who have been wrongly accused and/or convicted. Family relationships and presumed descendants can also be demonstrated by DNA samples, the most famous case apparently proving that Thomas Jefferson, whom Lincoln was so fond of quoting, fathered at least one child (and perhaps several more) with a slave mistress named Sally Hemmings. In this case, the DNA configuration of a known white descendant of Jefferson was compared to one of Sally Hemmings's descendants and a genetic match was found.

Although each human being has a distinct genetic profile, the genetic variations among humans are so widely distributed that the concept of race is clearly arbitrary, artificial, and mistaken, as Darwin had held. All human beings belong to a single species, and there are no such categories, biologically speaking, as superior or inferior races of humankind. Certain genetic resemblances among living things also suggest that all life forms are related and, as Darwin proposed, may be descended from the same organic particles from a couple of billion years ago.

Rapid genetic mutations of viruses also explain why some vaccines, such as those for influenza, have to be modified each year to try to keep up with the mutations that occur in the fast-evolving flu virus for which no immunities have yet been acquired in potential human victims. The overuse of antibiotics has also led to bacterial strains that have mutated in ways that make them resistant to a wide variety of antibiotics. For many scientists, this is compelling evidence that biological evolution is occurring in the here and now, as they research, write, and speak.

In the three decades after the Scopes trial of 1925, there had been little public controversy over teaching evolution in the schools. This was party because antievolutionists successfully pressured textbook adoption committees in certain parts of the country—particularly the South—to reject books that took a strong stance on evolution, forcing publishers to remove offensive materials. Hunter's *Civic Biology*, which John Scopes had used at the Dayton, Tennessee, high school, was among the texts that underwent considerable surgery. As late as 1942, less half the science teachers surveyed even mentioned evolution in the classroom.[5] Meanwhile religious fundamentalists had turned inward, giving up on trying to convince the American population as a whole and concentrating instead on educating their own flocks about the dangers of evolutionary thought and especially about Darwinian natural selection. These circumstances continued to allow religious modernists was well as most scientists to believe that they had won the battle over evolution in the United States.

This triumphal mood provided the context for a very successful Broadway play and movie, both titled *Inherit the Wind*. The play (1955) and the film (1960) greatly distorted the Scopes trial, portraying Bryan (Brady) as a pitiful ignoramus and bigot and Darrow (Drummond) as a champion of modern enlightenment, free speech, and civil liberties. These dramatizations also portrayed the citizens of Dayton (Hillsboro) as an angry mob determined to put Scopes (Cates) behind bars. The authors even invented a girlfriend for Scopes/Cates, the daughter of a fundamentalist preacher who has been fulminating against the defendant and the teaching of evolution in the local schools.

Unfortunately, most people who saw *Inherit the Wind*, and especially those who saw the movie, accepted it all as a true account of the Scopes trial—a modern morality play in which reason and tolerance triumph over hatred and persecution of the truth. There was nothing in the film or the play about how the case had actually been trumped up by the prosecution to gain publicity for a town down on its luck, about how the well-liked Scopes (who never spent even a second in jail) had cooperated with the whole scheme, or about how Bryan, once the most beloved politician and reformer of his day, had seen no inconsistency between his campaigns for political reform and his crusades against evolution. Some degree of invention is always necessary for presenting a historical event on the stage or screen, but *Inherit the Wind* was way over the top with contrived dramatization.[6]

Just a year before the movie, on the hundredth anniversary of *The Origin of Species* in 1959, Julian Huxley spoke of what he called "evolutionary humanism" at a scientific conference in Chicago. "The earth was not created," he said, "it evolved. So did all the animals and plants that inhabit it, including our human selves, mind and souls as well as brain and body." "Man's destiny," he added, "is to be the sole agent for the future evolution of this planet." This meant safeguarding the environment, celebrating cultural diversity, and emphasizing the quality of life over the unending consumption of material goods. Evolution's greatest gift was the "vision, first opened for us by Charles Darwin a century back, [that] illuminates our existence in a simple but almost overwhelming way."[7] For Huxley, this revelation was far more exhilarating than anything religion could offer.

When Huxley made these statements, Darwin's Down House had been open to the public since the British Association for the Advancement of Science took possession of the property in 1929. Various members of the family had contributed furniture to the project so that Darwin's study could be put back together exactly as it was when he worked there. Later the property was taken over by English Heritage. The Mount, Darwin's birthplace at Shrewsbury, now houses local government offices and awaits restoration.

The Lincoln home had been open to the public since the late 1880s, when it became the property of the state of Illinois. In 1972 the home was taken over by the US National Park service. The Lincoln birthplace at Hodgenville, Kentucky, became a national park in 1916. Three years later, the site of New Salem, Illinois, where Lincoln had spent a crucial half dozen years, became a state park, and over the next several decades, the village structures were researched and reconstructed. Indiana created a state park at Little Pigeon Creek, where Lincoln had spent most of his childhood, and in 1962 the National Park Service acquired the property.

As Lincoln sites were being preserved and opened to the public, politicians, writers, and historians continued to shape the Lincoln image. For decades after the Civil War, the Republican Party had monopolized the Lincoln heritage in politics, making his birthday on February 12 into a sort of feast day for the GOP. This began to change with the inauguration of Franklin Roosevelt in 1933. Every year on February 12, unless he had to be away from Washington, Roosevelt went to the Lincoln Memorial, where an aide laid a wreath in front of the seated statue. At the same time, Roosevelt did not forget the Democrats' "patron saint" Thomas Jefferson, prompting the administration to build the large neoclassical Jefferson Memorial not far from the Lincoln temple, with Roosevelt often referring to both Lincoln and Jefferson in his speeches.

Roosevelt admired Lincoln for his vigorous use of executive authority as well as for his pragmatism, approaches used by the Depression-era president to experiment boldly to restore prosperity and reform the economy. In a speech that he gave at Gettysburg in 1938 on the seventy-fifth anniversary of the battle, attended by dwindling numbers of Civil War veterans, Roosevelt wove together these themes of practical action as a lasting legacy for his New Deal, with a none-too-transparent comparison between himself and Lincoln: "A statesman deals with concrete difficulties—with things which must be done from day to day." Now the nation faced "another conflict, as fundamental as Lincoln's, fought not with the glint of steel but with appeals to reason and justice on a thousand fronts—seeking to save for our common country opportunity and security for its citizens in a free society. We are near to winning this battle . . . and through the years may we live by the wisdom and humanity of the heart of Abraham Lincoln."[8]

As Europe fell under the sway of fascists and war clouds began to gather, Lincoln became a symbol of freedom for the American people and of strong and determined leadership in the face of those who would destroy democracy. Nowhere was this more evident than in the 1938 Broadway play *Abe Lincoln of Illinois*, written by Robert Sherwood, and the 1940 movie version, both starring Raymond Massey as Lincoln. At the climax of this drama, the Lincoln–Douglas debates, Lincoln delivers a ten-minute peroration against slavery and the ongoing conflict over human rights, which the audience cannot help connecting to the horrors of modern totalitarianism. Once the United States went to war after Pearl Harbor, Roosevelt drew upon the awesome war powers first invoked by Lincoln, and in his formal acceptance speech for his fourth nomination in 1944, he ended by quoting the famous closing lines of Lincoln's "Second Inaugural Address": "With malice toward none; with charity for all. . . ."

Roosevelt died on April 12, 1945, in another Easter season, just three days short of the eightieth anniversary of Lincoln's death on April 15, 1865. With the war not yet over and Roosevelt's work left unfinished, clergymen and journalists alike drew the obvious parallel with Lincoln, who had died before he could preside over the coming peace. Roosevelt's body, like Lincoln's, lay in the East Room of the White House, though not on view to the public.

Lincoln's positive reputation continued to build in the years leading up to the sesquicentennial of his birth in 1959. For the first time, in 1955, the entire Lincoln home in Springfield, now restored and furnished with period pieces, was opened to the public. One of its more famous visitors was Governor Adlai Stevenson of Illinois, also the Democratic nominee for president in both 1952 and 1956. A strong admirer of Lincoln, Stevenson relished the honor of narrating composer Aaron Copland's *Lincoln Portrait*. President Dwight Eisenhower, who defeated Stevenson both times in his bid for the White House, was also a great Lincoln admirer. Eisenhower had a photographic portrait of Lincoln on the wall in his office, kept a set of Lincoln's *Collected Works* close by, quoted him frequently, and occupied the Lincoln family pew at the New York Avenue Presbyterian Church.

At mid-century, historians turned increasingly against the revisionist school. Just after World War II, young Arthur Schlesinger Jr. attacked the whole revisionist thesis of a "needless war," calling it pure sentimentality. Making an analogy with the recent war, Schlesinger believed the revisionists' claim that the slavery issue in the territories had been "unreal" was like saying that the Nazi's invasion of Poland, which touched off World War II in Europe, was equally unreal.

Harry V. Jaffa, in his *Crisis of the House Divided*, took on both Albert Beveridge and James Randall, who had played down any real differences between Lincoln and Douglas on the question of slavery in the territories. At the heart of Lincoln's argument, according to Jaffa, had been the Declaration of Independence and his insistence on the equality of all men to be free and to pursue their own happiness. Clearly, the differences between the two world wars had made a great impression on the historical community: while World War I had seemed like a tragic and colossal waste of blood and treasure to the revisionists, World War II had eliminated some of the worst regimes known in history.

David Donald, in his *Lincoln Reconsidered* (1960), reversed his earlier view that Lincoln had aligned himself with the conservatives and moderates in his party against the Radical Republicans. Not everyone who opposed Lincoln was a radical, Donald argued; neither were Lincoln's policies always at odds with the Radicals. Instead, the ever-practical Lincoln had cooperated with several factions within Republican ranks to achieve his ends.

Positive views of Lincoln from the 1930s through the 1950s are not difficult to explain. At a time when the country faced the ravages of economic depression, world war, and the challenges of international communism, Lincoln appeared to represent the qualities that Americans wanted to represent to the world: honesty, equality, hard work, careers open to talent, and faith in the wisdom of the common people. Darwin did not fare as well at a time when many commentators linked both fascism and communism with scientific materialism and survival of the fittest.

As war clouds gathered in the 1930s and then burst into World War II, Columbia University historian Jacques Barzun took Darwin to task for promoting a dangerous and simplistic materialism. In *Darwin, Marx, Wagner* (1941), Barzun compared Darwin's worldview with these other two famous men of the nineteenth century and laid much of the blame for fascism and communism on their intellectual shoulders. Karl Marx, as Barzun correctly pointed out, had been enthralled by the scientific materialism of Darwin's *Origin*, believing that it gave powerful support to his own theory of economic determinism, dialectical materialism, and class conflict. Marx had written to the German socialist Ferdinand Lassalle, "Darwin's work is most important and suits my purpose in that it provides a basis in natural science for the historical class struggle."[9] In

1873, Marx had sent Darwin an autographed copy of *Das Kapital*, which Darwin never read. He had no sympathy for communism and can in no way be blamed for the terrible excesses that accompanied the Russian Revolution more than three decades after his death.

Barzun's connections between Darwin and Wagner are even more strained and come down to his observation that Wagner, like Darwin and Marx, was essentially a materialist. As an example of Wagner's materialism and disregard for either romanticism or morality, Barzun cites the composer's opera *Tristan*, first performed in 1859, the same year that Darwin published *Origin*. The opera, he wrote, "enshrines and celebrates the biological act of [sex]. . . . It is a force of nature . . . that seizes them and ends by destroying them."[10] This materialist attitude toward sex, he insisted, continued in Wagner's subsequent operas: "This means that the material base of the Wagnerian art engages the whole of our attention."[11]

Echoing some of Barzun's criticisms nearly two decades later was Gertrude Himmelfarb, who published her *Darwin and the Darwinian Revolution* in 1959. Although Himmelfarb admitted that Darwin himself made no applications of this theory to society and politics—and indeed was both surprised and amused when others did so—she wrote that from Darwin's preservation of favored races in the struggle for life,

> it was a short step to the preservation of favored individuals, classes, or nations—and from their preservation to their glorification. Social Darwinism has often been understood in this sense: as a philosophy exalting competition, power, and violence over convention, ethics, and religion. It has become a portmanteau of nationalism, imperialism, militarism, and dictatorship. . . . The hero or superman, most recently translated as *Fuhrer*, is assumed to be the epitome of the fittest, the best specimen of his breed, the natural ruler who exercises his rule by right of might. . . . Recent expressions of this philosophy, such as *Mein Kampf*, are, unhappily, too familiar to require exposition here. And it is by an obvious process of analogy and deduction that they are said to derive from Darwinism.[12]

Himmelfarb made less of a case for linking Darwin to Marx than Barzun had done twenty years earlier. Still, she observed that both Darwin and Marx "insisted upon the basic fact of struggle and upon progress as its result."[13] She also quotes Friedrich Engels's eulogy of Marx: "Just as Darwin discovered the law of evolution in organic nature, so Marx discovered the law of evolution in human history."[14] However, Himmelfarb does not go on from here to link Darwin with Joseph Stalin and totalitarian communism as she had tried to link Darwin with Hitler and Nazism. In fact, connecting Darwin to either system was as unfair as William Jennings Bryan's earlier associating Darwin the man with the causes of World War I. Without a doubt, Darwin would have been appalled by both Hitler and Stalin and their monstrous regimes.[15]

Darwin's name, however unfairly and inaccurately, continued to be attached to social evolutionary theories. In 1944, historian Richard Hofstadter published his widely read *Social Darwinism in American Thought*. In his introduction, Hofstadter wrote, "In some respects the United States during the last three decades of the nineteenth century and at the beginning of the twentieth century was *the* Darwinian country."[16] This was not only because biological evolution was quickly embraced by the American scientific community following the publication of *Origin of Species*, but also because of the warm reception given to the social Darwinian philosophy of Herbert Spencer, who was far more popular in the United States than in his native England.

According to Hofstadter, Spencer's social Darwinism was a godsend to the captains of industry and the conservative politicians who represented them. It served them well, Hofstadter wrote, in two different ways: "Nature would provide that the best competitors in a competitive situation would win, and that this process would lead to continuing improvement. . . . Secondly, the idea of development over aeons brought new force to another familiar idea in conservative political theory, the conception that all sound development must be slow and unhurried."[17]

In other words, a political hands-off policy on business would promote economic competition and efficiency and social progress.

As Hofstadter was happy to point out, this approach to business and politics led to monopoly and oligopoly and the exploitation of both workers and consumers. Reformers were quick to turn the tables on the conservative social Darwinists and argue that government should pass social and economic legislation to help its citizens adapt to the vicissitudes of an urban industrial environment. Strong antitrust legislation, supplemented by business regulation, could also help to restore competition and level the economic playing field. To buttress his case, Hofstadter repeats the now-famous quote from Supreme Court justice Oliver Wendell Holmes's dissent in *Lochner v. New York*: "The Fourteenth Amendment does not enact Mr. Herbert Spencer's *Social Statics*."[18]

As to Darwin himself, Hofstadter concluded that there was much in his writings to buttress both the conservatives and the reformers, though he believed that Darwin gave more ammunition to those who stressed human cooperation and mutual aid. Darwin, he wrote, "believed man's moral sense to be an inevitable outgrowth of his social instincts and habits, and a critical factor in group survival. The pressure of group opinion and the moral effect of family affections [Darwin] ranked with intelligent self-interest as biological foundations of moral behavior."[19]

Still, whether it was conservatives or reformers who attempted to use biological concepts to explain or justify certain types of social behavior, Hofstadter concluded that these efforts were both futile and illegitimate: "Such biological ideas as the 'survival of the fittest' . . . are utterly useless in attempting to understand society; that the life of man in society, while it is incidentally a biological fact, has characteristics that are not reducible to biology and must be explained in the distinctive terms of a cultural analysis; . . . that social improvement is a product of advances in technology and social organization, not of breeding or selective elimination."[20]

Four decades later, Greta Jones, in her *Social Darwinism and English*

Thought, also discussed the ways that a variety of individuals and groups in Darwin's homeland had sought to exploit his work for their own ends. "For anarchists and liberals it showed nature and society required no intervention from without or from within. . . . To a wide range of social-ists [Darwinism] demonstrated the possibility of change in society and human nature and it acted as a challenge to religious authority."[21]

In the midst of continuing reflections over evolution, both social and biological, scientist and prolific writer E. O. Wilson suggested a truce and a new avenue of cooperation between Darwinists and anti-Darwinists. A former Southern Baptist, Wilson became a secularist who fully accepted Darwin's natural selection and rejected the Genesis story of creation. Although he found religious and scientific explanations for the origins and development of life to be incompatible, he believed that both the religious and the secular camps could find common ground through a commitment to what he called the stewardship of life: "How-ever science and religion wax and wane in the minds of men, there remains the earthborn, yet transcendental, obligation we are both morally bound to share."[22]

Wilson was already famous—or notorious, depending on one's point of view—for founding the new discipline of sociobiology. In his 1975 book *Sociobiology: The New Synthesis*, and in subsequent writings, he has argued that much of human behavior is biologically determined rather than learned. Such behaviors as altruism, mate selection, and aggression, he argues, are biological in nature and have been shaped by natural selec-tion as a result of their survival values. Wilson's critics, such as Richard Lewontin and Stephen J. Gould, have argued that sociobiology is a throw-back to conservative social Darwinism, since it deemphasizes the role of culture in shaping behavior and with it, the free will that humans have to shape their behavior. This was also the main objection that Hofstadter had made about social Darwinism three decades earlier.[23]

Darwin himself became the object of criticism in a best-selling novel in 2005 called *The Darwin Conspiracy*. In it, author John Darton spins a yarn that, if true, would rob Darwin of any claims to originality. Two modern scientists, Hugh and Beth, follow a number of clues appearing to show that the *Beagle's* surgeon, Robert McCormick, had actually formulated the concept of natural selection while still onboard ship but had conveniently died after falling into an erupting volcano that he and Darwin were exploring. Darwin, the novel suggests, might have saved McCormick from this terrible death and he later failed to give any credit to the dead man for his conclusions about natural selection. It was consuming guilt over these actions, the two sleuths conclude, that was the real reason for Darwin's mysterious illnesses throughout life.

In reality, McCormick did leave the ship after only four months, but he did not perish in a volcanic eruption. He died back home in 1890, at the ripe old age of ninety. Though the novel's conclusion has no basis in truth, it reflects a tradition that Darwin was not really the gentle, unassuming sage of Down House that he and his admirers portrayed to the public but a very ambitious man who may have given too little credit to the other scientists and thinkers of his time, whose ideas and work helped inspire and support his own accomplishments.

Twenty years before the publication of *The Darwin Conspiracy*, novelist Gore Vidal presented Lincoln as equally ambitious—and often unscrupulous. In *Lincoln* (1984) Vidal shows his protagonist to be a master politician who shamelessly uses patronage to get others to cooperate with him. According to Vidal, Lincoln also has no qualms about allowing bankers and stockbrokers like Jay Cooke of Philadelphia to grow rich while financing the war; this wealth allows them or their descendants to become the robber barons of the next generation. Vidal even has a drunk William Herndon telling John Hay that Lincoln had resorted to prostitutes as a young man and had become infected with syphilis (there is no real evidence for either charge).

Long before Vidal's book, Richard Hofstadter had already made a connection between Lincoln and the robber barons in his *American Political Tradition* (1948). Having written extensively about how conservative social Darwinists had used Darwin and Spencer to justify laissez-faire economic and governmental policies, Hofstadter attempted to show how these same selfish interests had exploited Lincoln. Pursuing this theme, he wrote, "Lincoln was a pre-eminent example of that self-help which Americans have so admired." This was an impressive example of "sudden ascent from relative obscurity to high eminence."[24] Throughout his life, he had subscribed to the Protestant ethic (as did Herbert Spencer and virtually all spokesmen for American capitalists) of hard work, frugality, and temperance. Employing such traits, even the most unskilled worker could supposedly become a capitalist. To prove his point, Hofstadter quotes from Lincoln's 1860 speech on labor at New Haven, Connecticut: "I take it that it is best for all to leave each man free to acquire property as fast as he can. Some will get wealthy.... So while we do not propose any war on capital, we do wish to allow the humblest man an equal chance to get rich with everybody else."[25] Only the advice did not hold up over time, Hofstadter charged, a failure that Lincoln did not live long enough to see: "Had he lived to seventy, he would have seen the generation brought up on self-help come into its own, build oppressive business corporations, and begin to close off those treasured opportunities for the little man."[26]

It might be supposed that the civil rights movement of the 1950s and 1960s would have raised Lincoln's stature still higher, especially since the organizers of the 1963 march on Washington purposely chose the Lincoln Memorial as a backdrop for their rally. Yet it was not Lincoln who became the iconic figure that day but the Reverend Martin Luther King Jr., whose "I Have a Dream" speech electrified the movement and inspired much of the rest of the country. When King was assassinated in 1968, he replaced Lincoln as the martyr for racial justice in the eyes of many African Americans. King also symbolized the desire of black Americans to take control themselves of the fight for racial equality and not to depend on white politicians, who could never entirely appreciate their situation or their perspective.

A number of black scholars—ironically and for different reasons from the earlier revisionist school—renewed the claim that Lincoln was really a Southern sympathizer. He had also been a moderate on the question of emancipation, they charged, had freed the slaves largely out of military necessity, had strongly favored African colonization, and had made various pronouncements about blacks not being equal to whites. For members of the black power movement, which emphasized black pride and black self-sufficiency, Lincoln was racist at worst and irrelevant at best.

Reflecting this view is Lerone Bennett's *Forced into Glory: Abraham Lincoln's White Dream* (2000). An African-American historian, Bennett writes, "There is overwhelming evidence that Lincoln was a wily and determined foe of equal rights and black liberation." Rather than being a major actor on the stage of black liberation, Bennett charges, Lincoln was merely carried along by the tides of history, which he did little to shape: "Lincoln was at best an incidental, accidental rider of a liberating wave that probably would have crested sooner—and higher—without him."[27] Four years later, historian Michael Lind, who is not African American, renewed charges of racial prejudice in *What Lincoln Believed*. Although Lind admits that Lincoln freed the slaves and supported the Thirteenth Amendment that made slavery unconstitutional in the United States, he adds, "An integrated, multiracial society was unimaginable to Lincoln. . . . A few brave and visionary white Americans in his day joined black Americans in opposing white supremacy as well as slavery. Lincoln was not among them."[28]

Concern about abuses of power by both Democratic and Republican presidents in recent decades has led to questions about presidential power in general and whether or not Lincoln had made himself into a virtual dictator during the Civil War. As early as 1948, political scientist Clinton

Rossiter, in his *Constitutional Dictatorship*, did not hesitate to call Lincoln a wartime dictator. Rossiter approved of Lincoln's actions during the Civil War, but he admitted that he had established dangerous precedents for future occupants of the White House. In the aftermath of undeclared wars in both Korea and Vietnam, Richard Nixon's creation of "an imperial presidency," and George Bush's decision to invade Iraq based on dubious intelligence and to revoke habeas corpus for "enemy combatants" made Rossiter's warnings seemed chillingly real and caused even liberals, who usually approve of a strong presidency, to reassess their position.

Arthur Schlesinger, generally an admirer of Lincoln, wrote in his *Imperial Presidency* (1973) that many of the war powers abused by later presidents had begun with Lincoln during the Civil War. "Throughout the war," Schlesinger wrote, "even with Congress in session, Lincoln continued to exercise wide powers independently of Congress" without a legislative declaration of war.[29] Lincoln's justification for these powers had been his role of commander in chief under the Constitution, an argument that Schlesinger believed "marked the beginning of a fateful evolution."[30]

As historians and commentators were continuing to debate the Lincoln legacy, there was a renewal of controversy over teaching evolution in the schools. In Darwin's England, the teaching of evolution has been compulsory for many years in the public schools, which are under the direct control of a national system of education. According to a recent National Curriculum Outline for England, science teachers are directed to cover how "organisms are interdependent and adapted to their environments" and how "variation within a species can lead to evolutionary changes."[31]

England's national curriculum also mandates the study of religion in the state schools, though parents can ask that their children be excused from these classes.

The outline for religious education directs, among other things, that "students should be taught to reflect on, express and justify their own opinions in light of their learning about religion and their study of religious, philosophical, moral and spiritual questions" and to "relate their learning in religious education to the wider world."[32] Given these generous parameters, students are free to express any opinions about science and religion and what they might see as conflicts between natural selection and biblical accounts of creation.

The presence of religious education in the English curriculum, where there is no legal separation between church and state (the Church of England being the established religion) may be one reason why there is little consternation over the teaching of evolution. Another reason has to do with the fact that England is a far less religious country than the United States, despite—and perhaps because of—its national church. In the United States, where an "establishment of religion" is strictly forbidden by the Constitution, each denomination has had the freedom to compete vigorously for members and to appeal to every taste. Great denominational variety has also been a product of mass immigration in the United States, with immigrants often seeing their church as a powerful connection to the old country and its culture.

The decentralization of American education, like American religion, had originated in frontier communities that established their own schools largely independent of state or federal influence. Dissenting religious groups that also emphasized local control of education have often had a great impact on the schools in a given area, and in rural areas and small towns, many of these groups have held to a fundamentalist creed that emphasized the literal and inerrant truth of the Bible, including the Genesis story of creation.

Even so, fighting over evolution in American schools had died down since the Scopes trial, mainly because in states where there were large numbers of fundamentalists, legislatures and school boards had continued to ban the teaching of Darwinism while the fundamentalist churches had turned inward with an emphasis on educating their own members about the dangers of evolution. In the absence of any federal court decisions to overturn such prohibitions, both the states and their local school districts could do more or less as they pleased when it came to teaching evolution. This status quo was badly undermined when, in 1957, the Soviet Union successfully launched *Sputnik*, the first artificial satellite to be put into orbit around the earth. In the postmortems over how the Russians had managed to pull ahead in the space race, educational experts and the press heaped much of the blame on American academic standards—especially in the sciences. One response was the creation and publication of the multimillion-dollar Biological Sciences Curriculum Study (BSCS), paid for by the federal government and sponsored by the National Science Foundation. The study and resultant classroom materials laid a heavy stress on evolution.

The new textbooks sparked a reaction from conservative religious groups at a time when the "mainline" Protestant churches, such as Episcopalians, Presbyterians, Congregationalists, Methodists, and mainstream Lutherans, which had generally come to take a more liberal and open-minded view of science and evolution, were experiencing stagnant or declining memberships. At the same time, more and more Americans were joining rapidly growing conservative congregations, sometimes labeled evangelical, such as the Southern Baptist Convention, the Lutheran Church (Missouri Synod), various Pentecostal groups, the Assemblies of God, and the Seventh-day Adventists. These denominations fared particularly well in the South and Midwest and succeeded in electing like-minded candidates to political office, most of them Republicans by the late twentieth and the early twenty-first centuries.

Members of these conservative churches established the Creation Research Society in 1963, the same year that the BSCS biology text was adopted by about half the public schools in the country and just over a century since the publication of Darwin's *Origin of Species*. The Creation Research Society's statement of belief, to which all members had to swear allegiance, held that "the Bible is the written word of God and because it is inspired throughout, all its assertions are historically and scientifically true." The statement also laid great emphasis on the biblical story of creation: "All basic types of living things, including man, were made by direct creative acts of God during the Creation Week described in Genesis." In an attempt to explain the extinction of some species and the appearance of new ones, the statement returned to the old idea, espoused for well over a century, that these could be explained by Noah's flood: "The great Flood described in Genesis, commonly referred to as the Noachian Flood, was a historic event worldwide in its extent and effect."[33]

Creationists considered not only Darwinian evolution to be false but also the source of virtually every modern evil. Writer and creationist Henry M. Morris declared that evolution had provided "the pseudo-scientific justification for almost every deadly philosophy and every evil practice known to man."[34] These included social Darwinism, racism, Marxism, and Nazism, along with the promotion of homosexuality, abortion, and the use of illegal drugs. The fact that Darwin had no use for socialistic schemes and that he would have been sickened and appalled by any totalitarian regime apparently made no difference to Morris. Since Darwin had also opposed birth control, there is little doubt that he would have been strongly against abortion.

Meanwhile the US federal courts, for the first time, became involved with the issue of evolution in the public schools. In 1968 the Supreme Court, in *Epperson v. Arkansas*, declared in a unanimous 9–0 opinion that a 1928 Arkansas law was unconstitutional for prohibiting the teaching of evolution as well as disallowing any textbooks that presented the concept of evolution. Included in the opinion was the conclusion that Arkansas had "sought to prevent its teachers from discussing the theory of evolution because it is contrary to the belief of some that the Book of Genesis must be the exclusive doctrine as to the origin of man." For this reason, the court reasoned that the Arkansas law amounted to an establishment of religion in violation of the First Amendment of the US Constitution.[35]

Creationists now realized that it would be impossible to keep evolution out the classroom altogether. Their new strategy was to demand equal time for what they called creation science, arguing that the preponderance of scientific evidence supported the Genesis story of creation and claiming that natural selection could not stand up to rigorous scientific analysis. Because the *Epperson* case had only overturned laws that banned the teaching of evolution—and had said nothing about teaching creationism—they believed that the court had given them an opening, however narrow.

Now the main tactic of creationists was to lobby the states to pass "balanced treatment" laws, which required creationism to be taught at the same time that evolution was presented to students. Arkansas again led the bandwagon when its legislature enacted a law in 1981 to require equal treatment for "creation science" and natural selection in the classroom. The following year, a federal district court ruled this law unconstitutional in a case called *McLean v. Arkansas Board of Education*, and in 1987 the Supreme Court disallowed a similar law passed by Louisiana in *Edwards v. Aguillard*. In the latter 7–2 decision, the court declared that the Louisiana act similarly violated the First Amendment prohibition against an establishment of religion, since it "impermissibly endorses religion by advancing the . . . belief that a supernatural being created mankind."

Despite this ruling, creationists believed that the Supreme Court had left room for yet another approach to the question. In his majority opinion in *Aguillard*, Justice William Brennan wrote, "Teaching a variety of scientific theories about the origins of humankind to schoolchildren might be validly done with the clear secular intent of enhancing the effectiveness of science instruction." More encouraging still was Justice Antonin Scalia's dissent in this case, where he held that Christian fundamentalists "are quite entitled, as a secular matter, to have whatever scientific evidence there may be against evolution presented in their schools."[36]

Following up on these enticing possibilities, creationists began going before school boards, state legislatures, and the courts, arguing that teachers should be allowed to explain why the theory of evolution causes controversy in science and society, meaning that teacher should be able to find fault with evolutionary biology so long as they used nonreligious arguments. Providing these arguments were individuals such as biochemist Michael J. Behe. A practicing Roman Catholic who believed in both the concept and reality of evolution, Behe nevertheless maintained that there were evidences of intelligent design in the living world. In his book *Darwin's Black Box* (1996), he argued that some organs like the eye were far too complex to have evolved through random natural selection, an objection that Darwin himself had anticipated. Behe's explanation was that any light-sensitive group of cells, no matter how primitive, would have given their possessors an advantage in the struggle for survival and that subsequent evolutionary improvements to these cells could have eventually produced a fully formed and functional eye. Nevertheless, critics have used this "complexity of eye argument" over the decades. Behe has made a similar argument at the molecular level: "Although Darwin's mechanism—natural selection working on variations—might explain many things, however, I do not believe it explains molecular life. I also do not think it surprising that the new science of the very small might change the way we view the less small."[37] More specifically, Behe asserted that the twenty or so interacting proteins necessary for blood to clot could not have come about through natural selection alone. In that case, he argued, the phenomenon of blood clotting required an intelligent designer, as did the evolution of the eye. In many ways this was an updated version of William Paley's two-hundred-year-old argument from design, which had so attracted the young Charles Darwin.

Critics of intelligent design (often abbreviated as I.D.), which included the great majority of the scientific community, held that I.D. is not real science but merely a thinly disguised religious argument, and that although its proponents do not invoke God by name, their intelligent designer is clearly a synonym for God. These critics also maintain that, no matter how sophisticated I.D. may sound, it is merely a stalking horse for creationism and lacks any valid scientific basis. In fact, Michael Behe's own colleagues in the biology department at Lehigh University in Pennsylvania have distanced themselves from his point of view in their official Web site: "While we respect Prof. Behe's right to express his views, they are his alone and are in no way endorsed by the department. It is our collective position that intelligent design has no basis in science, has not been tested experimentally and should not be regarded as scientific."[38]

Behe's own Roman Catholic Church had no problem with the most recent science of evolution and no objection to its being taught in Catholic schools. Although the nineteenth-century Pope Pius IX had condemned materialism, secularism, and scientific theories that went against church teachings, he did not single out Darwinism in his 1864 *Syllabus of Errors* or in subsequent criticisms of the modern world. In 1948, the church did belatedly add *Origin of Species* to its Index of Forbidden Books, where it remained until 1966, when the Index was abolished. But since the Catholic Church had never insisted on a literal interpretation of the Bible and had long held that tradition and the pronouncements of church councils and popes were as important as scripture, the hierarchy as well as Catholic scholars were not as boxed in as Protestant Fundamentalists. The church's official scholastic philosophy also held that there could be no conflict between faith and reason "rightly understood."

Pius XII became the first pope to address the subject of biological evolution in his 1950 encyclical *Humani Generis*. In it, he admitted that "the Teaching Authority of the Church does not forbid . . . research and discussions . . . with regard to the doctrine of evolution." Nearly a half century later, in 1996, John Paul II went much further in a speech to the Pontifical Academy of Sciences: "New knowledge has led to the recognition of the theory of evolution as more than a hypothesis. . . . It is indeed remarkable that this theory has been progressively accepted by researchers, following a series of discoveries in various fields of knowledge. The convergence, neither sought nor fabricated, of the results of work that was conducted independently is in itself a significant argument in favor of this theory. And if at first sight, there are apparent contradictions [with Catholic teachings] . . . we do know, in fact, that truth cannot contradict truth." This was a classic scholastic statement of how reason and faith cannot contradict each other. The pope also qualified his acceptance of evolution by rejecting a materialist explanation for the process and asserting that God had directed the unfolding of life and that biologists had simply discovered how that divine process had taken place.[39] This was an old compromise that went back to Darwin's own time but that he had rejected—and it was one that most modern biologists would also reject. In this sense, the pope and Michael Behe agreed, since Behe, too, accepted the main tenets of evolution, only arguing that there had been some degree of intelligent design when it came to humans.

Of course, religious fundamentalists did not agree, and as in the past, attempts to strengthen the science curriculum in the public schools alarmed them greatly. In the late 1980s and early 1990s, the states, in an effort to bring more accountability to the schools, started mandating curriculum standards in the various subjects, including the biological sciences. The adoption of these standards, which invariably called for the teaching of evolution, alarmed opponents of natural selection. These changes also gave them new venues to try to influence the groups charged with drawing up or approving the standards.

The new science standards became the subject of a case in US Federal Court in the autumn of 2005. The case stemmed from a decision by the school board of Dover, Pennsylvania, which oversees a district of thirty-six hundred students in a largely suburban part of York County, some twenty-five miles southwest of Harrisburg. In October 2004, the board became the first in the United States to mandate the reading of a brief statement about intelligent design at the beginning of a ninth-grade unit on evolution. The statement read in part, "Darwin's theory is a theory [and] is not a fact. Gaps in the theory exist for which there is no evidence.... Intelligent design is an explanation of the origin of life that differs from Darwin's view.... With respect to any theory, students are encouraged to keep an open mind."[40]

This statement and the policy behind it led the American Civil Liberties Union, on behalf of a group of parents, to sue the board in federal court, resulting in the case *Kitzmiller v. Dover Area School District*.[41] Defending the school board was the Thomas More Law Center, a conservative Christian advocacy group. One of the group's star witnesses was Michael Behe, who, as might be expected, testified on the side of intelligent design.[42] The *Philadelphia Inquirer* immediately dubbed the case, which went to trial in September 2005, as a "latter-day version of the Scopes monkey trial."[43] In reality, there were many differences between the two cases: While in the earlier trial the defense had argued that Scopes's First Amendment rights of free speech were being violated, in the Dover case it was the supporters of intelligent design who were claiming that their rights of free speech were being denied. There was no attempt in Dover, as there had been in Tennessee eighty years before, to forbid the actual teaching of evolution in the public schools; and this time, testimony by scientists was allowed, whereas the judge in the Scopes trial had excluded it. Another difference was demographic. While Dayton, Tennessee, had been a rural southern town with a struggling economy, Dover was a relatively affluent suburban community. Nor was there any of the carnival flavor of the earlier trial surrounding the Dover case.

Yet there was a unique twist to Dover. Among the twenty-seven writers and reporters covering the trial was Matthew Chapman, a great-great grandson of Charles Darwin, on assignment for *Harper's Magazine*. Chapman told the *Philadelphia Inquirer* that he was stunned at all the passion surrounding the evolution issue in the United States, since it "is such a nonissue everywhere else in the world."[44] For Chapman and many others observing the trial, it was amazing to realize that three generations after the Scopes trial and nearly a century and a half after the publication of Darwin's *Origin of Species*, the teaching of evolution remained a subject of heated controversy in some American communities.

Apparently many residents of the Dover school district agreed with Darwin's descendant when, on November 8, 2005, they voted out of office all the board members then up for reelection (eight of the nine) and replaced them with pro-evolutionists opposed to the requirement that biology classes begin with a statement about intelligent design. In reaction to this rout at the ballot box, noted televangelist Pat Robertson said on the air two days later: "To the good citizens of Dover: If there is a disaster in your area, don't turn to God; you just rejected him from your city."[45] Robertson's statement and the many outraged reactions to it showed just how divided the American people remained over Darwin's theory.[46]

Very revealing was American public opinion at large on the subject of evolution. According to a poll taken in July 2005 by the Pew Forum on Religion and Public Life, 60 percent of the American people believed that "humans and other animals have always existed in their present form or have evolved over time under the guidance of a Supreme Being." Only 26 percent agreed with Darwin that life had evolved through natural selection, and 64 percent fully supported teaching creationism alongside evolution in the classroom.[47]

In 2005, President George W. Bush, who had long campaigned for support from conservative Christians, weighed in on the subject of evolution when he responded to the most recent controversy over how it should be taught in the public schools, saying that both evolution and the concept of intelligent design should be part of the curriculum. During a news conference in August 2005, Bush said, "Both sides ought to be properly taught so people can understand what the debate is about."[48]

The end of the twentieth century saw a revival of interest in Lincoln among both scholars and the general public. There was a flood of new books and a number of television programs about both him and the Civil War. Historian James M. McPherson effectively summed up the revived interest in Lincoln among scholars. McPherson's own contribution to the growing list of books was *Abraham Lincoln and the Second American Revolution* (1991). In answer to those who disparaged the failure of racial equality after the Civil War, McPherson argued that the "counterrevolution" launched by former Confederates did not, in fact, succeed in reestablishing slavery and that blacks continued to have the right to own property and receive an education—definite advances over slavery days when they themselves were property and it was against the law to teach a slave to read or write. He added that the Fourteenth Amendment, which bestowed citizenship and forbade the states to deny due process and equal rights to any person, and the Fifteenth Amendment, which outlawed "race, color, or previous condition of servitude" as a basis for withholding the right to vote, were not repealed and were still in the Constitution many decades later when they were finally enforced.

Other recent books focused on a wide array of Lincoln subjects: newly available Lincoln photographs; the Lincoln–Douglas debates; Lincoln and civil liberties; the Gettysburg Address; the Ann Rutledge romance; Lincoln's psychology, religion, ethics, economic views, and sexuality; Lincoln as a lawyer, politician, statesman, and wartime leader; Lincoln and Reconstruction; Lincoln and American culture; and the Lincoln assassination, among others. In 2005, biographer Doris Kearns Goodwin contributed a large tome titled *Team of Rivals*, which focused on Lincoln's skillful handling of a cabinet of exceedingly ambitious men who had sought the presidency themselves or planned to succeed their chief. Douglas L. Wilson also plumbs the theme of Lincoln as master politician in his *Honor's Voice* (1998). Wilson writes that the man was not always as honest as his reputation: "It was folly to deny that Lincoln could be slippery and that he could, particularly where partisan politics were concerned, dissemble and deceive."[49]

The general public was riveted by Ken Burns's nine-episode documentary on the Civil War, broadcast by the Public Broadcasting System (PBS) in 1990. Although the series featured dozens of significant men and women, Lincoln was the undoubted star of the saga, with his rise from obscurity, his great native intelligence, his political sagacity and kindliness, his uncanny eloquence, his belief in Providence, his steadfastness in the face of crushing setbacks, and his tragic death at the very moment of triumph. In 1995, the History Channel broadcast a program on the Lincoln assassination, and in 2001, *The American Experience*, also on PBS, showed *Abraham and Mary Lincoln: A House Divided*, which featured the stormy Lincoln marriage. The bicentennial of Lincoln's birth in 2009 and the one hundred and fiftieth anniversary observances of the Civil War, beginning just two years after, promise even more attention to a man who remains at the center of what it means to be an American and the focus of an ongoing struggle over the meaning of the American experiment.

As more and more attempts to understand Abraham Lincoln were pouring fourth, there was also an avalanche of new publications about Charles Darwin. In 1985, Cambridge University Press began putting out a multivolume new edition of Darwin's correspondence. Two massive biographies, *The Life of a Tormented Evolutionist* (1991) by Adrian Desmond and James Moore, and the two-volume *Charles Darwin* (1995, 2002) by Janet Browne, both sought to connect their subject more fully and intimately to the world of Victorian life and culture.

The early years of the twenty-first century brought a continuing and escalating interest in the two rebel giants, as reflected in the cover stories of popular magazines.[50] In the fall of 2005, Darwin's name appeared thousands of times in newspapers all over the world as a result of the Dover School District case and once more became a household word among supporters and opponents alike.

Meanwhile, the Lincoln Memorial in Washington, often described as "America's soapbox," had again become a prime cultural image, as conservatives complained that an eight-minute orientation video shown to millions of visiting students was tilted in favor of liberalism, since it supposedly showed only liberal rallies at the site. According to one conservative Web site, the video "gave the impression that Lincoln would have supported abortion and homosexuality." In response, the National Park Service added footage of pro-gun and pro–Iraq war rallies staged at the memorial.[51]

The bicentennial of Darwin's birth and the sesquicentennial of his *Origin of Species* in 2009 may not attract as much broad public attention in the United States as the Lincoln bicentennial. But both men have left a legacy that continues to inspire some and to trouble others. Whether one agrees or disagrees with natural selection, Darwin's theory—like the ideas of Copernicus and Galileo, which demolished the long-cherished beliefs that the earth was at the center of the universe—questions the central importance of humankind. More disturbing still for some is the thought that human existence—and the existence of all life—was the result of some cosmic chance with no ultimate meaning. This might excite the existentialist, who could revel in the freedom to choose within the framework of cosmic circumstance, but for many people this is a frightening prospect. On the other side of the Darwinian coin, the realization that race is a figment of the human mind and not a biological reality has tremendous potential for bringing about an end to racial and ethnic prejudice. The parallel realization that all living things are related and part of a complex web of life can only support the environmental movement and its search for ways to save the planet

Lincoln's legacy is equally paradoxical. Like the DNA evidence of human solidarity, Lincoln's decision to free the slaves represented a revolutionary step toward realizing dignity, justice, and equal treatment for all people, regardless of race, color, or ethnic origin. Yet Lincoln himself made ambivalent and contradictory statements about racial equality that dramatize how far present-day Americans have yet to go in completing Lincoln's revolution. Just as troubling is the war that Lincoln waged to save the union and free the slaves, a conflict that consumed 620,000 lives and plunged millions of family members and friends into terrible grief. Lincoln ultimately decided that the war and all the attendant suffering were somehow part of God's purposes, yet many may be tempted to ask what kind of God would demand such terrible punishment; or if humans do indeed have free will, what guilt rests upon the shoulders of Lincoln and the others leaders who chose to go to war?

Whatever one might think of Abraham Lincoln or Charles Darwin, it would be a mistake to see them as superhuman, as individuals who had somehow burst the bonds of common humanity, despite their impressive achievements and great fame. Both knew the joys and sorrows that are inevitably part of the human condition: they fell in love and lost loved ones, enjoyed and worried about their children, were uncertain about their futures and doubted that they would succeed, reached out to others for understanding and gave encouragement and support to family and friends. Neither they nor their closest associates would have credited them with brilliant flashes of insight but instead would describe them as men with good, tenacious minds and steady work habits.

Timing was certainly crucial, since both men reached their prime years when transforming societies and momentous events gave them stages to perform at their best. Yet tens of thousands of other individuals were born in the United States and the British Isles in 1809—and in the several years on either side of that date—and had come into the world at an equally advantageous time. Thus an understanding of certain personal qualities and wider circumstances is needed to explain the great successes of these revolutionary figures.

A desire to prove themselves, or to go beyond their disapproving fathers, were important motives, as were driving ambitions to escape from mental depression through hard work and through contributing something important to the world. Both pursued self-education: Lincoln because he had no choice, Darwin because he found school wanting. This self-learning may have saved them from more commonplace views of the world and freed them to seek answers that men bound by more traditional educations would never have thought of asking. Although willing to question conventional views and practices, they also bided their time until a critical mass of other people were ready to receive what they wanted to say and do. Equally important, they used their political skills to gain the support of men who could help advance their plans.

Whatever the exact reasons for their great achievements, Abraham Lincoln and Charles Darwin have helped to teach the world what it means to be human—free, equal, and connected to the rest of creation. Debates over what they accomplished and what those accomplishments mean for each succeeding generation seem destined to go on for as long as anyone can imagine.

NOTES

1. In this discussion of how Darwin was vindicated, I have relied on Michael White and John Gribbin, *Darwin: A Life in Science* (New York:

Dutton, 1995), pp. 281–301; Ronald W. Clark, *The Survival of Charles Darwin* (New York: Random House, 1984), pp. 204–345; and Ernest Mayr, *One Long Argument: Charles Darwin and the Genesis of Modern Evolutionary Thought* (Cambridge, MA: Harvard University Press, 1991).

2. Clark, *Survival of Charles Darwin*, pp. 214–15.

3. White and Gribbin, *Darwin*, pp. 294–95.

4. Julian Huxley, *Evolution: The Modern Synthesis* (London: Allen and Unwin, 1942).

5. Clark, *Survival of Charles Darwin*, p. 336.

6. For a good discussion of *Inherit the Wind*, see Edward J. Larson, *Summer for the Gods: The Scopes Trial and America's Continuing Debate Over Science and Religion* (Cambridge, MA: Harvard University Press, 1998), pp. 239–46.

7. Julian Huxley in Clark, *Survival of Charles Darwin*, p. 249.

8. Franklin D. Roosevelt, July 4, 1938, quoted in Merrill D. Peterson, *Lincoln in American Memory* (New York: Oxford University Press, 1994), p. 321.

9. Quoted in Janet Browne, *Charles Darwin: The Power of Place* (Princeton, NJ: Princeton University Press, 2002), p. 188.

10. Jacques Barzun, *Darwin, Marx, Wagner* (Boston: Little, Brown and Company, 1941), pp. 260–61.

11. Ibid., p. 263.

12. Gertrude Himmelfarb, *Darwin and the Darwinian Revolution* (Garden City, NY: Doubleday, 1959), pp. 394–95.

13. Ibid., p. 400.

14. Ibid.

15. Among the most recent titles that connects Darwinism with the Nazis is Richard Weikart, *From Darwin to Hitler* (New York: Palgrave Macmillan, 2004).

16. Richard Hofstadter, *Social Darwinism in American Thought* (1944; repr., Boston: Beacon Press, 1955), pp. 4–5.

17. Ibid., pp. 6–7.

18. Ibid., p. 47.

19. Ibid., p. 92.

20. Ibid., p. 204.

21. Greta Jones, *Social Darwinism in English Thought* (Atlantic Highlands, NJ: Humanities Press, 1980), p. 77.

22. E. O. Wilson, *The Creation: An Appeal to Save Life on Earth* (New York: W. W. Norton, 2006), p. 168.

23. Wilson, *Sociobiology: The New Synthesis* (Cambridge, MA: Harvard University Press, 1975) and *On Human Nature* (Cambridge, MA: Harvard University Press, 1978).

24. Hofstadter, *The American Political Tradition and the Men Who Made It* (1948; repr., New York: Vintage Books, 1958), p. 93.

25. Quoted in ibid., p. 106.

26. Ibid., p. 106.

27. Lerone Bennett Jr., *Forced into Glory: Abraham Lincoln's White Dream* (Chicago: Johnson Publishing Company, 2000), pp. 43–44.

28. Michael Lind, *What Lincoln Believed* (New York: Doubleday, 2004), p. 24.

29. Arthur M. Schlesinger Jr., *The Imperial Presidency* (Boston: Houghton Mifflin Company, 1973), p. 58.

30. Ibid., p. 61.

31. National Curriculum Online, Science Outline, 2006.

32. Ibid., Religious Education Outline, 2006.

33. Quoted in Clark, *Survival of Charles Darwin*, p. 337.

34. Quoted in Edward J. Larson, *Evolution* (New York: Modern Library, 2004), p. 257.

35. For a good, brief article on this and other pertinent federal court cases on the teaching of evolution in the public schools, see David Masci, "From Darwin to Dover," *Pew Forum on Religion and Public Life* (September 2005).

36. Ibid., pp. 1–5.

37. Michael Behe, *Darwin's Black Box* (New York: Simon and Schuster, 1996), pp. 5–6. In 2007, Behe followed up this title with *The Edge of Evolution* (New York: Free Press).

38. Quoted in *New York Times*, July 1, 2007.

39. Ibid., October 2, 2005.

40. Quoted in *Philadelphia Inquirer*, September 25, 2005. See also ibid., November 21, 2004, and *New York Times*, October 2, 2005.

41. *New York Times*, October 2, 2005.

42. Richard Dawkins, "Inferior Design, " a review of Behe's *The Edge of Evolution*, in *New York Times*, July 1, 2007.

43. *Philadelphia Inquirer*, September 25, 2005.

44. Ibid., October 26, 2005.

45. Ibid., November 11, 2005.

46. *Newsweek*, August 15, 2005, pp. 27–35.

47. Masci, "Darwin to Dover."

48. Quoted in *Newsweek*, August 15, 2005, p. 28.

49. Douglas L. Wilson, *Honor's Voice: The Transformation of Abraham Lincoln* (New York: Alfred A. Knopf, 1998), p. 315.

50. For example, *U.S. News and World Report*, February 2, 2005; *Time*, July 4, August 15, 2005; *Atlantic*, October 2005, pp. 52–68.

51. *Philadelphia Inquirer*, July 1, 2005.

BIBLIOGRAPHY

PRIMARY SOURCES—LINCOLN

Basler, Roy, et al., eds. *The Collected Works of Abraham Lincoln*. 8 vols. New Brunswick, NJ: Rutgers University Press, 1953.

Wilson, Douglas, and Rodney O. Davis, eds. *Herndon's Informants: Letters, Interviews, and Statements about Abraham Lincoln*. Urbana: University of Illinois Press, 1998.

SECONDARY SOURCES—LINCOLN

Angle, Paul M. *Here I Have Lived: A History of Lincoln's Springfield*. Chicago: Abraham Lincoln Book Shop, 1971.

Baker, Jean H. *Mary Todd Lincoln: A Biography*. New York: W. W. Norton, 1987.

Bennett, Lerone, Jr. *Forced into Glory: Abraham Lincoln's White Dream*. Chicago: Johnson Publishing Company, 2000.

Beveridge, Albert J. *Abraham Lincoln, 1809–1858*. 2 vols. Boston: Houghton Mifflin, 1928.

Boritt, Gabor. *Lincoln and the Economics of the American Dream*. Urbana: University of Illinois Press, 1994.

———. *The Lincoln Enigma: The Changing Faces of an American Icon*. New York: Oxford University Press, 2001.

Burkhimer, Michael. *100 Essential Lincoln Books*. Nashville, TN: Cumberland House, 2003.

Burlingame, Michael. *The Inner World of Abraham Lincoln*. Urbana: University of Illinois Press, 1994.

Charnwood (Lord). *Abraham Lincoln*. New York: Garden City Publishing, 1938.

Current, Richard N. *The Lincoln Nobody Knows*. New York: Hill and Wang, 1958.

Donald, David Herbert. *Lincoln*. New York: *Quadrangle Books*, 1995.

———. *Lincoln Reconsidered: Essays on the Civil War Period*. New York: Vintage Books, 1989.

———. *Lincoln's Herndon*. New York: Da Capo, 1989.

———. *"We Are Lincoln Men": Abraham Lincoln and His Friends*. New York: Simon and Schuster, 2003.

Goodwin, Doris Kearns. *Team of Rivals: The Political Genius of Abraham Lincoln*. New York: Simon and Schuster, 2005.

Guelzo, Allen C. *Abraham Lincoln: Redeemer President*. Grand Rapids, MI: William B. Eerdmans, 1999.

Hamilton, Charles, and Lloyd Ostendorf. *Lincoln in Photographs: An Album of Every Known Pose*. Norman: University of Oklahoma Press, 1963.

Herndon, William Henry. "Analysis of the Character of Abraham Lincoln." Lecture delivered in Springfield on December 12, 1865. *Abraham Lincoln Quarterly* (September 1941).

———. *Herndon's Life of Lincoln*. New York: Da Capo Press, 1983.

Hobson, J. T. *Footprints of Abraham Lincoln*. Dayton, OH: Otterbein Press, 1909.

Holland, Josiah G. *The Life of Abraham Lincoln*. Springfield, IL: Samuel Bowles and Company, 1866.

Holzer, Harold. *Lincoln at Cooper Union: The Speech That Made Abraham Lincoln President*. New York: Simon and Schuster, 2004.

Jaffa, Harry G. *Crisis of the House Divided: An Interpretation of the Issues in the Lincoln-Douglas Debates.* Chicago: University of Chicago Press, 1982.

———. *A New Birth of Freedom: Abraham Lincoln and the Coming of the Civil War.* Lanham, MD: Rowan & Littlefield, 2000.

Keckley, Elizabeth. *Behind the Scenes: Or Thirty Years a Slave, and Four Years in the White House.* New York: Penguin Books, 2005.

Leland, Charles G. *Abraham Lincoln.* London: Marcus Ward and Company, 1879.

Lind, Michael. *What Lincoln Believed.* New York: Doubleday, 2004.

McPherson, James M. *Abraham Lincoln and the Second American Revolution.* New York: Oxford University Press, 1991.

Miller, William Lee. *Lincoln's Virtues: An Ethical Biography.* New York: Alfred A. Knopf, 2002.

Neely, Mark E., Jr. *The Fate of Liberty: Abraham Lincoln and Civil Liberties.* New York: Oxford University Press, 1991.

Nicolay, John G., and John Hay. *Abraham Lincoln: A History.* 10 vols. New York: Century, 1890.

Oates, Stephen B. *Abraham Lincoln: The Man behind the Myths.* New York: HarperCollins, 1984.

Paludan, Philip Shaw. *The Presidency of Abraham Lincoln.* Lawrence: University of Kansas Press, 1994.

Peterson, Merrill D. *Lincoln in American Memory.* New York: Oxford University Press, 1994.

Pickett, William P. *The Negro Problem: Abraham Lincoln's Solution.* New York: G. P. Putnam's Sons, 1909.

Quarles, Benjamin. *Lincoln and the Negro.* New York: Da Capo, 1990.

Randall, Ruth Painter. *Mary Lincoln: Biography of a Marriage.* Boston: Little, Brown, 1953.

Reep, Thomas P. *Lincoln at New Salem.* Petersburg, IL: Old Salem Lincoln League, 1927.

Sandburg, Carl. *Abraham Lincoln: The Prairie Years.* New York: Harcourt, Brace and World, 1926.

Shenk, Joshua Wolf. *Lincoln's Melancholy: How Depression Challenged a President and Fueled His Greatness.* Boston: Houghton Mifflin, 2005.

Strozier, Charles B. *Lincoln's Quest for Union*. Philadelphia: Paul Dry Books, 2001.

Tarbell, Ida M. *Boy Scouts' Life of Lincoln*. New York: Macmillan, 1925.

———. *In the Footsteps of the Lincolns*. New York: Harper and Brothers, 1924.

———. *The Life of Abraham Lincoln*. New York: Macmillan Company, 1928.

Temple, Wayne C. *Abraham Lincoln: From Skeptic to Prophet*. Mahomet, IL: Mayhaven Publishing, 1995.

Thayer, William M. *The Pioneer Boy and How He Became President*. London: Hodder and Stoughton, 1892.

Thomas, Benjamin P. *Abraham Lincoln: A Biography*. New York: Modern Library, 1968.

———. *Lincoln's New Salem*. Carbondale: Southern Illinois University Press, 1954.

Tripp, C. A. *The Intimate World of Abraham Lincoln*. New York: Free Press, 2005.

Vidal, Gore. *Lincoln*. New York: Vintage Books, 1984.

Walsh, John Evangelist. *The Shadows Rise: Abraham Lincoln and the Ann Rutledge Legend*. Urbana: University of Illinois Press, 1993.

Warren, Louis A. *Lincoln's Parentage and Childhood*. New York: Century Company, 1926.

———. *Lincoln's Youth: Indiana Years, Seven to Twenty-One, 1816–1830*. New York: Appleton-Century-Crofts, 1959.

Wesley, John. *Abraham Lincoln: Man of God*. New York: G. P. Putnam's Sons, 1920.

Williams, T. Harry. *Lincoln and the Radicals*. Madison: University of Wisconsin Press, 1972.

Wills, Gary. *Lincoln at Gettysburg: The Words That Remade America*. New York: Touchstone, 1992.

Wilson, Douglas L. *Honor's Voice: The Transformation of Abraham Lincoln*. New York: Alfred A. Knopf, 1998.

Winik, Jay. *April 1865: The Month That Saved America*. New York: HarperCollins, 2001.

Winkle, Kenneth J. *The Young Eagle: The Rise of Abraham Lincoln*. Dallas: Dallas Trade Publishing, 2001.

Wolf, William J. *The Almost Chosen People: A Study of the Religion of Abraham Lincoln*. Garden City, NY: Doubleday, 1959.

PRIMARY SOURCES—DARWIN

Barlow, Nora, ed. *Autobiography of Charles Darwin, 1809–1882*. New York: W. W. Norton, 1993.

Darwin, Charles. *The Correspondence of Charles Darwin*. Cambridge, UK: Cambridge University Press, 1985–(2005). To date, fourteen volumes of the Darwin correspondence have been published. This correspondence is also available from the Darwin Correspondence Online Database, http://www.darwinproject.ac.uk.

———. *The Descent of Man and Selection in Relation to Sex*. New York: Modern Library, n.d.

———. *Origin of Species: A Facsimile of the First Edition*. Cambridge, MA: Harvard University Press, 1964.

———. *Voyage of the Beagle*, New York: Barnes and Noble, 2004.

Darwin, Francis, ed. *The Life and Letters of Charles Darwin*. New York: D. Appleton and Company, 1896.

Wilson, Edward O., ed. *From So Simple a Beginning: The Four Great Books of Charles Darwin*. New York: W. W. Norton, 2006.

SECONDARY SOURCES—DARWIN

Allen, Grant. *Charles Darwin*. London: Longmans, Green, and Company, 1888.

Barzun, Jacques. *Darwin, Marx, Wagner*. Boston: Little, Brown, 1941.

Bowlby, John. *Charles Darwin: A New Life*. New York: W. W. Norton, 1990.

Bowler, Peter J. "Charles Darwin," in *Cambridge Minds*, edited by Peter Harman and Simon Minton. Cambridge, UK: Cambridge University Press, 2002.

———. *Charles Darwin: The Man and His Influence*. Oxford, UK: Basil Blackwell, 1990.

————. *The Eclipse of Darwinism*. Baltimore, MD: Johns Hopkins University Press, 1983.

Brent, Peter. *Charles Darwin: A Man of Enlarged Curiosity*. New York: Harper and Row, 1981.

Browne, Janet. *Charles Darwin: The Power of Place*. Princeton, NJ: Princeton University Press, 2002.

————. *Charles Darwin: Voyaging*. Princeton, NJ: Princeton University Press, 1995.

————. *Darwin's Origin of Species: A Biography*. New York: Atlantic Monthly Press, 2006.

Clark, Ronald W. *The Survival of Charles Darwin*. New York: Random House, 1984.

Darnton, John. *The Darwin Conspiracy*. New York: Alfred A. Knopf, 2005.

Darwin, Francis. "Reminiscences of My Father's Everyday Life," in *The Life and Letters of Charles Darwin*, edited by Francis Darwin. New York: D. Appleton and Company, 1896.

Desmond, Adrian, and James Moore. *Darwin: The Life of a Tormented Evolutionist*. New York: Warner Books, 1991.

Eldridge, Niles. *Darwin: Discovering the Tree of Life*. New York: W. W. Norton Company, 2005.

Himmelfarb, Gertrude. *Darwin and the Darwinian Revolution*. New York: Doubleday, 1959.

Hodge, Jonathan, and Gregory Radick, eds. *The Cambridge Companion to Darwin*. Cambridge, UK: Cambridge University Press, 2003.

Hodge, M. J. S. "Darwin as a Life-Long Generation Theorist," in *The Darwinian Heritage*, edited by D. Kohn. Princeton, NJ: Princeton University Press, 1985.

Hull, David L. *Darwin and His Critics*. Chicago, IL: University of Chicago Press, 1973.

Huxley, Thomas H. *Darwiniana: Essays by Thomas H. Huxley*. New York: AMS Press, 1970.

Jones, Steve. *Darwin's Ghost: The Origin of Species Updated*. New York: Ballantine Books, 2000.

Keith, Arthur. *Darwin Revisited*. London: Watts and Company, 1955.

Keynes, Randall. *Annie's Box: Darwin, His Daughter and Human Evolution.* New York: Riverhead Books, 2002.

Kohn, David, ed. *The Darwinian Heritage.* Princeton, NJ: Princeton University Press, 1985.

Lack, David. *Darwin's Finches.* Cambridge, UK; Cambridge University Press, 1947.

Mayr, Ernest. *One Long Argument: Charles Darwin and the Genesis of Modern Evolutionary Thought.* Cambridge, MA: Harvard University Press, 1991.

Moorehead, Alan. *Darwin and the Beagle.* London: Hamish Hamilton, 1969.

Nichols, Peter. *Evolution's Captain: The Story of the Kidnapping That Led to Charles Darwin's Voyage Aboard the Beagle.* New York: HarperCollins, 2003.

Poulton, Edward B. *Charles Darwin and the Theory of Natural Selection.* New York: Macmillan and Company, 1902.

Quammen, David. *The Reluctant Mr. Darwin.* New York: W. W. Norton Company, 2006.

Raby, Peter. *Alfred Russel Wallace: A Life.* Princeton, NJ: Princeton University Press, 2001.

Ralling, Christopher, ed. *The Voyage of Charles Darwin.* London: Ariel/BBC, 1982.

Sager, Peter. *Oxford and Cambridge: An Uncommon History.* New York: Thames and Hudson, 2003.

Scrapbook of the University of Cambridge Darwin Commemoration, June 22–24, 1909. Rare Book Room, Cambridge University Library.

Seward, A. C., ed. *Darwin and Modern Science: Essays in Commemoration of the Centenary of the Birth of Charles Darwin and of the Fiftieth Anniversary of the Publication of the Origin of Species.* Cambridge, UK: Cambridge University Press, 1910.

Vorzimmer, Peter J. *Charles Darwin: The Years of Controversy.* Philadelphia: Temple University Press, 1970.

White, Michael, and John Gribbon. *Darwin: A Life in Science.* New York: Dutton, 1995.

Wilson, David Sloan. *Darwin's Cathedral: Evolution, Religion, and the Nature of Society.* Chicago: University of Chicago Press, 2002.

SECONDARY SOURCES—GENERAL

Bannister, Robert C. *Social Darwinism: Science and Myth in Anglo-American Social Thought*. Philadelphia: Temple University Press, 1979.

Behe, Michael. *Darwin's Black Box*. New York: Simon and Schuster, 1996.

———. *The Edge of Evolution: The Search for the Limits of Darwinism*. New York: Free Press, 2007.

Blackett, R. J. M. *Divided Hearts: Britain and the American Civil War*. Baton Rouge: Louisiana State University Press, 2001.

Bolt, Christine. *The Anti-Slavery Movement and Reconstruction: A Study in Anglo-American Co-operation, 1833–77*. London: Oxford University Press, 1969.

Brown, Richard D. *Modernization: The Transformation of American Life, 1600–1865*. Prospect Heights, IL: Waveland Press, 1988.

Brown, Thomas J. *The Public Art of Civil War Commemoration: A Brief History with Documents*. Boston: Bedford/St. Martins, 2004.

Butko, Brian A. *The Lincoln Highway: Pennsylvania Traveler's Guide*. Mechanicsburg, PA: Stackpole Books, 1996.

Carter, Paul A. *The Spiritual Crisis of the Gilded Age*. DeKalb: Northern Illinois University Press, 1971.

Carver, G. S. *A Hundred Years of Evolution*. New York: Macmillan, 1957.

Chapman, Matthew. *Trials of the Monkey: An Accidental Memoir*. New York: Picador USA, 2000.

Cherny, Robert W. *A Righteous Cause: The Life of William Jennings Bryan*. Boston: Little, Brown, 1985.

Contosta, David R. *Henry Adams and the American Experiment*. Boston: Little, Brown, 1980.

Dawkins, Richard. *The Ancestor's Tale: A Pilgrimage to the Dawn of Evolution*. New York: Houghton Mifflin, 2004.

———. *River Out of Eden: A Darwinian View of Life*. New York: Basic Books, 1995.

Dupree, Hunter. *Asa Gray: American Botanist, Friend of Darwin*. Baltimore, MD: Johns Hopkins University Press, 1988.

Erikson, Erik H. *Childhood and Society*. New York: W. W. Norton, 1963.

————. *Identity and the Life Cycle.* New York: W. W. Norton, 1980.

————. *Young Man Luther: A Study in Psychoanalysis and History.* New York: W. W. Norton, 1962.

Foner, Philip S., ed. *The Complete Writings of Thomas Paine.* 2 vols. New York: Citadel Press, 1945.

Goertzel, Victor, and Mildred Goertzel. *Cradles of Eminence.* Boston: Little, Brown, 1962.

Grant, Alfred. *The American Civil War and the British Press.* Jefferson, NC: McFarland and Company, 2000.

Goldman, Eric. *Rendezvous with Destiny.* New York: Alfred A. Knopf, 1965.

Harman, Peter, and Simon Mitton, eds. *Cambridge Scientific Minds.* Cambridge, UK: Cambridge University Press, 2002.

Hofstadter, Richard. *The American Political Tradition and the Men Who Made It.* New York: Vintage Books, 1958.

————. *Social Darwinism in American Thought.* Boston: Beacon Press, 1955.

Howe, Daniel Walker. *The Political Culture of the American Whigs.* Chicago: University of Chicago Press, 1979.

————. *Victorian Culture in America.* Philadelphia: University of Pennsylvania Press, 1976.

Huxley, Julian. *Evolution: The Modern Synthesis.* London: Allen and Unwin, 1942.

Jones, Arthur. *Science in Faith: A Christian Perspective.* Romford, Essex, UK: Christian Schools Trust, 1998.

Jones, Greta. *Social Darwinism and English Thought: The Interaction Between Biological and Social Theory.* Sussex, UK: Harvester Press, 1980.

Kayle, Howard L. *The Social Meaning of Modern Biology: From Social Darwinism to Sociobiology.* New Haven, CT: Yale University Press, 1986.

Kazin, Michael. *A Godly Hero: The Life of William Jennings Bryan.* New York: Alfred A. Knopf, 2006.

Kelley, Robert. *The Transatlantic Persuasion.* New York: Alfred A. Knopf, 1969.

Kingsmill, Hugh. *The Poisoned Crown.* London: Eyre and Spottiswoode, 1944.

Kuhn, Thomas S. *The Structure of Scientific Revolutions.* Chicago: University of Chicago Press, 1996.

Larson, Edward J. *Evolution*. New York: Modern Library, 2004.

———. *Summer for the Gods: The Scopes Trial and America's Continuing Debate Over Science and Religion*. Cambridge, MA: Harvard University Press, 1998.

Liddon, H. P. *The Recovery of St. Thomas*. London: Rivingtons, 1882.

Lyell, Charles, Sir. *Geological Evidences of the Antiquity of Man*. New York: Dover Publications, 2004.

———. *Principles of Geology*. Abridged. New York: Penguin Books, 1999.

Mackenzie, John M., ed. *The Victorian Vision*. London: V&A Publications, 2001.

Malthus, Thomas. *An Essay on the Principle of Population*. Cambridge, UK: Cambridge University Press, 1992.

Martineau, Harriet. *Society in America*. Garden City, NY: Doubleday and Company, 1962.

Marsden, George M. *Fundamentalism and American Culture: The Shaping of Twentieth-Century Evangelicalism, 1870–1925*. New York: Oxford University Press, 1980.

Mayer, Henry. *All on Fire: William Lloyd Garrison and the Abolition of Slavery*. New York: St. Martin's Press, 1998.

McCloskey, Robert Green. *American Conservatism in the Age of Enterprise*. New York: Harper and Row, 1951.

McKinney, H. L. *Wallace and Natural Selection*. New Haven, CT: Yale University Press, 1972.

Olasky, Marvin, and John Perry. *Monkey Business: The True Story of the Scopes Trial*. Nashville, TN: Broadman and Holman Publishers, 2005.

Palmer, Charlotte, and Denis Palmer. *Slavery: The Anglo-American Involvement*. New York: Barnes and Noble Books, 1973.

Poole, Michael. *Teaching About Science and Religion: Opportunities in the National Curriculum*. Abingdon, UK: Chatham College Institute, 1998.

Repcheck, Jack. *The Man Who Found Time: James Hutton and the Discovery of the Earth's Antiquity*. Cambridge, MA: Perseus Publishing, 2003.

Ruse, Michael. *The Evolution-Creation Struggle*. Cambridge, MA: Harvard University Press, 2005.

Russett, Cynthia Eagle. *Darwin in America: The Intellectual Response, 1865–1912*. San Francisco: W.H. Freeman and Co., 1976.

Schlereth, Thomas J. *Victorian America: Transformations in Everyday Life.* New York: HarperCollins, 1991.

Schlesinger, Arthur M., Jr. *The Imperial Presidency.* Boston: Houghton Mifflin Company, 1973.

Scopes, John, and James Presley. *Center of the Storm: Memoirs of John T. Scopes.* New York: Holt, Rinehart and Winston, 1967.

Secord, James A. *Victorian Sensation: The Extraordinary Publication of "Vestiges of the Natural History of Creation."* Chicago: University of Chicago Press, 2000.

Spender, Stephen. *Love-Hate Relations: A Study of Anglo-American Sensibilities.* London: Hamish Hamilton, 1974.

Thistlethwaite, Frank. *America and the Atlantic Community.* New York: Harper and Row, 1959.

Thomson, Keith. *Before Darwin: Reconciling God and Nature.* New Haven, CT: Yale University Press, 2005.

Tocqueville, Alexis de. *Democracy in America.* New York: Ballantine Classics, 2000.

Uglow, Jenny. *The Lunar Men.* New York: Farrar, Straus and Giroux, 2002.

Vanauken, Sheldon. *The Glittering Illusion: English Sympathy for the Southern Confederacy.* Worthing, UK: Churchman Publishing, 1988.

Weikart, Richard. *From Darwin to Hitler.* New York: Palgrave Macmillan, 2004.

Wilson, David Sloan. *Evolution for Everyone.* New York: Delacorte Press, 2007.

Wilson, Edward O. *The Creation: An Appeal to Save Life on Earth.* New York: W. W. Norton, 2006.

———. *On Human Nature.* Cambridge, MA: Harvard University Press, 1978.

———. *Sociobiology: The New Synthesis.* Cambridge, MA: Harvard University Press, 1975.

Wilson, R. Jackson, ed. *Darwinism and the American Intellectual: An Anthology.* Chicago: Dorsey Press, 1989.

INDEX